BRIT
by Mass-Ob

BRITAIN
by MASS-OBSERVATION

ARRANGED AND WRITTEN BY
Tom Harrisson AND Charles Madge

New introduction by Angus Calder

THE CRESSET LIBRARY

London Melbourne Sydney Auckland Johannesburg

The Cresset Library

An imprint of Century Hutchinson Ltd

62–65 Chandos Place, London WC2N 4NW

Century Hutchinson Publishing Group (Australia) Pty Ltd
16–22 Church Street, Hawthorn, Melbourne, Victoria 3122

Century Hutchinson (NZ) Ltd
32–34 View Road, PO Box 40–086, Glenfield, Auckland 10

Century Hutchinson (SA) (Pty) Ltd
PO Box 337, Bergvlei 2012, South Africa

First published 1939
This edition first published 1986

Printed and bound in Great Britain by
Richard Clay (The Chaucer Press) Ltd, Bungay, Suffolk

British Library Cataloguing in Publication Data

Madge, Charles
    Britain by Mass Observation.—(The Cresset Library; 3)
    1. Great Britain—Social life and customs—20th century
    I. Title   II. Harrisson, Tom.   III. Mass Observation.
    941.083   DA566.4

ISBN 0 09 168771 3

Photographs © Humphrey Spender and the BBC Hulton
Picture Library

CONTENTS

INTRODUCTION TO
THE CRESSET LIBRARY EDITION

Britain by Mass-Observation is well-known to historians as an invaluable source of vivid material about life in the late 1930s. Yet its status as one of the most significant books of that decade has never been fully acknowledged – perhaps because it has not been seen out of the uniform red and white of the Penguin Special series of books which was intended to be above all topical. Though *Britain* was reported to have sold 100,000 copies in ten days, other Specials had equal popular appeal. We have tended to see the whole series as one of pamphlets, some brilliant, many distinctly left of centre, which are supposed to have influenced thoughtful members of the public to such effect that the Conservative Party suffered a landslide defeat in 1945. And *Britain* certainly shares with other Specials a sharply polemical tone and an air of desperate urgency. However, it retains its general interest as most don't.

Uneven though *Britain* is, it remains compulsively readable, a wonderful expression of the sheer energy of two highly-gifted young men who put it together racing against a deadline amid the Munich Crisis of autumn 1938. Furthermore, this was the first time that a work of would-be-scientific sociology had made such a popular impact. Just as its initial impulse had started to falter, *Britain* attracted numerous new recruits to the idea and practice of Mass-Observation, which it confirmed as a household word.

Was *Britain*, though, as innovatory as it seemed to many at the time? The idea that an anthropology of the British people was needed had been in the air for some years. When the leading American student of tribal

peoples, Frans Boas, proclaimed in the 1930s his belief
that 'the same attitudes prevail among ourselves that are
characteristic of primitive man', he was echoing in
academic circles a message conveyed by Joseph
Conrad's *Heart of Darkness* and T. S. Eliot's *Waste
Land*. To cite a few other relevant instances: in 1929,
Edith Sitwell had published her long poem *Gold Coast
Customs*, explaining that in it 'We see everything
reduced to the primal need – the "rich man Judas,
brother Cain", and the epitome of his civilisation, Lady
Bamburgher, are at one with the slum-ignorance and the
blackness and superstition of the African swamp.' *Left
Review*, the influential product of a brilliant group of
Communist intellectuals carried in its third number
(1934) a cartoon by James Fitton in which two naked
spear-carrying tribesmen are seen wearing 'old school
ties' in lieu of loincloths, to the horror of an imperialist in
solar topee and jodhpurs whose tie carries the same
pattern. Next year, a successful humourist, Charles
Duff, published an *Anthropological Report on a London
Suburb*, labouring what was already a well-known point,
and in 1936 Dr O. A. Oeser of the Department of
Experimental Psychology at the University of St
Andrews used the phrase 'anthropology at home' in a
methodological paper delivered to the British Association.

But *Britain* was the first widely-read book to put the
concept practically to work. M-O's commitment went
deeper than merely joking about the 'intense anthropological interest' of the scrap of paper which Chamberlain waved to the crowds after his agreement with Hitler,
'replacing the Golden Bough by a Paper Symbol'. M-O's
argument for regarding the Keaw Yed festival in Westhoughton as a 'slight case of totemism' is measured,

learned and surely rather convincing. That social traditions in South London have 'many features in common
with primitive dancing' seems well-established here by
careful observation. In this context the reaction of a
retired major to the Lambeth Walk, that it recalls erotic
festivities in the southern Sudan, seems more than a
mere expression of crusty prejudice.

Public opinion polling was certainly not M-O's invention. As early as 1915, A. L. Bowley had discovered
random sampling techniques which permitted accurate
assessment of the views of a given mass of people without the impossible labour entailed by interviewing
everyone. It seems that this had not been appreciated by
those who organized the gigantic 'Peace Ballot' of
1934–5 as a house-to-house canvass throughout Britain
which trawled in over 11.5 million replies to questions
about the League of Nations and disarmament. However, in the USA, from 1928, Dr George Gallup had
applied sampling techniques first to market research,
then also to politics. The accurate election predictions of
his American Institute of Public Opinion brought
Gallup prestige and profit. In 1936, Henry W. Durant
began to establish a British counterpart. Besides work
for commerce and industry it undertook, from 1938,
monthly surveys of political opinion for the *News
Chronicle*. From a voting population of nearly 30 million, BIPO used samples of 2000 to 15,000, and claimed
accuracy within 3 per cent. Meanwhile, from September
1937, the BBC had conducted 'Listener Research' using
a 'panel' of 2000 licence holders chosen by random
sample.

Britain's deployment of statistics to illustrate fluctuations of opinion before and during the Munich Crisis
would not have satisfied expert pollsters then and does

not bear close inspection now. Mass-Observation lacked funds to mount surveys with adequate samples. Its organizers later realized that M-O's real strength lay in other techniques, 'qualitative' rather than 'quantitative', and began to proclaim a high-minded scorn of polls. There are already signs of unease in the claim, on the original cover of *Britain*, that M-O's National Panel of self-chosen volunteers numbered 'some two thousand'. Responses to any one monthly questionnaire never reached a quarter of that figure, even after the success of *Britain* itself swelled the panel's numbers. It is hard to resist the conclusion that '2000' was hit on because that would match the BBC panel in size and correspond to the minimum sample used by BIPO. But if it was not rigorous, *Britain*'s use of statistics was vigorous, and must have excited the book's largely youthful readership, contributing powerfully to growing public acceptance of the usefulness of sample polls. (A mountain of prejudice had to be climbed – as late as 1945 the *News Chronicle* predicted that Churchill would win the General Election despite the BIPO evidence published in its own pages.)

Britain's authors were very well-equipped to convert others to enthusiasm for 'social science' because they were recent converts themselves. Both were Cambridge drop-outs. Charles Madge (born in 1912) had first attracted attention as a very promising poet. T. S. Eliot had suggested a job on the *Daily Mirror* (where a bibliophile friend of his was a leader-writer) and Madge, as a Fleet Street reporter, had become fascinated by the newspaper medium – its astrologers and vox pops, its shock-horror headlines and strange human interest tales. Tom Harrisson (1911–76) had published his first book while a schoolboy at Harrow. It was a guide to the birds of the area, and launched him on a career as a self-taught naturalist which took him to the New Hebrides in 1933 with an Oxford University scientific expedition. He lingered alone on the island of Malekula awhile, 'living with cannibals', and manifested himself as an 'anthropologist' with a best-seller, *Savage Civilisation*, which was published by the Left Book Club just as he and Madge came together, early in 1937, to found Mass-Observation.

Initially, Harrisson's role was to organize the survey of Bolton (Worktown) which he had commenced before he had learnt of Madge's converging interest. This produced a plethora of information about Lancashire life which Harrisson and his helpers never quite succeeded in marshalling into the four books whose imminent publication is prophesied in Chapter 9 of *Britain* – only *The Pub and the People* eventually appeared (1943; this will also be republished as part of The Cresset Library). Meanwhile, Madge set up the National Panel from his home in Blackheath, London. But by late 1938 Madge had worked in the North and Harrisson in London. According to his own recollection (interview with Nick Stanley, May 1978) it was, surprisingly, Madge, not Harrisson, who wrote up the Westhoughton Keaw Yed festival. Dividing the later chapters between them, they worked very closely together on number two, 'Crisis'.

Whatever reservations must be expressed about their use of statistics, this chapter remains extremely gripping. It surely provides the first comprehensive and sophisticated account of British public opinion in rapid flux. If it did not exist, BIPO polls of the day would tell us something about that stage of opinion – but Gallup techniques do not provide means for recreating, as *Britain* does so vividly, the atmosphere of the Munich period. The

women who say, even before the crisis, that they would
kill their children rather than see them bombed; the
reactions of well fed denizens of a Suffolk hotel to
Hitler's speech; the crowds in Whitehall on that same
evening overheard talking among themselves; later in
the month, a Tory MP besieged in his home by telegrams
and phone calls, Fascist demonstrators running from
angry crowds near Parliament, the horrific mass-issue of
gas masks exciting 'mass-fears', and the smile on the
Russian ambassador's face as he leaves the House of
Commons after Chamberlain, amid hysterical relief, has
received Hitler's third invitation to talk – these and
many, many other details convey a sense of depth never,
surely, attained by any social scientist or reporter before.
Despite the rise of TV and of 'insight' journalism, M-O's
achievement would be hard to match since.

Other sections of the book pioneered in different
directions. M-O's study of the Lambeth Walk craze was
perhaps revised in final draft by Madge, but certainly
owes much to Harrisson's unaffected zest for everyday
lowbrow amusements – it was certainly he who set John
Sommerfield and others to work observing the minutiae
of pub life in Bolton, and later inspired young volunteer
observers to heroic attempts to plot the incidence of sex
in summer Blackpool. In any case, the resulting chapter
here nobly anticipates, by some two decades, the first
large stirrings of 'serious' interest in popular culture. It
goes well beyond the inspired impressionism of George
Orwell's forays into such territory. It combines the techniques of journalist and folklorist. To vivid first-hand
observation, it adds 'oral history' – little practised then,
commonplace now. It lacks the theoretical insights of
post-structuralism as applied to musical fashion, say, by
Dick Hebdige in his *Subculture* (1979), yet still affords

solid food for thought. So does *Britain*'s treatment of all-in wrestling – now familiar television fodder, but discovered in its infancy by M-O's explorers in Lancashire, and reported from the changing British jungle to fascinated readers from classes and regions where its existence was unknown.

Mass-Observation was part of the broad movement, typified by Orwell, of conscience-stricken middle-class intellectuals trying, in days of wide unemployment, to meet and understand the working class. Though the air of 'slumming' and condescension which such an enterprise can convey still sometimes arouses prejudice against M-O, the motivations of those involved surely deserve respect. However, the very concept of 'mass' now seems dated and unhelpful. It is never wholly clear, from *Britain* or from other M-O publications, whether the primary aim was observation *of* the mass or *by* the masses. On the one hand, M-O seems to be addressing the 'political classes' and making them an offer they can't refuse – an improved understanding of public opinion. 'Market research' for political parties is now routine. Some politicians even in the late 1930s were beginning to recognize its potential. (Edith Summerskill believed, it seems, that M-O's involvement as 'scientists' in west Fulham when she won a by-election there for Labour in 1938 had actually contributed to her victory.) On the other hand, M-O often represents itself as a medium through which the Man in the Street can express himself, by-passing the MPs and pressmen who pretend to represent his opinions but don't. If there were few working-class M-O panel members, at least plebeian sentiments could be registered through street interviews.

The 'Lambeth Walk' chapter, as it concludes with

question begging speculation, demonstrates M-O's ambivalence. It has shown that the dance craze has involved complicated two-way interactions between commercial showbiz and popular self-expression. Yet it claims that:

It proves that if *you give* the masses something which connects with *their* own lives and streets . . . *they* will take to it with far more spontaneous feeling than they have ever shown for the paradise-drug of the American dance-tune [my italics].

Two dubious suggestions are conveyed. One is that 'the masses' are intrinsically innocent. 'These Lambeth Walkers are happy because they find that they are free to express *themselves* without the hypnosis of a jazz-moon or a Führer.' Contradicting this we have the implication that the book's reader, whose 'you' is distinct from the masses' 'they', should apply himself to thinking about what the masses should be *given*. The politics of 1938 explain the contradiction. Unless 'they' are *given* the right things (which include 'facts'), 'they' are naïvely vulnerable to the 'hypnotic' appeal of Fascism. It is more urgent that the 'masses' should be well-understood and well-directed than that they should speak for themselves through M-O.

The concept of a single 'mass-mind', which Madge and Harrisson deploy casually yet confidently, consorts strangely with their statement that 'Each and every person is automatically an individual, conforming outwardly . . . but underneath with repressions and furies which are partly "personal".' *Britain* exposes, without resolving it, a contradiction characteristic of the thinking of 1930s intellectuals – who were typically, the heirs of a liberal–individualist tradition in a period of 'mass politics'. Freudianism appeared to offer the chance of a new kind of liberal individualism based on appreciation of psychological differences between autonomous personalities. Marxism seemed to call on the intellectual to immerse himself in the 'masses' and the 'struggle'. Harrisson's politics, when he chose to name them, were Liberal (he worked on a volume, never published, for the Liberal Book Club). Madge had been a committed Communist. But both seem to have been relieved to retreat from the dilemma of their generation into the supposedly neutral position of the 'scientist', where consciousness could be neither 'collective' nor 'individual', but 'objective'. The social scientist, Madge and Harrisson argue, must find out 'what people do want, do get, don't get and could get to want', and must publish his findings in such place and form that the masses themselves will be able to read and check them. Mass-Observation's role is to describe rather than prescribe – not to agitate, but to mediate.

Angus Calder
Edinburgh 1986

I

ASTROLOGY AND
BRITISH ASS

"WHILE Europe was tensely watching the crisis over Czechoslovakia, Herr Hitler, accompanied by eight of his generals, paid a surprise visit to the French frontier to-day."

That is the way the newspapers talk about the world. These actual words were splashed across the *Star* on August 29, 1938. They are typical. But what do they mean? Europe is a continent, so it can't very well watch anything. Nor can the people in it watch a crisis in a literal sense. What is implied is that millions of people are on tenterhooks to know what is happening on the German border, in Foreign Offices and at Cabinet Meetings. It is naturally difficult for people to get to know the facts about these things, because secrecy is essential when bluff and counter-bluff are the order of the day. This is a democratic country, so we are supposed to have some idea of what is going on. For this we depend on wireless and newspaper presentation of news. But can we believe what we read and hear? People want inside information, they want to get behind the news. This is impossible for the vast majority, so they have to accept what the newspapers say, or else stop bothering.

Of course that is assuming that Britain, and the rest of Europe, really were at that time "tensely watching". But were they? How many were more tensely watching the racing news and daily horoscope? That is another kind of fact we shall not know without trying to find out.

One thing we can be fairly sure of, namely that most readers of this book want to know these facts, and all other relevant facts which will help them to play their full part in the world—unless they paid their sixpence by mistake or without thinking. Fact is urgent—we are cogs in a vast and complicated machine which may turn out to be an infernal machine that is going to blow us all to smithereens. In any case, life is short, and if we are at all interested in this world (instead of, or as well as, the next world) we had better hurry up and learn where we stand. We must have knowledge, at least sufficient for us to come to personal decisions.

There is an alternative view of things (not often openly expressed, more often implied or unconscious) according to which there can only be a handful of people who know the facts, it being their job to control the destinies of millions of other people. For these millions it is necessary only to sleep, eat, work, reproduce, and, if they have time to spare, amuse themselves. The question then arises: Do these millions, under the present order of things, have enough sleep, enough to eat, enough work, do they reproduce themselves enough, and do they get the amusements that they need and want? The most optimistic spokesman of this view of things could not maintain that this was the case. It is by no means seditious to state the reverse. The most conservatively-minded would admit that we suffer in England from malnutrition, unemployment, a falling birth-rate and a "leisure problem". This being so, if the Handful-who-know can't do anything about it, there comes a point when the Man and Woman in the Street start uneasily wondering if there is anything they can do to help themselves. It is the function of the 615 members of our democratic Parliament to voice the wishes, feelings, wants, needs, hopes, opinions, grouses, aspirations and criticisms of 45,000,000 people. But this democratic system has broken down in other countries, and may break down in our own, because the 45,000,000 do not feel sufficiently strongly that they are able to speak through Parliament. So they give it up as a bad job and resign themselves to being voiceless or get annoyed with the whole system. At least there is evidence pointing that way, as we shall see.

It is because of this situation—the urgency of fact, the voicelessness of everyman and the smallness of the group which controls fact-getting and fact-distributing—that this book came to be written. Other Penguin Specials have dealt with questions of international politics and the danger of war. This book aims to give the other side of the picture—to give both ear and voice to what the millions are feeling and doing under the shadow of these terrific events. Only by understanding this side can we, as individuals, hope to decide what *we* can do and, if there is anything we can do, then how to do it.

To understand, we must first have facts, and to get the facts a new kind of organisation is needed, or rather a new attitude towards getting facts and publishing them. There has been much talk about the social relations of science, the need for extending the Science of Ourselves and for studying the everyday lives and feelings of ordinary people, as well as the customs of primitive people and the feelings of neurotics. In America, much survey work has been done by the Universities, so that "sociology" is rapidly becoming more than a name for a science not yet born. That very large numbers of Americans want factual knowledge about *people* is indicated by the success of papers like *Life* and *Time,* circulations of which have quickly soared past the million mark, and by documentary films like *March of Time, The River,* as well as the great new drive of Worker Theatres and Federal Art Project.

There are numerous reasons why the Man in the Street feels he is kept in the dark. Books are expensive to buy and not always easily available in libraries. The language they are written in is often difficult to understand. Often, too, there just isn't time or energy left at the end of a hard-working day for going back to school, as it were, and being lectured by some writer who obviously moves in a world of ideas quite different from one's own.

Some writers of popular science books have done the job very well, but unfortunately there is often as much distortion in the reporting of scientific discovery as in other kinds of news. It is the "story", not the fact, that most newspapers or magazines aim at presenting. People like stories, and it is a natural and human tendency. Yet there is much evidence that a growing number of people want less stories and more facts. They want the facts, and they want them in a form that suits the times we live in.

The huge success of the Penguin and Pelican series is a proof of this. The 250,000 who read a Penguin Special are a drop in the ocean of possible readers, but they represent a big move in the right direction at a time when "an important book can sell no more than 200 copies".

Out of the ordinary man's bewilderment and desire for fact has grown also a new organisation called Mass-Observation. This consists at present of 1,500 amateur Observers, ordinary people who have volunteered to help in the making of factual surveys. Anyone can be an Observer, no special training is needed. In the two years of its existence M-O has been exploring new techniques for observing and analysing the ordinary. Through M-O you can already listen-in to the movements of popular habit and opinion. The receiving set is there, and every month makes it more effective. There is a staff of full-time skilled observers centred on London, Worktown and Blackpool.

In the concluding section of this book, some account will be given of the origins of Mass-Observation, the people who started it, its programme of work, and the extent to which it has succeeded. The main part of the book will be occupied with a full description of a number of Mass-Observation's surveys immediately relevant to contemporary problems.

The idea of Mass-Observation has definitely broken through. The newspapers with the biggest circulations already assume that their readers have heard of it. Moreover, since Mass-Observation started, similar ideas have been much in the air, partly because of M-O's example, and partly because M-O itself did no more than crystallise an already existing tendency. It is not a sect, and to be useful it must collaborate with all others who are working in the same field. And most needed of all forms of collaboration is collaboration with the Man in the Street.

Much lip-service is paid to the Man in the Street— politicians and newspapers claim to represent him, scientists and artists want to interest him in their work. Much of what they say is sincere, but it must remain ineffective while the Man in the Street has no medium through which he can express with equal publicity what *he* thinks of *them*.

The present position of the Intellectual Few is a relic of the times when the mass of the population consisted of serfs who could neither read nor write. Then a few people at the top could easily impose their beliefs and rule on the multitude. But the whole tendency of history has been away from this state of things. If only because industry requires an army of technicians and semi-technicians, universal education became a social necessity. Everyone can read and write now. Yet even so in many ways there is as much intellectual serfdom as ever. When there are social reforms, they are imposed on the mass from above. Not "what they want" but "what's good for them". And the people who decide what is good for the millions are themselves a tiny group, with different habits of mind, ways of life, from those of the millions they are catering for. It is the same in art, religion, science and politics. The people who happened to start Mass-Observation—one a poet and newspaper reporter, the other an ornithologist and explorer, both aged 25—had an inkling of the hiatus between the millions and their leaders; two years' observation has confirmed it beyond doubt.

The gap between science and everyman is particularly noticeable, and now one of the main problems of the survival of our civilisation. This gap is most striking in the field of the human sciences. Despite numerous professorships, endowments and fellowships in Social Science, Sociology, Political Science, etc., the social relations of ordinary life and the scientific principles underlying politics have remained matters of argument, conjecture and monstrous generalisation, from which no potent research drive has emerged anywhere outside America. In this country, some good statistical work and some excellent administrative sociological reports on areas have been done. But nothing on normal behaviour, and nothing which has approached the formulation of fundamental laws in social relations and human behaviour—though the work of a South African, Dr. O. Oeser, of St. Andrew's University, Scotland, marks a distinct advance in the direction of Social Psychology. One main reason for this is the extra-specially special sort of life led by university people who have a monopoly of scientific funds. But the blindness and lack of general sense shown by most scientists is inherent in their whole approach. Anthropologists, who have spent years and travelled all over the world to study remote tribes, have contributed literally nothing to the anthropology of ourselves.

Scientists at the British Association meeting at Cambridge in August, 1938, were saying, as they have so often said before, that science must concern itself with its own social possibilities. "Man can satisfy all his needs, can be happy and free. Science has made this technically possible; it has yet to be made socially possible." To make the satisfaction of man's needs socially possible is, from the scientific point of view, a technical problem comparable to making a gearless car. Knowledge, like motor power, has to be transmitted. A few people make the discoveries, millions of people should benefit. But in the process of transmission, the discoveries pass into the hands of another set of people whose aim is largely either to make a profit out of them or else to arm themselves with enormously powerful weapons of destruction. Part of the trouble is that the scientists themselves tend to become isolated in a vacuum of "pure" science, and artificial detachment from human problems. The result is that, as we shall see, the Man and Woman in the Street often look upon science not as their greatest potential ally, but as just another of the forces which exploit them and of which they know little or nothing. Astrology and Football Pools are nearer reality for them than Science and Politics. So at present if science has anything useful to offer, it tends to be imposed from above, and it may take the form of a gas mask.

Professor J. D. Bernal, F.R.S., who is also aware of these problems, thus summed up this year's meeting of the British Association:

"The Cambridge meeting of the British Association may well prove a turning point in the history of science, for it announced a discovery of an importance altogether different from any of the great discoveries that have been announced there in the past. This discovery was not in science, but about science. It was that scientists for the first time have become conscious of the need to concern themselves with the social consequences and possibilities of science.

The discovery itself is not new. Many scientists from the very beginning of modern science have pointed it out;

but it has never before been officially accepted, and, what is more important, has never been acted on by an organised body of scientists.

Up till very recently the pursuit of science for its own sake was the conscious ideal of the scientist. The results of science might be human welfare or destruction, but that was the concern of society, not of the scientist.

This ideal still found reflection in Lord Rayleigh's presidential address at Cambridge; yet in that same address he announced the acceptance by the Council of the Association of the proposal to form a new division, whose purpose was to study the Social and International Relations of Science. . . .

Up till now the scientist has been isolated. Now, coming together in his own Association, he can, for the first time, effectively demand that science should be properly used, and lend force to a popular demand that these evils should be no more, that science is made for all men and not for the profit of a few."

(Reynolds News, August 28, 1938.)

Such is the attitude of an enlightened scientist, but even he is thinking primarily of the scientist "coming together in his own Association", not of any link between the scientists and the huge mass of the population. He implies also that this mass is only waiting to welcome science with both arms. There is a "popular demand" for science, he says. Partially this is true, but we doubt if Professor Bernal realises the danger that the masses may become disillusioned with science as well as with politics, religion and all other solutions except personal or magical ones. There is no indication that any scientist knows (or cares) what the Man in the Street actually thinks about science, as shown in the following comments, all from ordinary people in the vast income-group which includes three-quarters of the population and in which the chief earner of the family gets less than £200 a year. The interviewers asked them if they were interested in science, what they thought

about it, and if they read about it; then let them talk
and kept a verbatim record. Nine per cent were definitely hostile to science, and 13% definitely in favour
of it. Thirty-nine per cent were partly in favour, partly
hostile, and another 39% expressed complete indifference. About a third of the women asked, and a
sixth of the men, said that they didn't understand
about things like that.

Here are some of the many recorded examples of
indifference:

1. *Woman of* 32. "I suppose they as does it know what
they're doin', I don't."

2. *Man of* 30. "Do you mean them crackbrained blokes
who write them books, no I never read them for years
since I was a kid, they do things I know, wot should we
know abawt it anyways, not in my line, chum."

3. *Man of* 25. "What's it got to do with us, I used to read
it a lot, they tell you at school, it's nothing to me, I think
it's a good thing that them clever men do it, they do a lot."

4. *Man of* 25. "I read somewhere about them having a
meeting, where was it now, no I didn't read what they said,
not in my line, pickin' dogs is what I do in my spare time,
give you a good 'un for to-night at Catford."

5. *Man of* 26. "They do a lot of talking, it's not for the
likes of us. Blimey, we don't know what they're going to
do next. Be a good thing if everybody had a good education,
then we'd know what they're getting at."

The main reasons for hostility to science were that it
made people lose their jobs, that it just helped a few
people to make big profits, and that it was used for
weapons of war. For instance:

1. *Man of* 26, *Joiner*. "You want to ask them why they're
always inventing things, some of 'em no damned use except
to make us work like bloody machines. No time for 'em,
chum, that's me."

2. *Unemployed man*, 34. "All they do is put you on
the street, they don't care a damn for us, never think of

it mate till you said it. . . . Bad enough with a wife and two kids to keep, I don't think they help us mate, they ought to be under the Government so as to stop 'em from making things to get rid of us."

3. *Grocery assistant*, 22. "It all depends on what you mean, I don't believe in it, they spend most of their time thinking about new ways of finding out what we can do without, some of them are making things like gas for us to get rid of the surplus population . . . they ought to be put in jail or shot for it, they will be one day. Course I know what you're talking about, I read about it all in the paper, used to read books about it, they've made a new car so's it's easier to drive, more profit for them isn't it, like Lord Nuffield. Wireless is all right though."

4. *Unemployed man*, 40. "Read all about it chum in the papers, they don't interest me 'cept they don't do anything like for the likes of us, they talk about what we should eat, why don't they see we get it. . . . Vitamins—bread and bloody jam is what we get. . . . They think about more ways of making bloody money for the capitalists. . . . It's all right if they'd keep men in their bloody jobs."

5. *Unemployed man*, 45. "I saw a lot in the papers, I didn't read it, it's too clever for me. The papers were full of it about a fortnight ago. I don't know that it's got much to do with us, it puts us out of work more than in work. Before they let 'em do it, they should see that everybody gets a fair share."

6. *Man of* 30, *Carter*. "That's nothing these days; what with them scientists and Mussolini and Hitler, the world'll be in a bloody mess soon, that's what I think."

7. *Woman office-worker*, 24. "They make these wars and all that, I know they don't do it on purpose though, aeroplanes and bombs to set fire to everything, they start this and don't know where it will stop, then they ask you to join the A.R.P. You ought to find out what the people want, they are satisfied with anything, that's the trouble. I'm sick of all this talk about What are we going to do. . . ."

The last-quoted comment is much to this point: *you ought to find out what the people want*. It is quite clear that to ordinary people the Scientist is a remote, unreal figure. "Everybody seems to think the scientist is a queer bird," said a man of 32. Another said: "People are frightened of science because there's all this war talk, but if you ask me mister, I think the ordinary man thinks the scientist is barmy." The scientist is a popular enough character in detective fiction; he is definitely eccentric, often mad. Wellsian visions of the future are also important in building up the ordinary man's picture of science, as can be seen in these comments:

1. *Man of* 50, *with a small lending library*. "I don't know much about it myself, but I know if you put them sort of books on your shelves they'd never go out round here. They want exciting stuff, thrillers and that kind of thing. Still, I suppose there's a lot of what you'd call science in 'em, fantastic things, they like that, but I know that that's not the real thing. That stuff about atoms and that kind of thing, it doesn't interest them, why should it? It's too technical for them."

2. *Shop assistant*, 19. "I saw that film of H. G. Wells'— *Things to Come*. Makes you realise what things are going to be like. They know what they're talking about. If you don't know anything about things like that these days you don't get very far, because everything's specialised like. I wish I'd had a better education. If you 'aven't had that you've got to stick in the same hole all your life. Course they tell you you can go to Night School and that sort of thing, but you don't get much chance when you work in a shop till eight o'clock every night."

3. *Woman of* 25. "I've read a book of H. G. Wells, he's good, I saw that film about Things to Come, it's good, never read about science, they do some silly things, they're always talking about what should be, nobody takes any notice. My brother works in an electric works, he says they're always making new things. Gosh, I wouldn't like to go back to them old days . . . no buses or that . . . they only do it to make money."

4. *Man of* 35, *on the dole, was a soldier*. "I've never bothered much, I saw a good bit in the papers the last week,

they made a new car, easier to run and cheaper, there's a lot more, they think it's important, I suppose it is. I saw a picture of H. G. Wells in one of them, he's a scientist isn't he? I saw that picture of his. . . . You don't know what's coming next, I can see it coming, they get ready for wars a long time before."

The most widespread positive attitude to science was that it is a good thing in itself, provided it is in the right hands. Here are some typical examples of this point of view:

1. *Sailor*, 35. "It's a good thing there is people who get down to rock bottom, there's a reason for everything I says, good luck to 'em, they ought to be damned sure they only make things easier for our sort before they should be let use it."

2. *Man of* 40, *Electrical worker*. "Never thought much about it, took it for granted. One thing it's done is make people's nerves on edge all the time, wars and all that, get sick of it. . . . Pictures you get used to, they're all the same. . . . You can get about easier. . . . I don't blame them as finds things out, it's them as is let use the things wot they find out. . . . I read a bit about that new car, don't know what it means though. They're always finding things out now. All right if we knew how to use them, first thing they do is to put men on the shelf before they're grown up. . . . Sometimes think if they had a rest from thinking how they can make more money out of us—that's what they do it for."

3. *Man of* 50, *engineering worker*. "No guvnor, I never read about them, there's some at our place, they're clever, it takes a good education to follow them things up, it's all right till they put men out of work, then it makes you think different, they ought to stop them from making gases and bombers, it's them as makes these wars, they should be stopped for a few years till we know how to use 'em for the best."

4. *Man of* 35, *Clerk*. "It's only since science came that we have got anywhere at all. Religion has kept it back for centuries, now it's winning, proving what we can do. I go to church but that doesn't mean I'm a fool. . . . I don't

believe they ought to turn over what they discover to the people who get away with the use of it. . . . Stop inventing new ways to kill, that's where it's wrong."

5. *Unemployed man*, 48. "It's changed the world, I can't say whether it's for the better, new things, new ideas, change all round, that's science, I think they can make our lives easier, they never will till there's a change in the social system though."

While these comments on science were being collected, people were asked in the same London working-class areas (Peckham, Deptford, Fulham) whether they read the horoscopes in the papers, and whether they believed in them. Newspaper astrology has grown up almost entirely in recent years and is to be reckoned with as a very powerful force.

Horoscope of the greatest Daily, on crisis day, September 30, day Chamberlain and Daladier signed up with Hitler, read:

"IF IT'S YOUR BIRTHDAY TO-DAY.

A rather uncertain year this. Many pleasant times will be yours, and despite some ups and downs you should be fortunate with money. Be discreet about your personal plans; take care in whom you confide. . . . See that you do not relay gossip."

Similar advice is given to those who have birthdays between October 24 and November 22 ("Be discreet"), November 23 to December 21 ("Don't repeat scandal"), January 20 to February 19 ("Take care you do not betray secrets through lack of thought"), February 20 to March 20 ("Rumour and scandal are abroad which you can ignore"), April 21 to May 20 ("Keep your own counsel about immediate plans"), May 21 to June 21 ("Pay no heed to rumours or scandal. It's more than probably false"), while the July 23 to August 22 folk received another form of this advice well suited to the times ("You can't depend on the accuracy of news or information").

There are always two or three pieces of such advice in every day's newspaper for each day of the year, classified according to your birthday. Popular on September 30 was: "Defer important decisions" (September 24 to October 23), "Take care what you put in writing" (November 23 to December 21), "Not a good day to sign a business agreement. Defer important interviews until another day" (December 22 to January 19), "Be on guard against fraud. You may make a new friend" (April 21 to May 20), "Defer important journeys if you can" (June 22 to July 22), "Not a good day to sign documents" (July 23 to August 22). The outlook, therefore, is black for democracy—on September 30 Chamberlain signed for "permanent peace" with Hitler. But he was born on March 18 (1869).

From the enormous horoscopic data of the 1938 Press it is possible to construct a whole ethic of contemporary England, and through these columns much editorial policy is promoted as advice for your future. It is no exaggeration to say that holiday travel, city investments, the success of advertisers, rumours of war, can be more powerfully influenced by the paper's astrologer than its leader writer or news editor. For the child there is always some bouquet, and on September 30:

"Children born to-day will be adventurous and imaginative. They will be affectionate and will ultimately be successful."

There is no need to emphasise the effect which this philosophy must have on those who believe in it. It means the acceptance of a fatalism fixed by the position of planets at the exact moment of your birth. Those positions determine everything else. And modern astrologers frequently predict international affairs in terms of Hitler or Hore-Belisha horoscopes. In order to find out how many people believe in these, we surveyed areas in London only. On *a priori* grounds there was

reason to suppose that people must pay attention to
the horoscopes, for they occupy so much space in the
papers which have the largest circulations. We found
the influence far stronger with women than men. A
third of those asked said that all the womenfolk believed
in it, but they didn't think the men did. This was borne
out by the fact that of the women asked, a third believed
in the horoscopes, another third partly believed, and the
remaining third did not believe in them; while of the
men, only 5% believed, 15% partly believed, and 80%
said they did not believe at all, though often they
complained that their wives and daughters did. A man
of 26 said: "I suppose there's something in it, I've
never bothered about it myself though. Nearly all the
girls, they do it, *Peg's Paper* and that sort of thing."
Other comments on female weakness for the "stars"
were:

1. *Man of* 19. "It's a dangerous thing, it's only done
to take people's minds off things, and there's enough harm
done without that. Both my sisters are mad on that sort of
thing, they look at the *Express* every morning. My mother's
always at 'em about it, though. She told them they'd be
nervous wrecks if they kept on swallowing that sort of stuff."
2. *Woman about* 38. "Whenever I open my mouth and
ask what do the stars say to-day, Harry, that's my husband,
is always telling me not to be silly. Course I only treat-it
as a joke."
3. *Man of* 50. "That horoscope stuff, all the papers are
doing it now, they wouldn't do it if there weren't a demand
for it. In my opinion it's for the women, you can kid them.
The reason why they get away with it is they never tell
anything definite. I don't think there's many men read
them, if they did they wouldn't admit it."
4. *Man of* 45. "No, I never bother with it, but there
are folks, especially in the football season, who use all sorts
of things like that for marking their coupons. The women
are crazy about it, that and spiritualism. Can't say as I
know why it is."

Here are some of the people who believe in it:

1. *Woman.* "I read where there's going to be a war soon, it said so in the *People*, they tell you what's going to be, there's *more* than something in it."

2. *Woman of 35.* "I've had lots of things told me that were true, and there's nobody can deny it. I used to look at them every day, I don't bother so much now because it doesn't make any difference."

3. *Woman of 38.* "I read them every Sunday, many a time it's been true, but they don't give you so much bad news. When it was my birthday they said I should get a surprise. I got one. It was a good 'un, mister. No, I'm not telling you what it was, that's my business."

4. *Woman of 32.* "Come to think of it, there's more of that sort of thing now than ever there was when I was a girl. I was brought up not to dabble in that sort of thing, but I don't know as I think the same now. There's things happening in these days make you wonder where you are."

5. *Woman of 36.* "I read them now and again. Sometimes I think they're right, sometimes you don't know what they mean, but you can see it after. Never given much thought to it, but I should say I believe it."

6. *Woman of 42.* "Yes, I look at them things about the stars, I believe in 'em, they tell you what's true if you know what I mean. . . . I go sometimes to a spiritualist meeting when things get too bad, I believe in it, there's more in it than you think . . . they told me my mother's name and described her, said my husband would lose his job, and he did, what d'yer think of that, it makes you think there's something in it."

7. *Woman of 45.* "I believe in it, I've been to lots of Circles (séances). There's a lot of comfort in it, there's nothing to be afraid of, I've talked to my Mother lots of times."

The last two comments disclose the borderland of superstition where anything can be believed if there is "comfort" in it. "When things get too bad" there are many who turn to magic. In a crisis, for example, like that of Sudetenland.

2

CRISIS

(a) What is a Crisis?

THIS word CRISIS has no very exact meaning, but it has come to be one of those things, like epidemics and earthquakes, which suddenly arrive to threaten the security of our ordinary lives. In the ordinary way, the interest of private people in public events is fitful and vague; at times of Crisis it extends and increases. The biggest of all recent crises—bigger than any of the scares of war—was the Abdication Crisis, although this did not threaten to affect the lives of ordinary people in the same concrete way as war or severe economic crisis would do. The attitude of the masses to Crisis is very imperfectly understood by the minority who control the sources of opinion. Baldwin steered through the Abdication Crisis, and Chamberlain through the War Crisis of September, 1938: how they were able to do it is a question worth more serious inquiry than it has yet received. If one was to believe, for example, all that was said by "intelligent people" about the state of public opinion at these times, the only answer to the question would be that a miracle happened in each case. But in fact these "intelligent people" have a deep-seated tendency to base their estimates of public opinion not on factual observation but on their own personal judgment. Their judgment is usually wrong, because they do not realise that their picture of the world is different from that of the mass of people:

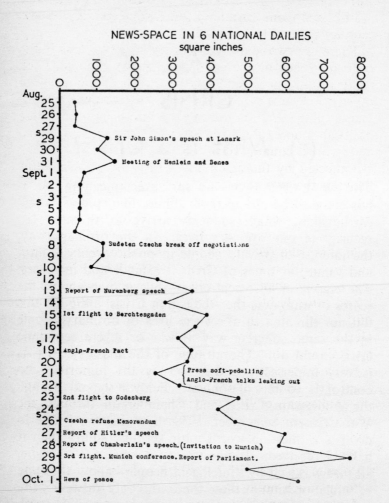

NEWS-SPACE IN 6 NATIONAL DAILIES
square inches

Sir John Simon's speech at Lanark

Meeting of Henlein and Benes

Sudeten Czechs break off negotiations

Report of Nuremberg speech

1st flight to Berchtesgaden

Anglo-French Pact

Press soft-pedalling
Anglo-French talks leaking out

2nd flight to Godesberg

Czechs refuse Memorandum
Report of Hitler's speech
Report of Chamberlain's speech.(Invitation to Munich)
3rd flight. Munich conference. Report of Parliament.
News of peace

Amount of column inches in national press devoted to foreign
politics, September 1938. This provides a good barometer of
crisis fluctuations.

from the very nature of their jobs and language they are isolated from "ordinary folk" who are the ultimate (voting) arbiters in a democracy.

There are two kinds of focus on society. One is the ordinary focus of the ordinary man or woman which centres round home and family, work and wages. The other is the political focus, which centres round government policy and diplomacy. What happens in this political sphere obviously affects the sphere of home and work; equally obviously, political developments are affected by the reactions of ordinary people. But between the two there is a gulf—of understanding, of information and of interest. This gulf is the biggest problem of our highly organised civilisation.

How far and in what way does and can the ordinary man share the responsibility for political decisions and events? Hitler, in a speech at Nüremberg, pointed to one possible answer when he said to 180,000 followers: "You can rely blindly on me, just as I can rely blindly on you. . . . You can make it easy for me to lead Germany." But even a dictator must try to convince his followers that he is leading them the right way, if their support is to be effective. And he must convince them that he is convinced; e.g., Hitler again: "I am the spokesman of the German nation and I know that every one of a people of millions agrees with my words and confirms my view."

Between one Crisis and another, diplomats and statesmen go on with their work, without limelight, without much notice being taken. But with the Crisis, a flock of other abstractions appear in the newspapers to perplex the public mind—"tension" becomes greater or less, the "situation" gets better or worse, the "problem" is solved or unsolved. To most people these abstractions are as mystical as the Voice of the Stars.

At the present stage of Western civilisation changes are taking place with such rapidity that there is in a sense a continuous crisis. In Fleet Street or Whitehall this is obvious enough, but the further you move from such centres, the less real does this conception of Crisis appear. The newspapers which cater for the administrative and professional classes occupy much space each day with foreign and political news, but the mass-circulation papers have a quite different emphasis. For them a 'plane crash in Edmonton is front-page news, when a war in Spain is crowded right out of the paper. To anyone who is only conscious of the headlines in the mass papers, it must seem that Crisis is something which comes along suddenly out of the blue and as rapidly disappears again.

In the last few years, events have become increasingly spectacular and crises more frequent. As a result, a great many people started being interested in foreign affairs and political issues for the first time. As one crisis succeeds another, one might expect that this interest would grow. But when M-O asked 460 people if their interest in Crises was increasing or decreasing, the results pointed quite clearly to a decrease of interest. This and other questions, which will be dealt with later, were asked at the end of August, 1938, when the Czechoslovakia Crisis was already prominent. These were the results:

	MALE		FEMALE		TOTAL
	Aged 30 & under	Over 30	30 and under	Over 30	
Interest	%	%	%	%	%
increasing	22	29	23	30	26
decreasing	42	36	43	38	40
stationary	23	14	8	16	16
negative	13	21	26	16	18

The important point to notice is that the largest group here is that which is feeling a definite decreasing interest in crises. Not only does this group outnumber

those whose interest is increasing, but it is larger than
the stationary and negative answerers put together.
The decrease of interest is most marked in those under
30, and about equal for men and women. Men
under 30 tend more to have a stationary interest than the
others; and women under 30 have the highest proportion of negative answers.

Here are some typical answers from those whose
interest is decreasing:

1. *Toolmaker*, 27. "Decreasing—for years we've heard
so much of them that we're a trifle wary."

2. *Mechanic (Territorials)*, 42. "Less—it's all a lot of
play and counterplay between diplomats and politicians—
incomprehensible to me."

3. *Insurance official*, 44. "Decreasing, realising the
futility of the ordinary man without organisation as against
big business and the financiers behind it."

4. *Typist, female*, 25. "Decreasing. There's always some
crisis. If it's not Spain it's Japan."

5. *Butcher*. "Makes me sick to open a paper or listen
to the news on the wireless."

6. *Textile warp-twister*, 33. "Decreasing. Not yet
uninterested, but getting callous and indifferent. Refuse
to be made ill and alarmed by horror reports."

7. *Science teacher, female*, 24. "Decreasing, so much
so that I dislike listening to the news. There was a time
when I hated to miss the news."

8. *Clerk*, 18. "I take little interest in any of the accounts
of crises—I am getting tired of people talking about wars
in Spain and China, and if people start talking about another
war I feel like saying 'For goodness sake shut up'."

9. *Deputy registrar, female*, 26. "Decreasing interest,
it's too blasted uncomfortable."

10. *Social worker, female*, 28. "Decreasing, because the
helplessness of the individual appals me."

This decreasing interest is highly significant as a
reflection of the stage our society has reached. It is
partly a defence against nervous strain, partly a kind of

fatalism, partly a mistrust of newspaper information.
Broadly speaking, it is a symptom of a serious breakdown
in the relation between the individual and society.

The analysis that follows is based on:

(*a*) A national survey made at the time of Eden's resignation in February, 1938.

(*b*) An intensive survey of a by-election of 1938, in a
London borough called "Metrop" which we study as a
typical constituent part in a great metropolitan area.

(*c*) Observations on reactions in the typical Northern
industrial town, Worktown, where Mass-Observation's
special survey is centred.

(*d*) A national survey on people's attitude to the war
danger, end of August, 1938.

(*e*) Study of how newspapers, radio, etc., treated Czech-
Sudeten crisis, August 25–September 30, 1938.

(*f*) Repeat observations in Metrop, September, 1938.

(*g*) Reports from London and elsewhere on reactions
to the Czech crisis, September, and observer reports on
Whitehall, Westminster, etc.

(b) The Making of Opinion

"This is the Chrysis of Parliaments; we shall know by
this if Parliaments live or die."

So said Sir B. Rudyard in 1627.   It is the first instance
recorded in the *New English Dictionary* of the use of the
word CRISIS in its political sense.   In 1775 there began
to appear a rare periodical called *The Crisis*, anonymous,
written possibly by Tom Paine.   The motto: *Potius visa
est periculosa libertas quieto servitio*—Better a dangerous
liberty than a tranquil slavery.   Numbers were as follows:

No. 1. To the People of England and America.
No. 2. A Bloody Court, a Bloody Ministry, and a Bloody
Parliament.

No. 3. To the King.
No. 4. Ye Conspirators. . . .
No. 5. To the People.
No. 6. To the Right Hon. Lord North . . .
etc.

No. 3 was burnt by the hangman at the Royal Exchange. "As soon as the fire was lighted before the Exchange it was immediately put out, and dead dogs and cats thrown at the officer." The matter was taken up by Lord Effingham in the House of Lords, where he said: "That the said pamphlet is a false, seditious and dangerous libel, subversive of the principles of the glorious Revolution to which we owe our present invaluable constitution, and of the rights of the people." The first number begins:

"To the People of England and America. Friends and Fellow Subjects, It is with the greatest propriety I address this Paper to you: It is in your Defence, at this GREAT, this IMPORTANT *CRISIS*, I take the pen in hand: A *CRISIS*, big with the Fate of the most glorious Empire known in the Records of Time; and by your Firmness and Resolution ONLY can it be saved from DESTRUCTION. . ."

In 1832 the Socialist Robert Owen published a periodical called *The Crisis*. The Prospectus to Volume I begins:

"It is now evident to everyone who observes passing events, and who reflects upon the new public opinion which is arising throughout the various Nations of the World, that some great Change in the condition of Man, either for good or for evil, is about to take place—in fact, that a *momentous* CRISIS is at hand. Be it our task to discern the signs of the times—to watch the progress of this Crisis, and to direct it for good instead of evil. . . ."

In the *Communist Manifesto*, drafted by Marx and Engels in 1848, there is mention of "crises that by their periodical return put the existence of the entire bourgeois society on its trial, each time more threateningly".

The idea of national or international crisis is one which we all accept as a feature of the times we live in. Crisis is a kind of melting-point for boundaries, institutions, opinions. In a crisis, public opinion, which at other times is largely inert, becomes a real factor. How is opinion made?

In the survey on the danger of war, 1,100 people were asked: "On what do you base your opinion?" Answers showed us:

	%
Newspapers	35
Friends	17
Radio	13
"Own opinion"	8
Recent History or travel	8
Books	5
Other factors (instinct, economics, observation, human nature, etc.)	10
Negative	4

Newspapers, therefore, easily lead in importance among the factors that make opinion. Yet dependent as they are on the newspapers for the data on which to base their opinion, at the same time they distrust them. It is like being led through strange country by a guide who may turn out to be a gangster in disguise. Hence most opinion, except the most fanatical, is tinged with uncertainty as to whether the ordinary man is in a position to have an opinion at all. This point has been illustrated already, but to clinch it, here are some comments from "Metrop" during the middle of the crisis of September 1938:

1. *Woman of* 33. "I read all the papers on it. I don't understand the politics of it, but they are all different. That's why people have less faith in the papers."

2. *Taxi-driver*, **40**. "There'll not be a war, it's all paper talk. It's serious, though, the papers make it worse. They have to give us something every day, though, it sells them."

3. *Man of* 38. "Got that I don't believe the papers now, they tell you all sorts, they're all different. When Hitler says nothing, it's guess-work."

4. *Youth of* 20. "Don't take any notice, mate. What's the good? If they want yer they'll take yer. They don't ask your permission like.

Got used to seein' it on the boards (placards). . . ."

5. *Shop assistant*, 25. "I stopped bothering about it . . . It's every day they say it's worse, then it changes, let it come, it'll be the end of everything . . . who cares?

It'll make things better while they want us, then if you don't get bumped off, well you can be a bloody hero for a while. They don't talk so much about it now, they've got fed up with having the wind up."

6. *Woman of* 35. "Of course it takes educated people to understand it all. They say we have to defend our country. I don't think Chamberlain wants war, of course we never know the truth. . . . The papers, you read them and you are more in the dark still.

I work in an office, but they don't talk now about it, they're all sick with fright of it."

7. *Woman of* 38. "We don't bother much about it . . . not because we are not thinking about it. Life's too short to keep on with war, war, war.

I don't think they will and I hope they don't. That's what I think. . . . It's too much to cope with, and we can't do anything."

8. *Man of* 53. "One day it's one thing, next day it's another. It gets you fed up."

9. *Woman of* 40. "Oh, when I see the paper I turn the page over. Suppose it's because I'm windy . . ."

10. *Woman of* 42. "It's for them as is in power, they're the people to ask. I think there will be one soon, don't you, but what's the good of worrying about it, that's no use now.

It's a crisis every day if you believe the papers. If Hitler wants one, well he'll have it, then we have a war whether we want it or not.

I'm not worried about other things in the political line. It's not an election, is it?"

Opinion is made in two ways. It is made by each single person looking at the facts, as far as they are available, and then framing his own judgment on them. It is also made by the reaction of each single person to the opinions of other people. Few people are so confident of their own judgment (whatever they may say) as to be uninfluenced by knowing what other people are thinking. It is here that the newspapers play an important role. For the newspapers not only state *their* version of the facts—they also state *their* version of the public opinion of the moment.

During the Czech crisis, in September, 1938, newspapers were continually saying "The entire public thinks this" or "The entire public thinks that". These pronouncements, which frequently contradicted each other, were not based on scientific estimates but on personal impressions helped out by personal wish-thinking. A detailed study of the six "populars" (*Express, Herald, Chronicle, Mail, Mirror, Sketch*) over several months showed this tendency to be an important factor in the building of crisis mentality. The fluctuations in the amount of space devoted by newspapers to the crisis are shown in the form of a graph on page 24.

A working-class man, aged 45, interviewed in New Cross on September 22, made the position clear when he said:

"I'm just a working-class man and I'm as entitled to an opinion as anybody else. We've let them down good and proper. That is the opinion of all working-class people. You should read the *Star* to-night and see for yourself."

The only means by which this man can tell what others like himself are thinking (apart from the few he meets and talks to) is through the newspapers and their estimates of public opinion.   It is their function to give these estimates, and they have an obvious responsibility to see that what they say about opinion is firmly founded on fact, and that it is stated as clearly as possible.   Unfortunately, although the papers are always playing up to the desire for this kind of information, they take little trouble to be factual about it.

The *Star*, to which the man quoted refers, published throughout the crisis articles by R. G. Cruikshank, its intelligent, progressive-minded editor, under the *nom de plume* of "The Man in the Street".   On the day when the remark was made, there appeared in the *Star* a striking article by the Man in the Street called "My Country".   He said:

"What do I mean when I say 'my country'?   It is one of those words that always call up pictures in the mind. When I hear it used, even in a hot political debate, I see some concrete image like the Sussex Downs sleeping in the sunshine, or the rich tangle of flower and leaf in a Warwickshire lane.

But beyond those gracious visions, what comes into the mind?   The big cities, many of them as ugly as the countryside is fair; the smoke and steam and tall chimneys of the industrial districts; the forgotten heroes of the Black Areas; and, above all, millions of simple, ordinary folk asking only to be allowed to go about their business and to bring up their families without interference.

What are they all thinking in these strange times?   By such tokens as come to me, through letters and by word of mouth, I gather that their feelings are as strangely confused as the times.   A deep yearning for peace is shot through by dismay at the humiliation of surrender.   Men's minds are harbouring the most contradictory thoughts.   The country is in a ferment as never before, not even during Abdication week."

In the past, editor Cruikshank has had long talks with mass-observers, with whose aims he was in sym-

B

pathy and with whose point of view he approximates in this article. But in making these key statements about public opinion, it is *not enough* to rely on personal impressions based on "such tokens as come, through letters and by word of mouth". Why cannot the great newspapers, with all the machinery at their disposal, make some effort to be scientific on this all-important question? By failing to do so, they forfeit their potential right to act as the voice of everyman—they have to be counted among the forces which make for confusion. In the same article, Cruikshank goes on to say:

"To those who are sick at heart—and I know that they are many—I should like to say, if they will let me, 'Keep steady!' The worst of all surrenders is to lose confidence in one's country. Remember that the people of England have not yet been heard from. They will speak in due season."

Why, one is bound to ask, shouldn't they speak *now*, if the newspapers were really prepared to let them do so?

Some light is thrown on the way that editors and other leaders of opinion form their own opinion and what "such tokens as come, through letters, etc.", really amount to, by these glimpses of them reported by an observer:

"In a —— Newspaper offices, Sept. 16, 1938, an Editor and the Syndicating Manager discuss the international situation, say it seems no better, that Chamberlain's move is a good one for him but no good internationally. After 5 minutes, Editor sums up: 'I don't think we know what's going on.' To which Syndicating Manager replies as he goes off: 'Yes, it's a very funny affair altogether.'"

"A labour M.P., on Saturday night, Sept. 17, talking to observer, complained that the people had no idea what was going on. 'Here am I, a Member of Parliament, a representative of the people, and I am impotent. There is NOTHING I can do.'

Reynolds News ring up and ask for a message on international situation. Writes out one about Beneš, who ought to be consulted, why have the Czechs been left out of consultation. Observer types it out and *Reynolds* send small boy down to collect it.''

"Tuesday night, Sept. 20. At house of prominent Conservative M.P. All listen to 6 o'clock news. From this source he gets his information. Three telegrams from constituents—none known to him—urge action to save Czechoslovakia. Phone call saying *Telegraph* have accepted his letter on Czechoslovakia. Says 'The *Telegraph* are coming round.' Is excited. Also says 'Good' when announcer says Czechs have NOT accepted Paris–London terms. Is then rung by *News Chronicle*, who ask for a letter. Drafts this, then asks wife to read this. She suggests 'common people' instead of 'people'. Then ring from Maurice Dobb, Cambridge leftist, saying huge meeting of Cambridge professors, etc., will he speak Sunday there. Then phone call from West Riding of Yorks, from a wool merchant, saying how worried everyone is in the clubs, etc., re government policy.—He imitates accent.

This in one hour. Also he phones friends to say may he come late to dinner, 8.30. O.K., he may.

He stresses his own feeling of impotence. . . .''

Yet the newspapers and public men speak confidently enough to the outside world. The swift sequence of events and statements and counter-statements by rival propagandist news-agencies make it more or less inevitable that what is printed as news one day should be denied the next, often in the same paper. Most people have come to expect this, though it isn't helpful in encouraging the masses to trust their own judgment. But there is less reason for the journalistic habit of making statements and assumptions about the public mind which it would be perfectly possible to verify. In some cases the falsification may be deliberate, but in most it is just a lack of objectivity, an easy attitude to fact, which seems to beset even those with goodwill enough to do better. Most of the papers have made some show of asking the "Man in the Street" what he is thinking, but though it probably takes many people in, it is unconvincing judged by any sort of scientific standard. It may have value as propaganda, but it is dangerous to treat it as fact.

The habit is illustrated in its crude form by statements such as these:

September 9:
D. Herald. Leader. ". . . the majority of people now feel that the Czechs have made their full contribution to the cause of peace, and that it is now the turn of the others. . ."

September 10:
D. Mail. Leader. "In this crisis the whole country will stand solidly behind the Government."
D. Mirror. Leader. "Humanity is facing the most dangerous week-end since 1914, but in a mood of solemn calm."

September 12:
D. Herald. Leader. "The British nation is completely united. They see no shadow of reason for anything but a frank and complete acceptance of the last Czech offer as a basis for negotiation."
D. Express. "Europe awaits Monday night at seven."
Star. Leader. "ENGLAND SPEAKS. The country remains admirably calm in these hours of deepening crisis. . . . It is the steady spirit of a nation that has made up its mind and faces the future unafraid."

September 19:
D. Mail. Leader. "The British nation unreservedly places its complete trust in the Prime Minister, Mr. Neville Chamberlain."

The point about these statements is not that they are true or false, but that it is *assumed* that there is no need to find out if they *are* true. More subtle are statements

which appeal to facts, but without establishing those
facts objectively. A. J. Cummings is typical of those
who accept the principle of observation—that we ought
to know what the man in the street is thinking—without
accepting the need for a technique to insure that our
findings are objective. In his "Spotlight on Politics",
on September 8, he wrote under the heading: The Facts
Break Through:

"The man in the street, exemplifying the entire British
nation, has made up his mind that Hitlerism stands for
war, that Hitler himself is to-day the supreme menace to
the peace of the world, and that until this menace is in some
way disposed of there can be no security for any nation
and no progress towards a more decent and humane
civilisation.

Go into any club, wayside inn or private house in the
land and you will find opinion in all classes crystallised into
this implacable view of the situation. . . ."

On September 14, John Bouverie in the *News Chronicle*
wrote:

"In the last 72 hours British public opinion, as expressed
in newspapers and in conversation among all classes, has
quite remarkably hardened. . . ."

By September 22, A. J. Cummings was telling off *The
Times* for saying it was a slander to pretend that Britain
had "capitulated to a German show of force". He
said:

"If the editor of *The Times* has any honest doubt about
the British view let him make inquiries among members of
his own staff.

Better still, let him take an evening off, go out into the
streets and put the same question systematically to a thousand
passers-by. . . ."

There is no indication that Cummings himself made
this experiment. If he had, he would not have sug-

gested that one man could get a thousand opinions
in a single evening. The same day, John Bouverie
wrote:

"At moments of supreme crisis democracy is not allowed
to function. The bosses simply say: 'It is too delicate a
situation to permit of our divulging the facts.'"

In contrast to this point of view, the *Daily Sketch* dis-
courages the inquisitive. On September 9, their leading
article:

"The situation is changing hour by hour in Czechoslovakia,
hopes are born only to be dashed, rumours arise and are
contradicted. Britons, normally uninterested in foreign
affairs, ask each other: 'What do you think will happen?'
—and the pessimist is, in his own melancholy way,
happy.
It is in this uncertain atmosphere that the calibre of the
individual, as of a nation, undergoes a severe test. On
the whole we are reacting to this strain upon the nerves
in a very creditable way.
Our duty at this time is to preserve both the appearance
and the reality of national unity. There must be no
wobbling. . . .
An old slogan is a good one: 'Leave it to the man at the
wheel.'"

On September 22, *Sketch* leader-writer Candidus pursued
the same theme under the title "Don't talk to the Man
at the Wheel":

"You cannot drive a car if everyone is shouting advice
to you all the time; the word of the captain of a ship is
final; and for the same reason a Prime Minister must be
allowed to choose his own time for making explanations and
seeking advice."

But though Candidus warns the masses not to be
inquisitive about facts, in another article he encourages
them to have "feelings" of a positively mystical kind:

"All sorts of people have said to me in the last few days that they do not 'feel' as though the present crisis over Czechoslovakia would lead to war; I have myself what I can describe as a 'feeling' that there will be no war."

He goes on to talk about "minds like wireless sets" and "half-heard mysterious harmonics of an imperfectly comprehended cosmos". In effect, he is advocating the same state of mind as that which Hitler recommends: "You can rely blindly on me, just as I can rely blindly on you." The *Daily Express* is more negative when it says that:

"We must grow accustomed to this state of strain and must understand that there is peace so long as there is no war. This attitude of mind should, of course, present no difficulties to a nation like ourselves, steeped in centuries of traditions of strength."

The *Daily Mirror* leader-writer, W. M., strikes a more popular line when he writes (September 23):

"What do we know this morning?
Not much."

The *Daily Herald* leader-writer, on the other hand, joins the hush-hushers, by implication, when he writes (September 10):

"Not to believe, not to spread, sensational or tendentious rumour or wild speculation is at this time both a national duty and a really valuable contribution to the cause of peace."

A week later the *Herald* announced as its front-page news-lead that the Sudeten party had split, describing it as an event of the highest importance. In their next issue, September 19, the leader-writer says:

"It is clear that the reports of a great rupture in the Sudeten German leadership are not well founded."

On its picture page on September 15, the *Herald*
printed, under the heading "What the Average Man—
and Woman—are Saying", six photographs and interviews with people in the crowd at Whitehall. One of
them was Miss Margaret Schimkaite, of Memel, Lithu-
ania; she said: "I do not think there will be a war."
In spite of this international touch, the general effect
of these interviews was not illuminating.

The *News Chronicle* repeated this experiment on
September 20[1]. Again, six people were questioned and
photographed. All but one thought that Britain should
have supported Czechoslovakia against Hitler. In this
case, M-O collected evidence which is given more
fully later. It shows a majority, including Labour
supporters, applauding Chamberlain's flight. Then,
when the London-Paris terms became known, an increasing anti-Chamberlain reaction, greater on September
21 and 22, than on Monday, September 19, when
Chronicle reporter had his interviews. But on these
two days, in every 100 people questioned 36 opposed
the Chamberlain plan, 22 in favour—other views
negative or mixed. There is a difference between the
observed ratio of 36: 22 and the *Chronicle* ratio of 5:1.
A couple of reporters could have collected better
data in a few hours, and made a contribution to
public knowledge.

(c) Bewildered

"It's a good thing to keep people in the dark. No panic.
If it comes it comes."

"I don't know what the Government is up to."

---

[1] On September 29, *N.C.* did it again, including this time
Scandinavian Sea-Scout Otto Nilssen. But they alone responded
to crisis by subsequently getting "exclusive rights" on Inst. of
Public Opinion ballots.

"I'm not sufficiently educated to say."

"I can't say whether they're doing right or not."

"I can't understand it properly, but it doesn't seem too good to me."

"I don't take that much interest."

"I don't support this Government or any Government. I would vote Labour. But when they get into power they always let us down."

"I don't understand so I don't like to express my opinions."

"It's a f——ing mêss, ain't it?"

"Don't know. You never know what they're hiding from you."

"No one knows what'll happen."

"The thing to do is to clear out. It's difficult otherwise to know what to do."

"We ain't got a chance. There's things going on we don't know about."

Thus did Metrops answer the question: "What do you think about the country's foreign policy?" when it was put to them in March, 1938. Of those asked, 35% did not answer at all. Of those who did answer, 28% were satisfied with the Government policy, 32% were not satisfied, and the remaining largest group of 40% were those who gave answers like the ones quoted above—uncertain, ignorant, bewildered.

Baldwin's sealed lips typified an era in which Those Who Know won't tell, and the newspapers tell whatever suits their book, with contradictory effect. Eden's resignation marked another phase in the thickening secrecy. Up till that moment our rulers were supposed to be of a single mind. If we didn't like what they were doing, it was because we didn't know what they knew. Trust Baldwin. But now here was one of them coming out into the open with his dissatisfaction. Certainly we couldn't see clearly what issues were involved— Mr. Eden did not help us very much on this point. But it was fairly obvious that there were two alternative views, that our wonderful Prime Minister held one of them and our brilliant Foreign Secretary the other. Was it possible that we ourselves might be given a chance of expressing our views as to which was right? But no attempt was made to ask for our views. With the greatest despatch the veil of secrecy was drawn close again, and the undivided front of the Government was maintained.

Eden's general popularity, especially with women, helped to make a sensational story of his resignation, and it reached through to sections of the population not usually touched by political happenings. This was apparent when of people all over the country asked by M-O if they were following the news on February 23, 82% were following it; but of these, 43% believed some but not all of it, and a further 21% did not believe any of it. So if the behaviour of the politicians made it difficult for the ordinary man and woman to understand what was up, the newspapers certainly didn't improve matters.

Asked "What ought Britain's policy to be?" the answers were roughly in the same proportion as the Metrop answers quoted above. A third had no idea at all. And two-thirds could give no answer when asked "What does Eden's resignation mean?"

The Eden crisis was surveyed in "Worktown" also. On February 21 when his resignation was announced in headlines everywhere, people questioned were unanimous in saying they had followed the news, but only one in fifteen believed all that was in the papers. Analysis of 15,000 conversations recorded in Worktown has established that on an ordinary day only 0.3% of the conversations are about politics; but on February 21 this rose to 4%, a tribute to Mr. Eden's popularity in Worktown.

On Saturday, March 13, Hitler marched into Austria, and this time the effect on Worktown was rather more noticeable. In conversation, politics reached a record of 6% on the Monday. Four young men were overheard saying:

1. "There's nowt in t'bloody paper?"
2. "How's Hitler going on?"
3. "Oh, Austria's buggered now."
4. "It seemed like it on Saturday."

As well as overhearing and recording 310 conversations, observers made 100 interviews, mostly in full detail, but one notably brief. Observer asked barmaid: "What do you think about the Austrian crisis?" She replied: "Oh, I'm not fussy."

Unlike the Eden crisis, considerable knowledge of the situation was shown. The questioners, unusually, never felt they were being a nuisance, but rather that they were providing pleasure in stimulating discussion. To the question: "What do you think of the Austria business?" the answers came:

Good
Austria is German territory **4**

Bad

Bad, pretty bad; looks bad	15	
Serious, might be serious; pretty serious. .	33	
Hitler's made a mess of things, what can you expect from Hitler	14	**69**
League of Nations should have kept together	3	
Black; very black	4	

Unsure

Don't know what to think	10	
Difficult to understand	2	**27**
Don't know anything about it; no concern of ours	15	

This time, instead of political intrigue which no one could fathom, the definite and clear-cut fact of Hitler's occupation of Austria gave the ordinary man something he could chew on. But when the further question was asked: "What can be done about it?" though only two have no opinion, and over half are sufficiently opposed to Hitler's gesture to say that something should be done about it, this time nearly all show bewilderment. One way in which to satisfy the feeling that something should be done was the calling of a protest meeting. Typically, it came off in the Co-op hall three weeks after the crisis, by which time the town was back to its usual 0.3% political talk. Total present: 100.

(d) What can we do that matters?

Eden's resignation was understood by many people to mean that the Government had reversed the policy on which it had been elected to power. This might have been in accordance with the wishes of the general public or it might not; without an election surely, impossible to tell. Individuals were faced with the question whether there was anything they could do about such a situation. When this question was put in the national survey at that time, it was found that 52% thought nothing could be done, and 11% gave no opinion.

For every 100 holding the former point of view, 42 thought the situation was not dangerous and therefore presumably there was no need to do anything. Another 17 gave no opinion on this point, but the remaining and most interesting group of 41 thought *both* that the situation was dangerous *and* that there was nothing to be done about it. Such a state of mind can only be described as despairing fatalism, and it is extremely significant as an indication of the individual's lack of faith in the society to which he or she belongs. This is the sort of answer in which it expresses itself:

1. "As ordinary individuals. No—except wait for the inevitable general election and for the first time in our lives really attend the platforms of the individuals we wish to vote for, and endeavour to make them realise that as a partly-educated people we insist upon the full publication of international correspondence in which we as a nation must be gravely interested. It is obvious that as we, the mass of people, progress in thought and reading, we no longer feel an absolute trust in the infallibility of a bickering set of political statesmen whose interests are of necessity the selfish interests of their own small group or clique, and not that of the vaster numbers of those who though far from wealthy or the representatives of the wealthy groups, yet contain probably 90% of the total intelligence of the country."

2. "No, inclined to feel that we are pawns in the professional politicians' game."

3. "No. We are helpless to prevent the Government doing as it will abroad. You can't trust any of them. Too much intrigue of which ordinary man knows nothing, so can never really judge for himself."

4. "Not much faith in anything I personally can do—of large enough number, yes. I suppose there is something we could do.
Puzzled to know what to do. Difficult to get together—a connecting link needed."

5. "Feel myself too old to take much interest in public affairs, that no one can do anything very much, individually; it is all very distressing, best to forget it if possible and talk of something else."

6. "Take very little interest in public affairs, so have no suggestion as to what I personally can do. Feel I must try to shut my mind to it all, because of state of nerves. Everything too worrying. Nothing much ordinary people can do."

These answers relate to the possibility of doing anything about the situation arising from Eden's resignation, and therefore by implication, though not directly, about the danger of war. When the question was asked at Metrop, it was related directly to the war danger, but bearing this in mind we can compare the two sets of figures. At Metrop in March 36% thought nothing could be done, and another 21% showed doubt or disinterest. If we add together the two latter groups, both negative, we get roughly the same proportion as in the other survey. Over half the total answerers lacked conviction that there is anything we can do about it. Here are examples of these attitudes:

SOMETHING CAN BE DONE.

Cabdriver, 55. "I'd like to have a go at f——ing Hitler meself." Goes on to say that he would not mind a war if it gave him a chance to act in the way specified.

Woman, 40. "We should take a firm stand."

Woman, 40, *lower middle class.* "Christianity is the only hope."

Chauffeur, 40. "Keep out of entanglements, that's the best. Old England's the best country in the world."

Worker, 35. "Just keep on arming as long as the others do."

Man, 30, *middle class.* "Stop him next time."

Man, 45, *middle-class Jew.* "Bump Hitler off. Only: no good. Another would take his place, I suppose."

It will be seen that many of these who think something can be done are not, really, very helpful.

NOTHING CAN BE DONE.

(21% of the 36% who thought nothing could be done about the state of the world, thought of the matter personally.)

Man, 35, *lower middle class.* "There's nothing we can do about it."

Worker, 55. "Don't see what we can do."

Worker, 50. "Have to fight, I suppose. We'll probably get conscription."

Worker, 25. "Go out and get shot, I suppose."

Worker, 30. "We've got to fight if we've got to fight."

Man, 55. "Don't think we'll have the chance to do anything when it comes."

Man, 45. "Nobody knows when it breaks out."
Woman, 50, *lower middle class.* "No one strong enough
in the opposition to take over. The country's in the hands
of the Jews."

As will be noticed, many of these link on to the
bewildered group, below.

DOUBT AND DISINTEREST.
Worker, 67. "I don't know. These bloody Fascists. It's
the women and kids I'm thinking of."
Woman, 55, *lower middle class.* "Heaven knows."
Man, 40, *worker.* "I'm not interested."
Man, 35, *lower middle class.* "Don't know what can be
done."
Man, 20, *worker.* "Don't know what we should do."

Here again the overwhelming impression is one of
fatalism and apathy. From the 460 answers to the
general survey on the war danger made at the end of
August, 1938, we can see how the attitudes are crystal-
lising in face of new crises and dangers, war preparations
and counter-preparations. Two questions were asked:

A. What do you suggest the ordinary man or woman
should do, if anything, in face of a danger of war ?[1]

[1] The answers to Question A can be divided into four groups,
namely:
    (i) *Work for peace,* including organisations such as the
Peace Pledge Union; educating opinion; conscientious objecting;
political action; changing Government; support for democratic
countries.
    (ii) *Co-operating with authorities,* supporting present Govern-
ment, joining A.R.P. or Territorials; "Do as Told"; "Be
Prepared".
    (iii) *Status Quo,* business as usual, keep your head, be under-
standing.
    (iv) *Negative,* nothing, don't know, die, get out of the way,
look after self.

The answers to Question B show a significant change. If war
did break out, what should we do ? This time there are five main
groups:
    (i) *Co-operate with authorities.* Join up with Army, Navy,
etc., volunteer for special jobs, medical, scientific, etc., volunteer

B. What will you actually do if war breaks out ?

Question A.

Age :	MALE 30 and under	MALE Over 30	FEMALE 30 and under	FEMALE Over 30
	%	%	%	%
Work for peace	30	22	18	19
Co-operate authorities	28	30	37	29
Status Quo	15	19	17	17
Negative	27	29	28	35

Here again (in Question A) there are about half and half of those who feel active and those who feel passive, in face of the war danger. But there is a slight increase on the positive side of the balance, and the action which it is suggested we *can* take has now found a more positive form. The most negative-minded are the women over 30. Most ready to co-operate with the authorities are the men over 30, and keenest on peace work are the younger men.

Question B

Age :	MALE 30 and under	MALE Over 30	FEMALE 30 and under	FEMALE Over 30
	%	%	%	%
Co-operate authorities	47	46	56	37
Qualified co-operation	13	9	15	4
Oppose	14	4	8	4
Negative	15	29	9	43
Individualist	11	12	12	12

---

for general usefulness; A.R.P. and defence; do as told; carry on as usual.

(ii) *Qualified co-operation.* Expecting to be conscripted; strictly humanitarian work; support if in agreement; follow conscience.

(iii) *Oppose.* Conscientious objection; passive resistance; revolutionary action.

(iv) *Negative.* Don't know.

(v) *Individualist.* Get out of way; look after self.

The most striking feature in Question B is the big increase in those who would co-operate with the authorities. Including those whose will to co-operate is qualified, this amounts to 58%, or well over half, as compared with 31% who are prepared to co-operate in face of the danger of war, but before it has started. The swing over to co-operation therefore amounts to 27%, or over a quarter of all who answer. What effect does this have on the other groups? The proportion of negative and individualist answers is roughly the same for Questions A and B, but the opposition group is reduced from 23% to 8%. The semi-indifferent Status Quo group of Question A answerers disappears in the real emergency, though it is replaced by those who carry on as usual as a form of patriotic co-operation; there are 12% of these included in the question B co-operating group.

Two curious but revealing answers to Question B:

1. *Business man*, 33. "A.R.P. Warden. Been in it from the start. Stick at my post till done for. Some use helping people not to panic. Think shall not panic myself. Expect to enjoy feeling useful. Life all along has seemed rather pointless. Hope that the end, if that was the end, might be worth while."

2. *Wife and mother*, 42. "I have been collecting poisons for some⸀time with guile and cunning. I have sufficient to give self, husband and all the children a lethal dose. I can remember the last war. I don't want to live through another, or the children either. I shan't tell them, I shall just do it."

This suicide talk is the last stage in the collapse of belief in any future. The same undercurrent runs through the replies to questioning in Metrop:

1. *Man of* 45. ". . . I'd rather see my two boys dead. I'd poison them if I thought it was coming."

2. *Woman of* 50. "I'd rather see my girl, who is my only one, killed outright than suffer it."

3. *Woman of* 33, *2 children.* "I want to see my children dead before I am if there is to be a war, and I'll see that they are if they bomb here."

4. *Woman of* 35. "I'd rather see the men dead by any means than to think of them lying blown to bits. . . ."

5. *Woman of* 45. "Want to know if there'll be a war? What sort, that's what matters. If there is one, well let's all get killed off in a lump. . . ."

6. *Woman of* 45, *3 children.* "You can't believe all the papers say . . . get my children out of it . . . rather see them dead first."

7. *Woman of* 34. "I'd sooner see kids dead than see them bombed like they are in some places. . . ."

To sum up the results arrived at so far, we find first of all a resistance to the idea that war is coming, and that this resistance grows as the danger of war is brought nearer. Secondly, that although most people are anxious and would like to know more about issues that they know to be a matter of life and death, they are discouraged and bewildered by the official secrecy and newspaper contradictions. Thence, thirdly, comes the sense of helplessness which makes it seem to one in every two that there is nothing we can do about it. Though it is only one in every three that thinks there is nothing we can do when war has actually begun.

"What do you think is the best thing that could happen in the present situation?" This question was put with the others in the national end-of-August survey, and the replies are extremely varied and in some cases obviously fantastic. It was no easy task sorting them into categories, and there remained at the end an irreducible 2% which was classified as "Peculiar", and which included:

"A new Leader for England, not a Dictator."

"The newspapers and the cinemas and the B.B.C. to preach the desirability of giving money and land to foreign peoples."

"Have Hitler examined."

"An earthquake."

"No crisis, no holidays with pay for M.P.'s on holiday."

"Shoot all power maniacs."

"The best thing is to get all the armament and war mongers together, and then painfully exterminate the lot, next best is to put the countries on a diet till they become democratic."

"If the City could be miraculously exterminated, things might be eased a little."

"Stop whiffle-whoffling."

"That a substantial comet should blow this planet to smithereens."

"That Chamberlain, Halifax and Simon, etc., should be assassinated."

"Treat Germany as though she did not exist."

"A few improvements in aircraft and explosives which would insure the entire extermination of both sides, especially the Governments."

"Let the situation talk itself out."

The "vagueness" of these answers is only an exaggeration of a genuinely existing muddle. We are in a mess, we are up to our necks in it and there is no sort of agreement as to how we can get out, if at all. Of all the wished-for ways out, that heard most often is the death of Hitler and Mussolini, resentment easily attaching itself to a single individual. Like this:

"Mussolini and Hitler want shooting."

"One or two of the dictators ought to be killed off."

"Kill Hitler and chloroform the Japs."

"That the European dictators should die in their beds."

"Bump off the dictators."

"Sudden death of Hitler."

"Someone should place a bomb on top of Goering, Hitler and Mussolini."

"Hitler to be killed or die."

"Hitler to be assassinated."

"That the three tyrants, Stalin, Hitler and Mussolini, should die."

"Pot shot at Hitler and Mussolini."

"I'd like someone to put a bullet in him (Hitler)."

"Spectacular and terrifying simultaneous bumping off of Hitler, Mussolini, the Japanese officers and Mr. Chamberlain."

"Somebody ought to shoot Hitler and all the other sods that are causing it all."

"Somebody to bump off Hitler."

"Paralytic stroke for Hitler and Mussolini."

"Mussolini and Hitler, together with Franco, to commit suicide."

"Shoot Hitler."

"Shoot all dictators and their adherents."

"A couple of shots (for Hitler and Mussolini)."

The next most frequently offered solutions are more "sensible": change of government in the Fascist countries, alliance between democratic countries. More than a quarter can offer no solution at all.

(e) Who's Afraid of the Big Bad Wolf?

Hanging over all our heads for years now has been the threat of another general European war. Practically every grown-up person in this country must have been conscious of this threat at one time or another. Since it is so much a matter of life and death, they must have some definite attitude about it.

How many people think there is going to be a war? One might have expected that the continuous bad news and the obvious preparations for war, rearmament, A.R.P. and the rest of it, would convince everybody that war was imminent. So it is interesting that the day after Hitler's Nuremberg speech on Monday, September 12, 1938, when war news filled the papers and the B.B.C.

was issuing special bulletins, questioning in working-class streets in Metrop showed a dominance of "there won't be a war" statements (A). Six months before, after Eden's resignation, but before Hitler marched into Austria, similar questioning in Metrop had shown under half saying there would be no war (B), while the national survey by M-O at the end of August, 1938, when the Czech crisis was already being taken seriously, produced results very similar to this (C).

	A	B	C
Said there would be no war	55%	42%	40%
Said they expected war	15	34	35
Were vague or did not know or care	30	24	25

Finally, at the time that Eden resigned (end of February, 1938), the national survey asked the question: "Do you think the situation is dangerous?" with the result that:

31% said it was not dangerous.
43% said it was.
26% were vague or did not know.

It is clear from these figures that so far from there having been an increase in the number of people who thought war was likely, less people said they thought so than earlier in the year. The most striking indication of this is in the two sets of figures from Metrop, which can be compared directly with each other, and which show that when the question was asked the second time, in the middle of the most serious crisis thus far, 13% more people said there would be no war and 20% less people said there would be a war.

Of course this is what people *say* they think. We cannot assume that it is what they actually think. But what people say is an important part of their total attitude. It certainly represents a vital part of the way they react to the danger of war. A possible explanation is that the worse things get, and the nearer the danger comes, the more necessary it is for people to put up a psychological defence in order to carry on with their daily lives. They *have* to hope for the best.

At Metrop in March, 1938, the people who said there would be no war can be divided into two groups, those who are absolutely certain there won't be a war, and those who qualify their answer into uncertainty, saying there won't be a war now, but there may be one sometime. The emphatic group of NO war, certainly not, are the smaller group, and speak as follows:

Man, 60, *lower middle class*. "No possibility of a war. We're building up huge army, etc., only for defence."

Woman, 45, *lower middle class*. "No possibility of a war."

Worker, 70. "No war. I don't think nothing ever happens."

Worker, 50. "I think the present policy will keep us out of trouble."

Curate, 30. "We are quite safe."

Woman, 45, *lower middle class*. "Halifax will keep us out of war."

Worker, 55, *worker*. "There won't be a war. Chamberlain is seeing to that."

Man, 65. "There won't be a war now. Situation has died down."

Now the type who say there won't be a war and then in some form admit the possibility:

Worker, 17. "Reckon we're in for a war."

Woman, 40, *lower middle class*. "Don't think there'll be a war for another three years."

Worker, 55. "I don't think we're in immediate danger of war."

Worker, 50. "There's trouble brewing. These armaments are not for nothing."

Man, 35, *lower middle class*. "I think we shall have another war sooner or later, not yet."

Worker, 25. "Not yet. If Czechoslovakia is invaded there will be a war."

Man, 25, *lower middle class*. "Think we'll muddle through."
Worker, 50. "Mussolini only kills blacks. Won't touch us."

There is a definite tendency for middle-class people to belong to this group, to say there will be peace, or peace in our time. There is no doubt that working-class people are more fatalistic about the whole business and do not rationalise their fear so much. Most of the women questioned had a less clear-cut idea than the men, and only half a dozen women admitted the war danger specifically. Here are some examples of the uncertain-bewildered-uninterested group:

Man, 45, *landlord of pub*. "I can't think. I hope it comes to nothing."
Woman, 40, *worker*. "If your name's on the bomb, it's all up with you. That's that. I don't read the newspapers."
Woman, 40, *lower middle class*. "They only do it to scare us."
Man, 45, *lower middle class*. "If things don't brighten up we shall see some trouble."
Man, 35, *worker*. "Over-population's the real trouble."
Woman, 50, *lower middle class*. "The country's in the hands of the Jews. My husband's as red as can be."

Twelve observers asked 125 Metrops this question, so that though the sample was too small, the distortion due to bias on the part of the observers was pretty well eliminated. In fuller detail:

	Percentage of total who gave this answer	Percentage of this type aged over 45 (approx.)	Percentage of this type who are women
Will be war	34	47	6
Won't be war (anyway yet)	42	29	17
Vague or don't know	24	27	55

Thus we see that older people tended more to say that there is sure to be war now. Many of these, over 45, were in the last war.[1]

The national survey also asked the question: "If you think war is coming, about when do you expect it?" Replies showed that:

18% expected war in the immediate future.
19% expected it next year (1939) or the year after.
27% in the next five or ten years, or not for some time.
20% thought it was remote or would never come.
16% did not know.

This indicates that the War-likely group can be divided into two roughly equal halves, one of which thinks war may come any day, while the other expects it to be postponed for some months at least. In the latest questioning at Metrop, only 15% said they expected war, though the newspapers were by that time taking a much more serious view of the crisis. It looks as if this 15% is the equivalent of the 18% in the national survey who think there is immediate danger of war. In that case many who previously would have said that

[1] The answers to the same question in the national survey at the end of August, 1938, worked out as follows:

| | MALE | | FEMALE | |
	30 and under	Over 30	30 and under	Over 30
	%	%	%	%
War likely	36	33	30	43
War unlikely	46	42	37	31
50–50 chance	14	18	22	10
Negative	4	7	11	16

In this sample, the women over 30 have the greatest expectation of war and also the greatest proportion of negative answers, i.e., don't know what to think. The men under 30 are least negative and also most sceptical about war danger.

war was coming have now, in face of a threatening crisis, taken up the line that "there will be no war".

We may suggest that there is an important conclusion to be drawn from all this: that as the danger of war comes nearer, so are people less able to admit it, partly through their own wish-thinking, partly through the increasing scarcity of facts. As we shall see, this was the source of the enormous sense of relief when it was known that Chamberlain was flying to see Hitler.

(f) Soaring, Sinking

While dramatically in Central Europe troops mustered and dictators thundered, all through September, 1938, in Britain the longest of all the crises was stirring up the soggy mess of public opinion. The stirring brought to the surface issues as important as those of war, annexation, minorities. The issue here was between leaders, news-givers and masses.

There were four peaks of crisis-interest—Nuremberg Night, Chamberlain's flight, the Further Demands and the Commons Hysteria. All but the third were essentially newspaper stories, with a strong personal angle; people who were not able to grasp difficult geographical and political realities could be made to respond to the personality-magic of Hitler and Chamberlain, the blood-thirsty bogey and the Old Man Who Goes Up In The Sky.

The third peak of interest, judged from M-O evidence and from the graph of space occupied in the papers, was about September 23. This time there was no dramatic figure in the limelight. What happened was a great movement of mass-opinion, moving faster than newspapers, instead of lagging behind them through exhaustion (as shown on page 75, etc.)

Hitler's speech.   From the point of view of publicity, there could have hardly been a better advertised show than the star turn on Nuremberg night.   Everything had to wait till Hitler had spoken.   But no issue was clarified when he did speak.   From that point of view the speech was a failure.   Nobody was any the wiser by next morning.   The disappointment tended to make people more than ever sceptical of "crisis".   The newspapers did their best, but the B.B.C. announcer pricked their bubble with his statement soon after the speech was over that it contained "nothing very new or sensational".

Next day, the *Evening Standard's* Londoner queried:

"Was Hitler Night greater in news value than Abdication Night ?

Not in England, though it was certainly an important night.   The *Evening Standard* printed 149,000 copies of a full special Hitler Speech Edition.   At 10.15 p.m. fewer than 3,000 remained in the publishing house.

On Abdication Night 240,900 extra copies of the *Evening Standard* were sold.

Did Hitler speak to the largest audience in the history of the world last night ?

Again, no.   Greater Germany heard him, and many of the Germans still outside what may become Greatest Germany.   Also a vast number of non-German-speaking listeners tuned-in to the Nuremberg noises.

But I estimate that an English broadcaster attracted a wider public.

The broadcaster had that day become Duke of Windsor.

But his theme was even more interesting than Hitler's. It was Abdication.   And if ever that should become Hitler's theme I have no doubt as to who would hold the record."

Observers in Whitehall on Nuremberg Night heard people discussing the Abdication.   The relative power of crises on the public mind is illustrated by these two quotes from a Hospital-Nurse observer, the first during the Eden crisis, the second on the night of Hitler's speech:

(i) "A Hospital Nurse spoke to-day to the Night-Sister, 'What do you think of Mr. Eden's resignation?' Night-Sister: 'H'm—don't bother my head with politics. My life is serious enough without worrying over things like that, so I don't read the papers—only read d'Alroy and Ann Temple. Anyhow—if there's a war I shall be in it, so it doesn't make any difference.'

Housekeeping pupil (voluntarily) reading the paper over my shoulder yesterday morning. 'I suppose Eden thought they'd go on their knees to get him not to resign. If there were many like him, there'd soon be a war.' At that moment, just as I was about to speak, another sister said: 'What's your star—Venus? Here's your fortune for to-day.' Another sister: 'Yes. For goodness sake forget politics. Don't get Tutor started.' Me: 'I'm not given to wasting words thanks.'"

(ii) "It *must* be a crisis!

I went into the dining-room to-night at 9 p.m. to serve Nurses' supper, and as I went in I asked someone if they had an evening paper. I was immediately bombarded with questions :

'What do you think is going to happen?'
'Do you think there will be a war?'
'What time is Hitler's speech?'
'Is our loud-speaker all right?'
'Isn't it like when we were all listening to the Abdication?'"

An observer at the Cliff Hotel, Felixstowe, records that:

"After to-night's report of Hitler's speech, the following remarks came from various occupants of the lounge—all middle-aged and bourgeois, male and female.
'Not too bad.' 'Not too good.' 'Awful.' 'Dreadful.' 'He's not ready yet.' 'He's bitten off more than he can chew.' 'He'll only have Italy on his side.' 'Awful to contemplate.' 'Awful to contemplate.' 'No one wants war.' 'I think I'll dig a little hole in the cemetery and get into it before war begins.' 'Perhaps they'll have a plebiscite and it'll all fizzle out.' 'Wish he'd fizzle out.' (All the preceding remarks came from women.)

'Fortifications ready at the end of the year? But what's happening now, that's what we want to know.' 'Is *anyone* ready?'

A 70-year-old Colonel Blimp said loudly and jokingly: 'Let's go out and find some Germans to shoot,' and later: 'We'll be having a reunion dinner in a cellar before long.'"

Meanwhile in Whitehall, an observer records that:

"5.30 p.m. Downing Street. No more than 300 people in the length of the street, from the Whitehall end to the piece of grass at the back of the Houses.

In the Street, the police are moving all the people along there, there is casual sauntering, looking across at No. 10 when they get opposite it; standing in the roadway with their faces to the house are three Police Inspectors, they move round now and again to inform the people, 'Come along, please, there's nothing to see.' Spasmodic efforts on the part of the police to get the people moving, there are lots of smiles; people, these mainly the middle class, go to the Inspectors to ask 'Is there anything happening?' and the Inspectors 'No, nothing yet'. A smile from both and these would move along back down the street, but to give another look or two as they got half way down to Whitehall again.

The people who are sticking around are mainly workers of better class, they move slowly and hesitate as they get to the point opposite No. 10, will then talk to the people they are with and many of them smile, then go slowly on to the top of the steps leading to the way out to St. James's Park.

Here are about 150 people, of ages from 20 up, in all to be seen about there are no more than 3 in their working clothes. One fellow of 25 is in a dirty blue sports shirt, no jacket; he has got in a group there, stands with his arms folded, his face healthy and brown, one of the few who look likely to be of the young soldier type if it comes to need, and he agrees with them to go.

There are old women of 70, in old-fashioned clothes, these are single figures and move about watching the faces of the others who are talking, as though to catch the drift of the talk.

Clerk types of all ages, in the smarter clothes, these do not stay long, they are passing up and looking at the doors.

They get near to the groups and listen to the talk, but are not the ones who take part in it.

The women of the working class are the ones who get into groups. Here there is some talking. This is not much at first. It starts in one group of a young lad of 18, a man of 48, man of 40, a woman of 40 and a group of 2 other men on the ring, all these are against the war, talk is started up, young lad asks: 'Have they done anything yet?' He is answered 'no, there'll be nothing till to-night.' They get into a talk of what the soldier has to go through, then the wages of the soldier; this starts a talk on what people can manage to live on. The youngster then says that an old person can manage to live on 10s. a week if they are careful. This brings the wrath of all present as to how he thinks it can be managed. He blushes and holds forth on how easy it is for his Granny in the country, Somerset, to live in a cottage on £5 a year, she has 3 acres of land. It is got from him that she has a husband and a son, these are earning between them £4 10s. a week so he gets it in the neck. 'You ought to bloody well have to go and try to do it in Stepney.' He was told very forcibly that he had a lot to learn, that he must have been reading or listening to Oswald Mosley. Arguments then began on the price of butter, how they would have to live on scraps to manage on 10s. a week. Asked how much he earned he replied £1 a week, this was then laughed at; a man and woman then asked him how he had the 'bloody cheek to suggest that old people who had given of their best in life could live on 10s. a week.' He then drew in his horns and said: 'Well I only says they could manage.'

Another group of men, with 3 women, then began to talk of the last war, how they had to put up with potato bread, line up for food in the worst parts of the war. A woman: '*They* didn't do it, *they* always get what they want.'"

The talk went on, in other groups, about butter shortage in Germany, concentration camps, Russian timber, Russian oil, Crozier on shooting officers, Gallipoli, Versailles Treaty:

"Wherever I went on this path from Whitehall to St, James's Park the scraps of conversation were about Germany,

Hitler, the last war. In all the talk groups where they were
of mixed company, built up from those gathered around,
the talk came down from the crisis to how they lived in the
last war and the present conditions.

At about 5.45, when the office workers began to leave
the offices, we saw a crowd begin to gather on the river
side of Whitehall, this slowly from the 20 or so at 5.35 p.m.,
went on increasing until at about 9 p.m. there would be
no less than 9,000 in and about Whitehall.

Every motor car which went up Downing Street was
closely scanned by the police and the people peering at
it. . . . When the red van of the G.P.O. appeared there was
some excitement. A woman: 'They're bringing dispatches.'
Answered by a man: 'Naw, lady, them's his love letters.'
Laughter, followed with one from a woman: 'Who'd fall
in love with Chamberlain's front teeth, not me, I want
something to look at. . . .'

Up at the theatre at the top of Whitehall, 'Glorious
Morning' is being played. We pass and see the dressed ones
leave their cars, a crowd of 40 watching them enter. We
hear 'They've got a nerve on a night like this to be going
to the theatre, haven't they?' A man of 40, ex-soldier:
'Nuffing ever will worry them, it's all the same whether he
has a war or not, they come out all right, mate.'

Then into Piccadilly. Here we see the first of the vans
with the placard on the side; it screeches as it brakes to
the kerb. The sellers make a drive to the back of the van,
twelve of them all waiting to grab their bundles. The men
are not slow to stand behind them, no asking for either of
the three papers, they take the one it happens to be, it's
the *Evening News*. The sellers shout 'Here you are, lady,
all about the Great Speech', then calling out at the top
of their voices 'Hitler threatens the Czechs', 'Hitler will
fight', 'Here it is at last, Hitler's great speech', 'Read the
yellow dog's speech', then to one of the men a seller said,
'The bastard.'

They are selling very fast, people are stopping, you can
see that the people on the pavement are not moving about
the same. The Commissionaire at the Criterion Café is
excited, he is looking over the shoulder of a man in evening
dress to see what it is.

People are buying the papers and then stopping, moving
on to the pavement edge to read them. Others, and these
are the greater number, are stepping up to the windows,
others into doorways to do the same. There is the same way
of holding the papers, we see the papers held sideways,
they are all reading the Stop Press news. This finishes at
the point where Hitler is threatening the Czechs. Many
of the same people are then moving back to catch the new
papers, this time the *Star*, they do the same. Others are
moving slowly along reading the papers sideways. Then
the performance is repeated when the *Standard* arrived. . . .

A man of 45, well-dressed, said viciously to the seller,
'Shut up', as he called 'Hitler's Sensational Speech'. Then
he walks on and observer followed to ask why. Reply,
'I'm fed up with these sensation-mongers, they make it a
lot worse than it is, in any event they don't help any.'

As I walk about with the paper open, others, mainly the
younger women, can be seen looking at the back of the
paper, they then go and buy one.

Six-foot man, well-dressed, to the evening-kitted man
on the door of the 'Criterion'. 'Well, what's he got to
say?' Reply: 'Oh, nothing, only it looks bad, he tells
us what he thinks. It's a lot of angry phrases. I don't think
anything will happen unless it's in the later editions.'

In a group of 56 people, Observer counted those with
and without papers; 39 had them, all of them the special
editions. . . . This was on the Criterion side, in a space of
less than 4 minutes."

Nüremberg Night was on September 12, and when
the Great Speech fell short of expectation, there was
a general feeling that another Crisis had spent its force
and would rapidly ebb away. But it soon became clear
that this one was due to grind on its course, and the
news got steadily blacker. Everyone was fed up and
longing for the thing to stop when there came the
wonderful news that our Prime Minister, Chamberlain,
was going to fly to see Hitler. It was emphasised that
he was 69 and that he had never flown before. The
combination of his age and his sky-journey made him

a father-deity. But his self-sacrificial abasement in going to Hitler made him like the son-deity who descends among the wicked to save them. The piled-up suspense and anxiety could only be dispelled by a gesture of this super-human kind, by a piece of myth-making. The whole Press applauded, including the *Daily Herald*, though the *News Chronicle* sounded a faintly warning note. Only the Communists struck a discordant key in the happy family clustering round the knees of Father Chamberlain. Nothing was known of what took place between Premier and Führer, but it was noted that on his outgoing flight Chamberlain's refreshments were ham sandwiches and whisky; on the return flight, chicken sandwiches and claret.

Immediately, on September 15, there was a sensational swing of opinion in favour of Chamberlain. On the evening of the 15th, an observer questioning people in a Metrop working-class pro-Labour street on what they thought were the chances of war, got from every second person questioned a spontaneous pro-Chamberlain tribute:

1. *Woman of 40.* "Things will be a lot better now, thank God. Chamberlain's done it this time for once, hasn't he? This'll stop it."

2. *Woman of 38.* "We're Labour here, we believe in what they do. . . . All this street is Labour, always has been. . . . Chamberlain seems to be doin' a good thing about this lot. I hope he tells Hitler what I would tell him. It's only bluff and it's playing with lives while he does it."

3. *Man of 34.* "If there's no catch in it, it looks as if the whole thing was over now bar shouting. He's a very clever man is Chamberlain."

4. *Man of 40.* "There'll be Labour men in the Government after this. Old Chamberlain not so bad after all. . . . This'll help 'em to get things runnin' again proper won't it?"

5. *Woman of 50.* "There'll be no war now, Chamberlain has put a stop to it. All the papers say so. It's in the *Herald* too, my husband said."

The direct question: "Do you think Chamberlain flying to Hitler will help peace?" was also put to a hundred people in this district on September 15 and 16. Results showed that:

70 thought it was a good thing
10 thought it a bad thing
20 were not sure, did not know, or would not say.

The size of this swing can be judged from the answers to a question put at the time of the Metrop By-Election campaign, end of March, 1938: "What do you think about the country's foreign policy?" At that time:

28% were satisfied with the Government's policy
32% were not satisfied
40% were vague or did not know.

By his flight, therefore, Chamberlain would seem to have scooped in 20% who were previously vague and not very interested, and also another 20% who were previously hostile. A close study of the pro-Chamberlain answers of September 15 and 16 shows that in 20% of them there is some sort of qualifying word, e.g., "quite good", "rather good", "I don't know what to think, but it's a good thing I think", "It's a good thing in a way", "Suppose he will do good in his own way", and so on. There was a margin of scepticism here which turned against Chamberlain again as soon as the meaning of the London-Paris terms had sunk in.

The first reaction was that the threatening danger had been moved, as by magic—the magic of the old man on wings:

1. *Woman of* 45. "What about the war? Is that over for good? That's what worries folks like us now. They all say Chamberlain's as good as settled it now. I wish him luck, bless him for it."

2. *Woman of* 40. "What a relief! They said it wouldn't be, that's my husband, I didn't believe him. I'm thankful now for this. It looks as if it's all over."

c

3. *Woman of* 40. "They should never have given us a scare like this last lot."

4. *Woman of* 40. "I don't bother about it now. We were only talking about Chamberlain being brave to go and see that swine Hitler. . . . It all seems a lot better now for it."

5. *Woman of* 55. "Oh, mister, it scared my wits out, thinking of the last war. They said it was going to be this week, and I heard the milkman say this morning that we can say the worst has passed now. He's a Conservative, he says Mr. Chamberlain's done it by going in an aeroplane to Hitler. It was all over the paper. It's a good thing we have men like that isn't it?"

6. *Woman of* 60. "I don't understand all this talk about war. There's no need for it. We should have seen what the last was. I was told the chances were better now and it won't come off. Thank God for that, we ought to say."

This is a woman's attitude, and there is a marked tendency for the women to stick to it over the following days, when their men are once more saying that Chamberlain was weak and we should have stood up to Hitler. Apart from all rights and wrongs, they want peace, and they hate having to give up the wonderful sense of relief which Chamberlain had given them:

1. *Woman of* 40. "He's a brick, the poor old man to go over there like that, at his age in a hurry. . . ."

2. *Woman of* 35. "It's the best thing that could have happened, we were only saying this morning. It hangs things up so they won't be at their throats so soon. He's very brave to have gone, we were saying."

3. *Woman of* 45. "I don't know what to think, but it's a good thing I think he went. It's brave of him, don't you think so, mister? It's going to put things off."

4. *Woman of* 50. "Wonderful man—splendid. Never been in a 'plane before. He comes from Birmingham and so do we! So he must be all right."

5. *Woman of* 55. "I think he's a marvellous man to have taken it on. Trying to bring peace—don't know—but only hope and pray (please God) he will."

6. *Woman.* "Hope it will help, don't you? What else can we do? We pray so. The One Above can do more than all the organisations in the world to touch his (Hitler's) heart."

The pro-Chamberlain *men* are more wary and more ready for fighting if Hitler goes too far:

1. *Man of* 20. "It's a good thing in a way, only speaking for myself I think they will fight in the finish. . . . It's a bluff of Hitler, he's got no raw materials or nothing to fight with."

2. *Man of* 30. "It's a damned good move. Either it comes off or else we know it's got to be war. Chamberlain will have told him that now. You can't help but give him respect for it when he took the risk."

3. *Man of* 24. "It's good, at least I think so. He's formed public opinion in what might have been a very serious thing. We might have been at war by now."

4. *Man of* 55. "He's done the right thing. He tried to mediate and that was what was wanted by everybody. Who wants a bloody war? Let 'em fight it if they do."

5. *Man of* 45. "Every Englishman should be proud of being an Englishman, he is safe wherever he goes for it. . . . I think Chamberlain's move was all right providing he don't give in. They should have trod on Hitler's toes a long time ago. . . . He wants to be boss and it's not what it used to be, these wars, it's the women and kids. . . . If it's in anybody's power to stop it then they should."

6. *Man of* 20. "It took everybody by surprise, didn't it? I wish the Labour Party had thought of it. Now Chamberlain will go down to history for it. I used to think he was a twister, but this makes you think twice."

The minority who are anti-Chamberlain tend to be those with detailed opinions on the foreign situation:

1. *Man of* 28. "I don't think it was a good thing. The Czechs won't give way, and Hitler is going to carry on in his way just the same. Nobody'll stop him. Did the same in Austria. . . . Chamberlain did it to try, but Hitler may take us too cheap through it. . . . It all depends on what Chamberlain tells us. . . ."

2. *Man of* 35. "I haven't time for a lot of thought, but I know what I think like. I don't think he should have humbled us and himself by going to see Hitler like he did. I suppose it's conducive to peace though, but who's it at the expense of, the Czechs? . . . I got my ideas like, but I'm no bloody good at explaining them, see what I mean, I wish I could. It's different when you're educated."

3. *Man of* 20. "I don't want you to think I'm a Communist but think it would have been better if he had approached President Benes instead of Hitler. This would have done much more good. Rather afraid he will do same with Czechs as with Austria—and that will mean trouble with democratic people in England. They might not stand for it."

4. *Man of* 70. "I think he's doing wrong. He should have gone to Benes first. We don't know what his objects are and we can't tell till we do. I think he has no right to go there and the rest of the Government should give him a good hiding. I'm an old soldier. Why shouldn't the Czechs fight for their country? Why should we allow a bully like Hitler to dominate Europe? Let's fight him and finish with it."

Then, more quickly than had been expected, Chamberlain flew home. Press photographers, film-camera operators, television and microphone technicians were there to welcome him when the fate-laden 'plane taxied into Heston airport. Millions were eager to see his photographed smile, hear his wax-recorded voice, in the hope that they could guess from them whether the issue would be peace or war. Newspapers, news reels and B.B.C. were quick to satisfy this curiosity. They combined to fix a powerful image on the public mind. In the *Listener* (September 22, 1938), Hugh Gray commented:

"This week as never before during the whole history of broadcasting the people of this country have listened in for news and information. Two speeches stand out. They are the recorded statements of Mr. Chamberlain before leaving for Germany and on his return. In a time of conflicting rumours and divergent opinions, and in the natural

absence of any comprehensive official statements, they
did something which revealed once more the possibilities of
wireless. They allowed us to gather impressions from the
tone of the speaker's voice. . . . But what else are we being
given ? Certainly less than we might reasonably have
expected. I do not suggest for one moment that we should
ask for news that could not wisely be given. I do not ask
for propaganda or personal statements. Surely, though,
it should be possible to broadcast even one talk explaining,
as simply as possible, the facts about the Czechoslovakian
problem. Isn't this where broadcasting should come to
our help at a time when each individual is called upon to
make up his mind on vital matters, and to come to a decision,
the consequences of which are unpredictable ? Five minutes
in the street, or in the Tube, listening to people talking are
sufficient to show that the majority are extremely vague
about the issues involved in Czechoslovakia. What is the
value of a democratic vote when the demos is ignorant ?
The newspapers provide some information. But the simple
spoken word is infinitely clearer and more instructive. . . ."

Here, in the official organ of the B.B.C. is a striking
admission of failure to provide facts; instead of facts,
the wireless gives splendidly the half-magical sense of
sharing in events. The optimism of Chamberlain's
voice kept millions comforted who a few hours later,
when they knew some, if not all, of the facts that *he*
knew, would turn against him with increasing fury.
(Though it would have taken Hugh Gray more than five
minutes in the street to get the full blast of what the
"demos" thought about it—and if he did his listening
in the Tube, it is unlikely that he would hear anything
at all. Just you try it, Mr. Gray.)[1]

[1] *Premier's Recorded Broadcast.* "Listeners to the B.B.C. news
bulletins on Saturday evening heard a recorded version of Mr.
Chamberlain's brief speech at Heston on his return from Germany.
    Those who, as I did, heard this as well as the direct broadcast
from Heston earlier in the day must have been struck by the
curious contrast between the speech itself and the recorded version.
    In the original broadcast Mr. Chamberlain's voice was entirely

An article in *L'Europe Nouvelle* has disclosed that all German newspapers will be suppressed in time of war and news transmitted only by radio. Presumably because "the simple spoken word is infinitely clearer and more instructive". *World's Press News*, (September 22, 1938) states that:

"The British Broadcasting Côrporation has formulated sensational plans to be put into operation in the event of war. It has been provisionally decided, *W.P.N.* learns, on any outbreak of hostilities involving this country, to discontinue normal programmes and instead to broadcast regular news bulletins at 15-minute intervals throughout the whole 24 hours of each day."

Though no official confirmation or denial was forthcoming, this suggests the further "possibilities of wireless" in relation to crisis.

When the first news reels were shown of the Chamberlain-Hitler tea-party, observers recorded that Chamberlain was cheered and Hitler hissed. A few days later, Hitler was still getting his hisses, but Chamberlain was received in silence.

On Saturday, September 17, when the terms proposed by Hitler and accepted by Chamberlain were first made known, though not officially, the newspapers published a still smiling Chamberlain leaving Downing Street on his way to see the King at Buckingham Palace. An observer saw him go and thus records the mechanism of the smile to which the nation looked for reassurance:

---

calm, as though he were feeling no undue fatigue from his journey. The recorded version sounded quite different.

As I have noticed in other broadcasts of recorded speeches, the tone of the speaker's voice was completely altered. The whole speech seemed to be pitched two or three notes higher than the original.

This, to listeners familiar with Mr. Chamberlain's voice who have not heard the real broadcast, may have conveyed an effect of strain and breathlessness which was entirely absent from the speech as delivered."—(*Daily Telegraph.*)

"Observer went through the line of police, then through to the pressmen. They have gathered in a semi-circle round the car which has drawn up to the door of No. 10. They are expecting Chamberlain to come out.

There are at least twenty camera men all equipped with flash. They wait, all eyes on the door. One of the camera men gets in front of a camera man who has taken a perch in the middle of the street. He calls 'Hey, Charlie, do you mind, you're spoiling me'. The interloper replies 'Damn, I'm sorry Jack' and moves. There are only about three of the reporter-type men about. These have note-books open and pencil in hand. They stand on the ends of the half-circle. At the rear five yards away are two Inspectors.

The door of this house opens. A man appears and opens the door of the car. The camera men are now alert and on their toes. They are all eyes on the door. One says 'He's here this time' . . . The door begins to open, and we see Chamberlain begin to come out. He hesitates before he does. Here I see that his face is set, there is no smile on it, only something serious, and, Observer thinks, deter-mined. . . . Then he steps out to the half-light of the lamp from above the door. Here he begins to smile. This means he shows his teeth. The flashes of the camera men send the street a powerful green, and behold I am looking at what I am to believe is the Prime Minister of Great Britain, but this man might easily have been the Devil to the Observer. The green of the flashes gave height to the illusion, and the continued grin through all the flashes, and some of them went off twice. He, Chamberlain, kept his hat in his hand as he stood there.

One of the camera men called out 'Just a moment, Mr. Chamberlain', and he did wait, then got into the car, the same grin, and another flash went off. . . ."

The smile was to last, but on Monday, September 19, the newspapers were subdued. They appeared not to know the terms. This sort of thing:

"For the moment, until we have full official confirmation of the nature of the proposals, it is better, after making that fact clear, to reserve comment. In a critical international situation hasty comment without all the facts can but make a critical situation more critical." (*Daily Herald.*)

"The unavoidable absence of official information leaves the field open to rumours and conjectures which may be disturbing. Despite this, Britons go about their business and their play as usual, perfectly satisfied that their best interests are represented and safeguarded by those who have won their trust. . . ." (*Daily Sketch.*)

"Trust Chamberlain." (*Daily Mail.*)

The *News Chronicle* is non-committal. John Bouverie thinks it necessary to open his remarks by saying: "Would it be considered indelicate if at this point in this crisis one put in a word for the Czechs?" Considered indelicate by the public, or by officials anxious to preserve the sunshine of Chamberlain's smile? The short leading article includes a phrase: "To put the matter on the lowest ground, if bad news has to be broken, it is better broken in easy stages."

This time the newspapers underestimated their public. Next day they were still soft-pedalling. But by now the fat was in the fire. Following the *News Chronicle's* example (see page 40), an observer asked six people picked at random in various parts of London, "What do you think about Czechoslovakia?" Subsequently the same question was asked of 350 others, but these first replies were interesting:

1. *Bus Conductor, age* 30, *Lewisham.* "I should think they should reject them. What the hell's he got the right to go over there and do a dirty trick like that? It'll have the whole world against us now. Who'll trust us? It's like throwing your own kid to the wolves. We helped make it a country and then Chamberlain comes along and wants to buy that swine off. There'll be a war sooner or later, then there'll be nobody to help us. America won't lend us a bloody cent then. It's a cert if they've any guts they'll not give in."

2. *Postman, 45, on London Bridge.* "It's a damned shame when you realise what he's done about it. He must think we're all frightened of Hitler. Are we, that's what I'd like to know now. It looks like it. If that's all he went to see Hitler for, and he agreed in one day, then he never did them Czechs any justice. They took a lot longer to give 'em Home Rule in Ireland. He goes and throws them away to save their own skins inside 24 hours, and threatens them he won't have anything to do with France if they won't agree. I'm not sure which is the worst Blackmailer now, whether it's Mussolini or Neville Chamberlain. I was a Liberal. . . . Oh this lot stinks and will do the world over."

3. *Clerk in Paymaster's Office at Woolwich, 36.* "Think? What can you think about it? After all if they are looking for excuses they could find one. They promised to have a plebiscite in about 1920, they didn't have it, so what can you expect? Still it's a let down for England. Tastes nasty for all that, arranging something for the other chap and he doesn't know what it is. It's made England look a real coward in my opinion."

4. *Packer at the "Evening News."* "Why didn't he say straight out six months ago that he wasn't going to do anything about anybody except our own coasts? It seems to me that when Hitler and Mussolini begin to ask for our Empire he'll give it to 'em bit by bit so long as they don't touch us, till we've no Empire left. It's a bit dirty in my opinion when you won't tell the small chap what you're going to do when you've more or less promised that you'll not see him robbed."

5. *Unemployed Scotchman, on the edge of Trafalgar Square, 24.* "The dirty so and so, that's what he is, selling 'em like that. He's done the same to all the others now. Only a ruddy Englishman could act like that. He flies to see Hitler, then he comes back and tells the papers that peace is near. He thinks he's going to keep England out of a war. Let the other fellers fight and he'll sell them the arms to do it, is that the big idea? I'll bet he goes to church like his wife does. They'll never be any use to the working class. It's money they're after, or something. I'd join up in any Foreign Legion the Czechs start now."

6. *Woman, aged 32, in Whitehall. Lives in Pimlico.* "It's not fair. At first I thought it was all right. Now it seems it's a low-down dirty deal. He might have given them the chance to say what they were prepared to do. It gives lots of them Czechs over to Hitler now for him to pay out as he likes and won't he just do it if we know anything. . . . I think people are changing round now, they thought last week that it looked like peace. Now it looks as if he is going to get everything he wants because everybody is frightened to stop him."

Statistical analysis of the 350 answers to the question: "What do you think about Czechoslovakia?" is misleading unless one takes into account the complex mixture of feelings in the minds of those who answered, contrasting with the simple way in which they expressed them. The difference of opinion between men and women was very striking—often enough there was disagreement between them in the same house. The men reacted against the idea that we were being bullied by Hitler, so they took the stronger line. The women, on the other hand, felt confused about the issues in central Europe, and though they admitted that the terms were unfair, their first thought was above all how to keep peace and stop their men from having to go to fight. Many of both sexes did not justify the Chamberlain terms, but thought he was playing for time. The reaction against Chamberlain was definitely greater on September 22 than on September 21. Of all the men questioned on September 22, not one thought Chamberlain was absolutely right.

The four groups can be distinguished:

(i) *Indignant.* Czechs treated unfairly, Chamberlain policy wrong, we should stand up to Hitler.

(ii) *No war.* May be unfair, but we want peace above everything.

(iii) *Pro-Chamberlain.* He is a good man, he is playing for time, he has saved peace.

(iv) *Don't know.* Indifferent, do not understand or care, won't say.

	M & F Sep. 21	M & F Sep. 22	F both days	M both days	Total both days
	%	%	%	%	%
(i) *Indignant*	36	44	22	67	40
(ii) *No war*	14	6	16	2	10
(iii) *Pro-Chamberlain*	25	18	27	14	22
(iv) *Don't know*	25	32	35	17	28

Those of the men who give a definite opinion are nearly five to one against Chamberlain. The women are much more divided in their views. There are many more women than men in the "Don't Know" group, and they make up nearly the whole of the "No War" group, which represents an uneasy hovering between the attitude of their militant menfolk and their own hopes that Chamberlain may save peace after all.

Out of these quotations it is possible to build up a composite picture of the state of mind in which women reacted to the threat of war in September, 1938, before Flight 3:

1. *Woman of* 60. "Prime Minister a brave man and a good one. Perhaps war must come." But her son, aged 30, said: "Prime Minister has betrayed Czechs."

2. *Woman of* 65. "Chamberlain's a good chap. Wait and see." But her son, aged 30, said: "Prime Minister should have stood up to Hitler."

3. *Woman of* 50. "Men know more of these things than women. Not worth while fighting for Czechoslovakia."

4. *Woman of* 30. "If we knew more about it we could form an opinion. Chamberlain did a grand thing. Best thing is to forget all about it."

5. *Woman of* 40. "My husband says it's a bad thing, but we don't want any more wars, we're not ready for one."

6. *Woman of* 30. "I can't think what to say, it's hard when you look at it when you don't want war. They

were saying at the meeting on the end of the street last night, the speaker said we ought to be thankful but all the men were against him for saying it, they said it was a shame to let them Czechs down like that."

7. *Woman of* 45. "Not thought about it much. If the men were in they'd talk about it a lot. They're always saying as Chamberlain has swindled them, but I think he's for peace."

8. *Woman of* 30. "If there's one thing we want, it's no more war. But I can't see what we are going to do when he keeps on wanting things that he says, like that Czechoslovakia. I know what I'd do if I had him. My husband says, and we agree, that we will have a bigger war now sooner or later for this."

9. *Woman of* 40. "I am sure I don't know the real rights of it all, but the men in this house say that he should never be allowed to get away with it."

10. *Woman of* 35. "We are all grumbling about there being no gas masks for us in this district yet. . . . We don't want war till we have to, then we have to be prepared. It's the children we must think of."

Next, in contrast, consider the warlike attitude of the men:

1. *Man, painter.* "I used to feel proud to be British but now I am ashamed of my own race."

2. *Man,* 50. "We've let them down."

3. *Man,* 25. "Neville ought to be shot, letting them down like that."

4. *Man of* 40. "It's a damned shame, Chamberlain has took a liberty with them."

5. *Man of* 34. "For once in my life I'm damned well ashamed to be an Englishman. I think the worst possible thing has happened to them Czechs now. It puts me in mind of a song they used to sing during the last war: 'You can send who you like, but for God's sake don't send me.'"

6. *Man of* 30. "I'm in the Territorial Army, I have to go, but I don't believe in this giving way all the time to Hitler. He'll want our colonies next."

7. *Man of* 45. "We ought to help the Czechs. It looks as if they have been sold by us and France this time all right."

8. *Man of* 40. "It's all wrong what they have done to them, giving him too much rope. There'll soon be nothing left. Hitler's swelled headed."

9. *Man of* 40. "We sold the Czechs for what we don't know. France and Chamberlain let them down. They won't let them stop at this."

10. *Man of* 40. "It's a bloody rotten shame what he has done to them. We can't understand it at all. Why, it's not playing the bloody game, is it ?"

11. *Man of* 30. "I feel very indignant about it all for once in a while."

12. *Man of* 40. "What'll he want to get away with next, I think, where's he going to stop ? Chamberlain's making us stink in the eyes of the world."

13. *Man of* 38. "It makes you damned well wonder what the world's come to when a German can do all this, twenty years after we licked them. We should have gone through when we had the chance."

14. *Man of* 30. "Stop Hitler now I say, before he takes away Czechoslovakia. We don't know what Chamberlain will be giving away in the end."

15. *Man of* 20. "I'd give Hitler hell for this lot. He's going to get it too before long, you bet he will."

16. *Man of* 42, *ex Royal Navy*. "I know what it's like. They should never have let Mussolini have get away with Abyssinia, that's what started it all off. We're supposed to be democratic, but where's our Parliament now ? . . . I like getting other people's opinions, but I think we have let them lads who dies, let them down. Now they will never stop till they either beat us or we do it to them. I'm for stopping them now."

17. *Man of* 35. "I think it's the bloody limit when we give what's not ours away. Besides they seem to think we are cowards now. Chamberlain's to blame for this, and we'll not let him forget it either."

These were the two viewpoints on the eve of possible war. The joy with which the masses welcomed Chamberlain's peace-flight, the speed with which the men turned against him when his terms became known, and their readiness to fight Hitler rather sooner than later, are in themselves striking enough examples of the rapidity with which popular feeling remoulds itself. They show clearly enough that the reason why the mass-mind is changeable is not any inherent fickleness, but simply that the masses are not given the facts, or are deliberately misled. Government spokesmen, and newspapers supporting the Government policy, kept on saying that there were reasons why the facts could not be made known to the masses. Was this because they were engaged in manœuvres to which the masses would have strongly objected if they had known about them? Whether this was the case or not, the lesson which a sociologist or social psychologist could hardly fail to draw from events was that an uninformed public is more variable, more uncontrollable, than an informed public. One consequence: that Chamberlain and Hitler were now held up three days by feeling which had to be overcome by feeling.

(g) Hub of the Universe

Right up to Chamberlain's return from his *second* visit to Hitler, no one really knew what was happening. Everyone knew there was a crisis. And so an enormous frustration boiled up into a simmering mass of doubts and fears and furies. For the first time since the Abdication, an observer spending an hour in any town would have been almost sure to hear at least one conversation about politics. This was a crisis not only of leadership and diplomacy but also in terms of every literate European. Bewildered as usual, but this time also certain that something was seriously wrong, reactions found expression in overt behaviour. There were daily demonstrations in Hyde Park and Trafalgar

Square, while Whitehall became the apparent focus and soul of all that was happening to people who, lacking facts, had to judge on feelings. Thus September 20, 8 p.m.:

"Up on the edge of Trafalgar Square are congregating some forty members of the University of London Labour Club, all under 21, with double placards of white stating SAVE CZECHOSLOVAKIA and SAY 'NO' TO HITLER. They lined the pavement facing Whitehall, then at the word of a police inspector they were allowed to cross over in a line. They were so slow in getting across that the inspector stood on the island site and shouted 'Come on now, please, please get a move on,' and waved his arm. As they got to the edge of Whitehall they began to sing, the words and tune unrecognised. The police stepped in, stopped them. They walk slowly on, start to sing again. This time the police spoke more sharply. One of the young women in glasses stopped and argued. This held up the rest of the line. Onlooking lads passed ribald comments, e.g.

'Who's this lot? Hey, Jenny, how'd you like me on your back instead of that board?"

The girl replied with a smile,

'What do you mean, carry you? What for?'"

Even more ineffective was a Fascist effort on September 23,—between Godesberg and Munich.

"7 p.m. About 600 people being kept on the move by the police. One woman got angry and argued. Policeman replied 'I'm sorry mum, I only know I have my orders, they are People have to keep on the move now. Yes I know there's lots could have done better than Mr. Chamberlain, that's what they all say, they ought to have a try, now come on please, will you.'

Six police across the end of Downing Street and two inspectors. Man of 40 says to observer:

'It's not the Germans they ought to tackle. These psychological people that ought to be shifted, they're the cause of all the trouble, go into all your hospitals, you find them there, there are one in three of the whole population who get into an institution in the course of a lifetime. . . . It's these doctors, they live on us right from the time they leave their school, all out of us, you want to stop them broadcasting them waves, they've done it every day for years, I've had my wife dead drunk on the floor three times this week and that's been in the morning, she never touches drink, it's them waves that do it.'

Another man overheard and remarks:

'Blimey mate, I wish I could get drunk on them waves all free and cost me nothing.'

Two men of 45 and one of 40 argue fiercely on the degree of blame on Chamberlain. 'He's only looking out of his class and thought he could get out of the mistake that Grey make in 1914 but it's crazy when you're dealing with men like Hitler; Chamberlain's only a commercial traveller, and Hitler don't need his stuff now.'

A line of Fascists now appear with boards held aloft. A young chap with a Communist badge went across and spoke to one of them 'Moseley mugs.' One of the walkers turned and said: 'Get down on your hands and knees, you Communist rat.'

Two women pin the cartoon from the *Star*, 'Coming Sir', of waiter Chamberlain bringing a cooked bird on a plate to Hitler, on to one of the trees at the bottom of Downing Street. The inspector saw it after fifteen minutes, and rolled it into a ball, threw it on the ground. The people on the pavement, a solid mass of eight thick, produced shouts:

'What about keeping the streets tidy?'

'Is that no litter?'

'Oh you can see what he is all right, it's Chamberlain's bodyguard.'

At 9.44 p.m., when observer was going home, he saw Fascists with the placards come into Trafalgar Square in broken order. Down Whitehall they come. A youth yells at them: 'Yah, Fascists.' To which one of the walkers replies: 'You needn't think my legs are wobbling because you said that.' At the edge of the crowd of four or five thousand at the junction of Downing Street, howls, hisses and groans began. This was taken up all over Whitehall. Into the placard bearers came the crowd, from both sides of the street, two thousand of them at first, splitting the crowd into two parts. Placards of the second part are seen waving in the air, while police break in and struggle with one man, and another takes the boards and breaks them with his hands.   Up comes a van-load of police and twenty on foot to guard the Fascists and they now march beside them.   They march down into Parliament Square, and the crowd goes down there too, swarming across the Square from all directions with shouts of 'Don't let them get away boys', 'Pull them boards down', 'Down 'em boys'. The marchers suddenly start to run as fast as they can go carrying their boards. One Fascist, over six foot, strikes a smaller man, as he goes, making him reel on to the pavement, holding his jaw. An officer leaps from the van shouting 'Break it up there, break it up there', as he rushes around holding his arms across his chest and using both elbows to crash into the sides of people, followed by constables. 'Throw a cordon across' and there was quickly a double line of police across King Street. The police stop, laughing as they wipe their faces and say 'Phew, that was hot.' Just before that, they had taken a man holding both shoulder and wrist rushing him into the van."

On the other side of Parliament Square, at Westminster Abbey, a distance of some fifteen yards east of the tomb of the Unknown Warrior has been roped off and flanked with kneeling chairs. The western doors have been specially and unusually opened. A nurse from the Westminster Hospital is in attendance night and day at a small prayer-desk west of the tomb. On the tomb a bunch of simple flowers in the form of a circle, at each corner are candlesticks and in the centre a long spear with fleurs-de-lis on it. In one hour's observation, 5.45–6.45 p.m. on September 23, 30 men and 106 women entered the Abbey, and prayed; 91 of these were over 30 years old. Seven were considered to be upper-class, 25 artisan or working-class, the rest distinctly middle-class. The Abbey authorities issued a special leaflet for the occasion which starts:

"Suggestions for Silent Intercession during these days of crisis.

1. Place yourself in the Presence of God. 'Spiritual silence is the turning of the soul in quietness to a power beyond itself.'

'My soul, be thou silent unto God, for my expectation is from Him.'

'The Lord is nigh unto all them that call upon Him— yea all such as call upon Him faithfully.

'He will fulfil the desire of them that fear Him: He also will hear their cry and will help them. . . .'"

"An urgent appeal" was made on September 27 by the Federal and National Free Church Council to open all churches for prayer on September 28 and especially during the proceedings in Parliament. Already the previous Sunday the *Sunday Dispatch* placards had smeared all over Britain:

WHEN THE PRIME MINISTER WAS A FAIRY PRINCE

On the same Sunday, in the *Express*, Godfrey Winn had observed:

"Praise be to God and to Mr. Chamberlain. I find no sacrilege, no bathos, in coupling those two names.

While in the *Sunday Chronicle*, the other God-conscious but not-Godfrey columnist Nichols put it:

"Mrs. Chamberlain, at the very moment that her husband was soaring through the clouds, was kneeling at the Tomb of the Unknown Warrior in Westminster Abbey. That is one of the pictures that make history beautiful."

Beautiful history was made each morning at 10, when an observer reports that "Mrs. Chamberlain comes to pray with a detective who doesn't."

The Queen, too—the Royal family were conspicuously out of most of the news—launched her totem ship on September 27, with a message from the King:

"He bids the people of this country to be of good cheer in spite of the dark clouds hanging over them. . . .

He knows well that as ever before in critical times they will keep cool heads and brave hearts. He knows, too, that they will place entire confidence in their leaders, who, under God's providence, are striving their utmost to find a just and peaceful solution. . . ."

Implied in the launching was Almighty's intervention when the ship mystically started to take to the water before she had pressed the button or christened it. While in another respect the Queen was less fortunate than Mr. Chamberlain, for just as she was about to deliver the King's message on the National Programme, she was faded out in favour of a B.B.C. French lesson to schools.

It is perhaps not too far-fetched to say that many people were praying as much to Mr. Chamberlain as to the Almighty, in a typical sympathy-magic. No wonder that when the Premier announced that he was off to see Hitler a third time, the Archbishop was given air in the middle of the B.B.C. news to say:

"Surely this so sudden and unexpected lifting of the burden which weighed so heavily upon us this very morning is itself an answer to the great volume of prayer which has been rising to God. . . .
None of us can tell or measure the power of prayer. It is one of the great mysteries of this universe, and the very humblest of us can know that in his prayers he is helping this country and the world."

A letter to *The Times* (October 3, 1938) from Wilson Carlile, Hon. Chief Secretary of the Church Army, headed "Keep open the Churches" begins: "Sir, Thank God for the Miracle of Munich; a prophet of the olive leaf has been raised up. . . . "
Prayer peak was reached when Chamberlain's return combining with Harvest Festival, put an end to fear and summer. On this Sunday (October 3) some central

London churches, uniquely, were full. News story was the City Temple because one of the choir-men there wore a gunner's uniform under his blue robes; City Temple's preacher was Britain's No. 1 religious writer and broadcaster, Leslie Weatherhead, who said:

"Do you feel a little uneasy, as though you had made friends with a burglar on condition that if he took nothing from you or your immediate friends, you would say nothing about what he took from somebody else?

I feel like that. I hope the burglar can do as much good as a converted imperialist like John Bull."

The Times leader next day saw Munich in this way:

"Here it is enough to praise GOD that He has crowned with success the efforts of good will, thereby saving the world from the illimitable catastrophe of a general war. Whatever else may be doubtful this is certain, and this supplies an ample theme for all the praise we can offer."

And the *Sunday Pictorial* praiseworthiness in its editorial; this typical piece of English crisis journalism deserves to go on permanent record, and it is our privilege to put it here:

"Let us now praise ourselves!

This is an exercise little practised by the British people. It is an art at which we are not adept. It is good that this is so.

Yet on occasion when outstanding praiseworthy things have been done, it is well to state them.

Not with empty vanity, nor with nervous shoutings. But with honest, sober truth.

Let us then praise ourselves. The peoples of Britain.

For the last few weeks we have walked in the Valley of the Shadow.

And we have been unafraid.

We have looked squarely in the face of evil. And we have seen it vanish.

We have been calm when panic called.

We have been united in the face of danger. We have stood shoulder to shoulder like a phalanx.

And we have come through the ordeal with dignity and added courage.

We have seen trenches dug in our cities. We have seen deep gashes slashed in our village greens, turning the pleasant land into a battle-front.

We have seen our children and old folk made hideous by gas masks.

But we have not broken.

We have seen many of our youth march away in uniform to what, we knew not.

And we have been quiet.

No generation of our race has yet endured exactly what we have during the dying days of this summer.

Others have had swift explosions and wars, but none has seen the Four Horsemen ride so menacingly day after day, week after week, until the strain became almost unendurable.

But we have kept control. We have kept our self-discipline.

Let us, then, praise ourselves, for we have done a praiseworthy thing.

We have stood behind our chosen leader, giving him strength and knowledge that we were content in him.

Without us he could not have succeeded.

But for him, and but for us, thousands would have been blasted to Hell this Sabbath morning. For, make no mistake, the guns would have spoken to-day."

Hitler himself, entering Czechoslovakia for the first time in his life, on the Monday, spoke to the thousands in Eger:

"Not only you are overjoyed. The whole nation shares your joy. Your happiness is that of 75,000,000 people, just as your sorrow a few days ago was that of all of us.

In this hour I want to thank the Almighty for having blessed us in the past, and pray that He may also bless us in the future."

Three hours later Mr. Chamberlain informed the House of Commons that his achievement had been made possible by "the prayers of millions". The pedant might find difficulty in locating the exact position of the Deity and the objective distribution of His favours, while the doctrinaire would undoubtedly have noticed that during the preceding week Christ was exceedingly seldom mentioned in the major utterances. Potent, no doubt, in the prevailing confusion was the fact that Mr. Chamberlain was himself not a Christian but a deist, Unitarian. On this prayerful Sunday, there being no suitable chapel near Chequers, he went for a walk with a sheep-dog. It had a ribbon round its neck, red, white and blue.

But while thousands were praying, millions were thinking. Indignation was rising. One piece of fact, an oasis in the desert of chaos, the Czech Penguin Special sold out its first edition of fifty thousand in 24 hours, speedily followed by another hundred thousand. By now tension, which many were already finding almost unbearable, and which had really got into full swing on the evening of Monday, September 26, when the late newspaper placards announced that Hitler would march if he didn't get what he wanted by October 1, was acute. War was regarded now as inevitable by Press and M.P.'s. An M-O snap-survey over a number of towns showed that the public agreed to an unprecedented degree. Out of 206 people whose answers had so far been received, 105 thought there would be war definitely on or before Saturday, 15 that there would be a war in a few weeks, 9 that there would be war in a year or two, but 56 still believed that there would be no war at all, and 21 say they don't know or care. 158 of these said what they'd do in the case of war, and their choices ranked as follows:

Carry on	58
Do as told	37
Help in some peaceful way . .	18
A.R.P.	14

Get away   13
Hide   6
Refuse service   6
Don't know   6

In Worktown, war fever was marked also. New forms
of greeting were popular: "Have you got your gas
mask?" "Have you not measured for your khaki
yet?" "Have you got your gun?" "Have you got
your papers yet?" A minority of 15% of men questioned were firmly decided not to fight in any war, but
more typical were sentiments such as these, emphasis
on the wish to have a go not at Germany but at Hitler:

1. *Man of* 30. "Yes I am prepared to go and fight. Hitler
has gone too bloody far this time, he needs teaching a lesson
and I for one am prepared to give it him."
2. *Man of* 30. "Yes I would fight. I'm a Britisher and
proud of it. I'll fight to my last drop of blood. Some of
these bloody pacifists want an operation and inject some
British blood in them.
3. *Man of* 24. "I don't want to fight but I will go to
defend my mother, you see there is only she and myself.
Hitler is a big braggart, that's what I think, I think we can
still call his bluff, All my pals are war minded now, it's the
general topic now I think."
4. *Man of* 40. "Yes I will fight now. He wants his bloody
clock knocking round. We shall have to show him who is
boss. They talk about nothing else at work, it's a bloody
pain."

On September 27 the mechanism of A.R.P. began its
turgid rotations and within 36 hours many areas had
run out of the smaller sizes of gas masks, while no masks
for small children were available. In Oxford City
Council, a member rose to make a protest against masks
not fitting, produced a mask from inside his coat, held
it up above his head. Shouting from several quarters
symbolised increased technical knowledge of the past

week. "Eh! you can't hold it up by its straps like that." On Lancashire moors, Sept. 27, farmers were chasing cows in the afternoon with large masks, while the gold-fish problem was solved by an A.R.P. warden who told a distressed woman bringing her bowl of goldies to the depot, "Oh they'll be all right ma'am, put them in your mask along with you." Cellophane sold out in London; it had been recommended for stopping glass splinters in explosions. Hammersmith Borough alone took on 2,000 unemployed to dig trenches, which now remain as earth-mounds, wrecking most of London's open spaces; suggested by wags as memorials to Chamberlain's Peace with Honour. Observer in a pub overheard landlord asking one still-unemployed man: "Why aren't you digging?" Said the man: "I am a painter." Said the landlord: "A painter. Why that's a disease not a job."

It was at this stage that mass-fears began. As one observer put it, "With distribution of gas masks began real fear. All over the place one heard: 'To think that one man is responsible for all this!' 'War! It doesn't bear thinking of.'"

Gas masks brought the war danger home to everybody and to every home. It was democracy inverted— everyone had the vote, now everyone had a mask. Especially among the women and the elderly, fear grew almost to panic, as can be seen from these reports from all over the country:

"Quite a dozen persons (men and women) told me they were suffering from diarrhœa and nervous indigestion. Most people I met apparently lived on tea and similar beverages. Food catered for this period was just thrown out."

[1] We can only present a minute fraction of the material which M-O has been collecting at high pressure during the last days of September and after. This book had to go to press in October. Much of the earlier material on A.R.P., anti-aircraft, Territorials, etc., is not particularly relevant for the present theme and will be made full use of in another publication.

"Elderly people are apparently suffering with stomach trouble owing to the anxiety of listening or reading reports of the crisis. I have come in actual contact with more than half a dozen so affected."

"After lunch I went to be fitted . . . I was horribly sick after a half-minute, through the smell of the rubber, and have been feeling nauseated since, during the afternoon. . . .
Two colleagues of mine were fitting masks, and they said they had a dreadful morning, with babies and toddlers crying and screaming. Quite a number of elderly folk looked ill, an expectant mother fainted, an old lady had a heart attack."

"One lady dashed hers off before she had got it on; she has a bad heart, and seemed to be about to faint. Poor lady, she is very nervous, and has spent the time since in trying to get into a hotel in the country; but they are all full."

"A neighbour who lives alone and is rather timid opened the door last night to a man with a gas mask. She was so frightened that her knees shook for half an hour after his visit."

"On Sunday a man called from the A.R.P. with gas masks. Eileen opened the door to him. She went quite white when he told her what he had called about. . . ."

"Some children thought the gas was in the defence valve and said they could smell it. Actually it was the Izal used for disinfectant."

"I was sitting in an A.B.C. having my lunch during the time when the war strain was at its highest. Suddenly there was a crash as a waitress dropped a pile of plates. Normally this would have gone unnoticed, but on this occasion the effect was electrical. Strangely enough it was the men who were most affected, not so much surprise as actual anticipation of something dreadful was registered on their faces."

"Four of us, including myself, were sitting at a long writing bench facing an open window in the laboratory after the tea interval. P remarked about three airplanes which had just passed overhead. Soon after a smell very much like chlorine was noticed. S said: 'That's chlorine isn't it?' looking a little alarmed. We others agreed and looked round in the lab, but could not see any likely source. The smell grew stronger and appeared to be coming from the open window. I do not know who made the suggestion that a gas attack had been launched, but all four of us for a moment thought it had. This is a fact, because we talked it over afterwards and admitted we were alarmed. . . ."

"Met a friend on the way. She looked haggard and worn. Reported she, husband, etc., has been out in car till past 12 midnight (Tuesday night) in pelting rain looking for accommodation in country. Everything was crowded out. Money was no object—but all they had was a vague possibility of a tiny two-bedroomed cottage which three families hoped to share. The white-faced girl of 12, holding a shopping basket with trembling hands, said: 'There's one thing good about it . . . it was so hard for us to find it that perhaps it will be equally difficult for them (the enemy) to discover us.'"

Along with fear goes hate, concentrating itself on a single figure:

1. "Everyone rages at Hitler. He will grace a good many bonfires on November 5th."

2. "A young English girl said: 'I'd like to dig my scissors in him and twist it round and round' (illustrating her method)."

3. "Talked with a woman who had been to the illuminations at Morecambe. The whole atmosphere of the journey, which should have been a pleasant one, was marred by talk of war and Hitler. Even more of Hitler than war, it seemed to be all Hitler, particularly four old ladies refused to discuss anything else, only war and Hitler. They created a morbid feeling among other passengers, and when passing through Lancaster, someone suggested paying a visit to the home of Dr. B. Ruxton the murderer. They all agreed to this. The driver had a job to get some back in the coach. It was only a double-fronted house in dilapidated condition, and one woman suggested it should have been Hitler instead

of his wife. Strange to say, this person was quite glad of the visit to the house of the murder. . . .

The party stopped at a public house for a drink and the landlord asked them generally their feelings about the situation. A few of them said they would like to shoot Hitler, but up and spake one young woman and said shooting was too good. She suggested taking Hitler into a room, and experimenting on his anatomy with unmentionable refinement. This was voted by the whole party as a good idea and one or two of the bolder ones hoped that they would be selected to go in. . . .

Hitler was discussed all evening and then again on the journey home. . . ."

On that evening, September 27, from No. 10 Downing Street the Prime Minister spoke through radio stations all over the world. He found it a "horrible, fantastic, and incredible thing, that we should be digging trenches." Speaking in an intimate manner utterly different from his usual speeches and with a frequent sob in his voice, for the first time he gave some account of what he'd been doing, told how he had done "All that one man could do to compose this quarrel", said that Herr Hitler had assured him "that this is the end of Germany's territorial claims in Europe", went on to say that on his second visit to Hitler he "was taken completely by surprise" when informed of Hitler's further demands, and so now decided "I see nothing further that I can usefully do". Then went on to say that it seemed inconceivable that they should undertake a war because of a quarrel in a far-away country between people "of whom we know nothing", that "it must be on deeper issues" that this country should go to war, issues which involve the rule of force, when "life for people who believe in liberty would not be worth living".

The B.B.C. then translated the speech very slowly and with many pauses into German, then Italian. For by now a new angle had been developed. Undoubtedly affected by the long delay in informing the British Public about what had really happened—and even now Chamberlain's phrases were far from clear—the Press were clamouring that the real problem was how to get the German public to realise that England was solid against these concessions and that Hitler's demands meant war. Innumerable rumours were circulating in Fleet Street about riots and mutinies in specified portions of Germany, and it was universally pointed out that the German Press had not reprinted the first of Roosevelt's elaborate cables. The *Mirror* had a heavy leader (September 28):

"PAST HITLER?"

Who will help us to get past Hitler to Germany?
In order to tell Germany what?
. . . (3) That from the President of the great American Republic has sounded the multitudinous voice of all America of a hundred and thirty million who regard war with detestation. Is it credible that Germany will not be allowed to hear that voice? . . .
. . . (7) That the moment of bluff and of threats is over. The time for haggling over concessions is ended. The policy of yielding for the sake of immediate peace has led us to the ultimatum of Saturday.
. . . (8) That such a peace, purchased for a moment, would be merely a moment's peace."

In response to this situation, yet another sort of E eryman was invented by the *Star* (September 28):

"WHAT IS THE MAN IN THE STREET THINKING IN BERLIN, IN PARIS, IN PRAGUE, IN ROME?"

The only answer provided was that there was "a new spirit of optimism among the Italian people", and that in Paris "the general feeling is that events are fast getting beyond the control of the statesmen". But from Berlin a Special Correspondent reports:

"Herr Hans Schmidt, Germany's 'John Citizen' who, as described in the *Star* yesterday, knew practically nothing about what was going on in the crisis, has had his eyes opened a little. He went to work this morning a little. shakily after watching a night of uncamouflaged troop movements which said more to him than anything else has done for some days past."

In France even "reactionary" M. Flandin, former French Premier, pointed out in *Le Journal* (September 28):

"Even Hitler states his policies before a monster political meeting. . . .

It is common knowledge that parliamentary circles in France are not in agreement as to the best plans for proceeding, and it is difficult for the average Frenchman to understand where France lies.

It has never had communicated to it officially the text of the Anglo-French accord at Berchtesgaden, nor the Hitler memorandum, nor has there been made public . . ."

The *Daily Herald* had already a new high for reportage with a photo illustrating a leading article, caption: "The average German does not want war. Scene in typical German café." The picture showed people carelessly enjoying themselves and with no sign of war-lust. No wonder, for according to the *Daily Express* and the *World's Press News*, in the centre of photo was *Daily Express* staff reporter Dennis Clarke, with Belgian wife, a picture taken by *Express* cameraman Harold Clements.[1]

In this fearful confusion, the main facts that emerged were about the exact times of the movements of Cabinet Ministers all over the world. Enormous emphasis was given to 2 a.m. cables, midnight Cabinet Meetings, M.P.'s arriving at 7.10 a.m., 2 p.m. German mobilisation (splashed in headlines all over the Press and immediately officially denied from Berlin). As Bernard Shaw put it, "All he knew about the international situation was innumerable items of the comings and goings of eminent gentlemen, so that now he was not

[1] The same picture was used in the same way by the *Daily Mail* on November 21st.

Shaw but Bradshaw." Whenever anything happened at an unusual hour, it got a special sort of mystical news value. The Postmaster General appealed for shorter phone-calls and a limiting of non-essential conversations, essential conversations being defined as those where "if there was no telephone you would have sent a telegram saying: Essential receive money by first post", as opposed to a letter beginning "Dear Aunt Martha". In fact, the telephone system became disorganised owing to the tremendous number of calls. The number of quick marriages at Registry Offices jumped 500%. Sale of Wills at several stationers interviewed leapt to three dozen a day, and W. H. Smith's sold out widely, while Deed Boxes and metal cash boxes boomed too. A leading publisher told an observer that sales of new books that should have been averaging 1,600 a week dropped to under 300. And the manager of a chain library said:

"Lots of people come in to say they'll be going away and won't be needing any more books. Just like the holidays. The groceries are full. People are buying up provisions. People are too distracted to read now. This is different from when the business man or politician reads fiction to take his mind off his troubles. But we sell papers all the time. And there's one sort of book we sell—the A.R.P. handbook. We can't get enough in. When we ask for twenty the Home Office supplies two. People are buying a lot of brown paper and paste and labels—that's for the school children: they're to be labelled."

In the London Borough of Metrop, 16 shops visited reported business was slumping, except sugar and newspapers, which had doubled. Tobacco as usual and beer perhaps slightly down, sweets down 50%, cinemas as much as 60%. Motor coach booking offices doing plenty of business, especially single tickets. Said one agent: "There are lots of people going away long distances. I don't blame them. I'd do the same if I could", while another said: "There are lots of people going away. They take single tickets. They're going for the duration of the war." Petrol touched £3 a tin in Kensington. On the 27th the Pound slumped on all centres, particularly Brussels, Geneva and New York, where it reached a new low since 1935, at 4.73⅛ dollars as against 4.82³⁄₁₆ dollars a week before. It was not till the happy 29th, after falling no less than 12 cents, that the Pound jumped 9 cents in a bump.

Spectacular were the rumours which came through every few hours. Typical stories included:

(i) Goering under preventive arrest for attempted mutiny.

(ii) Goering shot in the leg at Munich by an Austrian.

(iii) Hitler's double shot dead.

(iv) German troops have mutinied, mass demonstrations in Munich and elsewhere in Germany against war.

(v) "An advertising agent who returned from Germany yesterday saw a military parade. A private car collided with a tank—and went right through it."

(vi) Chamberlain was going to offer his resignation in Parliament, to be followed by that of Lord Halifax, because of their pro-German tendencies.

(vii) Conscription to begin on September 28.

(viii) R.A.F. is many times stronger than is generally believed and would successfully repulse any enemy attack.

(ix) (From Wales.) "A load of ammunition has just gone through and it is going to be hidden in a coal pit." "They are stopping all the lorries and taking them."

(x) A typist working in a London office rang up the office to say that her mother had refused to allow her to go that day, as there was to be an air raid at 2.30 p.m.

(xi) 200,000 S.S. men mobilised to keep the German civilian population quiet.

(xii) Hitler a neuropath, showing all the symptoms of an orgasmic death-wish.

(xiii) Hitler the only individual in the whole of the Reich who wanted war.

(xiv) German roads crumbling to pieces, because when they made them they had not thought about tanks.

(xv) Germany had 2,000 aeroplanes ready at a moment's

notice to fly on London and we only had 20 that could safely take the air. (This story was spread by a Labour leader who said he had it direct from a Cabinet Minister in the strictest confidence. It paralysed much of Transport House for a whole day.)

All these are wish-fulfilments or fear-fulfilments; as war came closer the stories which indicated the collapse of Germany spread throughout the country, though never officially sponsored. Observers who kept their heads during these days found that they were constantly being informed of absolutely specific facts, times and places, which nearly everyone who heard them immediately accepted and which never turned out to be true. Apparently the centre of these stories was in London, especially Fleet Street, the Stock Exchange and junior personnel in Whitehall. Absolutely typical was the action of one of a Cabinet Minister's secretaries who rang up all his friends and entreated them to leave London at once, as that same day one or other of the two highly secret German plans, the one to abolish London or the one to abolish Czechoslovakia, would probably be put into immediate operation and they didn't know which one it would be. The B.B.C. had to broadcast an official denial of the rumour that the Government was going to take over the railways, thus checking a panic of advance booking and rail congestion. Many of the people one met had unique inside sources of information, and a prominent Liberal Peer gave us the most emphatic assurance that we could do *nothing* against Hitler, owing to the weakness of our defences. This had been explained to him and others at a lunch given at the Carlton that day by "a very very rich American, who insisted on remaining anonymous, even to us". And threatened abdication of King of Italy has apparently not been denied. Perhaps he's abdicated. . . .

Estimated cost of crisis to this country, £40,000,000; to France, now slumping to ruin, £43,000,000.

(h) Opposition . . . .

Unfortunately treaties are made by politicians and leaders, not by ordinary people or anthropologists. Every social scientist, or rather the few social scientists that there are, has realised for the last twenty years that the Treaty of Versailles is a cultural impossibility. And in the Labour Party, Arthur Henderson wrote in 1919: "Millions of Germans are placed under Czechoslovak rule (and Polish and Italian rule). This will create irredentist populations as considerable as those which provoked the Serbian agitation before the war." In 1920 the Labour Party stood for the right of German areas in Czechoslovakia to determine their political future. By 1938 the threat of Hitler and world-wide Fascism had led Labour to take a very different view, and throughout September they insisted that Chamberlain should stand firm and say No to Hitler. It was, however, exceedingly difficult to find out what Labour was doing during the crisis, for like the Conservative Party they seldom think it worth while taking the public into their confidence or issuing any full statement of what happened at any meeting. Certainly Labour made no use of the crisis to enhance party prestige, and when Mass-Observation rang through to a key propaganda official and asked what Labour was doing during the period of maximum anti-Chamberlain feeling, the reply was:

"What are we doing? Oh Hell. Everything. A great mass meeting in the Empress Hall. Sold out three times."

This meeting was on Monday, September 26. Loudspeaker vans all over London had been announcing it for three days, circular letters and Press advertisements, speakers Attlee, Greenwood, etc. At a time

D

when bewilderment was at a peak and feeling not yet transferred from anti-Chamberlain to a national anti-Hitler, Labour's Empress Hall meeting was only half full. At no stage in the crisis did the Opposition show that they really understood what was happening. As they were not in a position to know what was happening in Chamberlain's mind, nor bound by party loyalty to support him, while he was going against their whole policy, it might have been supposed that they would have turned with especial vigour to the other type of information which it was open to them to get, information about public opinion. They did not do so, and as far as our observations go they consistently misjudged public opinion throughout the crisis, were always about two days late.[1]

During the period September 27 to 30, when the whole country was faced with war, opposition would not have been consistent with the situation perhaps, but by the 30th feeling was swinging once more round to the view that we had let down the Czechs and bought peace with shame. But Labour did not attempt to give a lead or crystallise this feeling. On Friday the 30th a Labour spokesman said:

"We can do nothing till the feeling of relief subsides. We may be able to put something over on Monday. You needn't be afraid there will be another national Rat Week. There will be a definite stand, but we must wait and see."

Labour had been clamouring for some weeks past that Parliament be called. Correctly, they insisted that in a democracy the nation's representatives should have an opportunity to discuss the issue. When war seemed inevitable, Chamberlain called Parliament for Wednesday, September 28. The evening before, he made his personal broadcast on all the wave-lengths. By now,

[1] Only positive propaganda was through publisher Victor Gollancz who independently distributed 1,850,000 leaflets in three days, titled *The Great Betrayal*; 5s. a thousand; effective.

the long bewildered public opinion, which had twice
swung dangerously anti-Chamberlain, had been re-
focused by the external actions of Hitler, who had
welded English public opinion together in a way that
has certainly not happened since 1918. When Parliament reassembled on the Wednesday afternoon, the
country was the first time in such a state as might have
justified some of the newspaper generalisations previously
noted as demonstrably false, e.g., "England is thinking",
and so on.

Talking to a Labour M.P. in the lobby before going
in, he told observer:

"Tell you the truth, lad, you know I went through the
last war as a C.O. Well this time I feel that it all has to go
by the board, if it's a case of war between democracy and
the Fascists, then we shall have to safeguard the little we
have left. It's a dirty business, none of us know where we
are in this lot, it's only the Germans and Chamberlain who
know where they are.

I was surprised to hear when I got up to Lancs. that the
men are for stopping Hitler, they know what it means
later. It's the women who are frightened of the chance
of a war now.

We can't tell what will happen over this. They've not
been telling us the truth about things."

Chamberlain then made his speech, in which for the
first time he gave full information of what happened
at his conversations with Hitler. In the middle of his
speech came Hitler's third invite, which brought the
House into a state of hysteria, already fully expressed
in the Press. Once more the Opposition have nothing
to say and the House is adjourned without debate.
Members pour out into the lobbies:

"A young member rushes out, shouts: 'You're not going
to be called up now, you needn't worry', followed by six
others who wave their hands and laugh and shout the news.

Out comes Strabolgi and replies to observer: 'The only
thing we can do is to keep quiet for a day or two, then
see what happens and let go. It's a complete surprise.'
Then Rhys-Davies of Westhoughton comes out and starts
speaking to the observer in Welsh. Observer asks him what
it all means, he says: 'There are some people who are
sorry there is to be no war. Czechoslovakia had to go, it
was only a question as to how and when. Now it's started.'
Then out comes the Archbishop of Canterbury lifting his
head, his eyes red and filled with tears. John Strachey
strides in from outside the Hall, passes the police. They
are taken aback, but he is through and in the Inner Lobby,
too quickly for a policeman to follow him. He reappears
with Maisky, who is smiling. . . . Grandi comes out, a
raincoat slung over his shoulders like a cape; he switches
on an electric grin. . . .

Then out come the Cry, it rings through all the corridors,
and each official takes it on from the next, shouts it, echoing.
It is 4.30 p.m. 'Who goes home?' Everyone looks at the
officers."

In the streets everywhere men rushed screaming:

CRISIS POSTPONED

While next day the channels of Fleet Street and Foreign
Office opinion flooded once more with Premier praise.
The *Daily Sketch* front page simply consisted of a huge
head of Chamberlain gazing into the distance, cap-
tioned:

"How well that faith in Mr. Chamberlain has been
justified: his firmness of spirit and gentleness of heart have
raised humanity to a new level.

Refusing to bow to fatigue, refusing to give way to dis-
couragement, refusing to be intimidated by opposition or
ridicule, he went relentlessly on until his spirit stood alone
between the waiting armies of the two sides."

And on the same afternoon, real public opinion about
the Culture Hero, in Metrop and adjacent boroughs
stood at:

	M	F	Total
	%	%	%
Pro-Chamberlain	46	59	54
Anti-Chamberlain	20	4	10
Mixed, sceptical	16	7	10
Vague, don't know	16	30	26

We have therefore seen Chamberlain swing through 10% anti (after his first flight, September 15–16), then 40% anti (after his terms became known, September 21–22), then again 10% anti (after his Peace Pact at Munich, September 29–30). And at the moment of writing, antis are tending rapidly to build up again, while among men—and in the long run these are much the most important in terms of the expression of public opinion through voting, where nearly three-quarters of about six thousand women studied by Mass-Observation's Worktown survey, vote according to the dominant male's decision—this build-up is more than among women. At every stage in the crisis the women have proved the conservative, peace-at-any-price and pro-Chamberlain element, and what is more, in each one of our snap surveys the results obtained during the day by interviewing women are significantly different from such research when continued during the evening after the men have come home from work.

The crisis has been postponed. In the last hours of this memorable September, Chamberlain, first circled in a fire-brigade spotlight on the verandah of Buckingham Palace, then from an upstairs window at No. 10 Downing Street, brought news of and waved in one hand a scrap of paper on which were typewritten three paragraphs of intense anthropological interest. The middle one:

"We regard the agreement signed last night, and the Anglo-German Naval Agreement, as symbolic of the desire of our two people never to go to war with one another again."

"It's peace in our time," said the Premier, ignoring Spain, China, Poland, and Palestine. "I advise you to go home to your beds," he said, replacing the Golden Bough by a Paper Symbol. This was the scene in Downing Street:

"5.50 p.m. Pavements of Downing Street full and those of Whitehall for about 20 yards from each corner and opposite its entrance. Not much increase in numbers till about 6.15, additions being discounted by those leaving on account of rain. Sellers of flags ('don't forget your waver') and photos of P.M. doing no business. Only three or four children seen with flags. Later an evening paper seller ('Public hero No. 1')—papers did a brisk trade, the papers being used as protection against rain."

7 p.m. Observer estimates rather under 5,000 people in Downing Street and Whitehall.

"Car with Kingsley Wood in it drives up Downing Street. Much cheering and the car is mobbed. It has to stop and people swarm round it and on to it. It is then discovered it is not the P.M. and it proceeds to No. 10 with a good deal of cheering. Young man, working class, cap and smart blue suit says, 'Well they all deserve a cheer.' One or two boos heard but source is not traceable. From near No. 10 man begins to shout loudly, 'We want Chamberlain.' Taken up by crowd. Then crowd chant 'For he's a jolly good fellow.'

7.5. A mail van gets through. Someone says 'Telegrams'. Crowd begins singing 'O God our help in ages past'. Then more of 'We want Chamberlain' and hoorays.

7.9. 'Land of Hope and Glory.' Woman says "e ought to 'ave a decorated car, didn't 'e.'

7.17. A car drives up amid cheers. Chamberlain's car follows. Tremendous cheering, from 80%. About one in every four wave arms with papers, hats, umbrellas, etc. At 7.27 Chamberlain appears at first-floor window. Now

practically 99% are cheering. P.M. stretches out his arm
for silence. Several in crowd appear to take this for a
Fascist salute and stretch forth their arms likewise. Then
follows P.M.'s speech as correctly reported in the Press.

Thus at this climax in national history, and although
the time of the Premier's arrival had been announced
over the wireless, there turned out under half the number of people that can be counted on for a routine Communist rally in Trafalgar Square (and there are 16,000
members of the Communist Party).

No second division football club could survive on a
Chamberlain gate. Nevertheless next morning the Press
arranged photos and headlines which gave the impression
of enormous crowds; with captions typified by the
Mirror's : "The enthusiasm of the nation was led by
the King, who . . ." and so on.

Next day Hitler started marching to occupy what he
wanted in Czechoslovakia, as a result of these discussions
at which the Czechs had at no time been represented.
Four undergraduates of Sidney Sussex, Cambridge,
at breakfast at October 1, eating the new Disney cereal,
Snow White, summed it :

"I know we've let them down like hell, but then we're
always swines, aren't we ?"

(i) General Electors

THE month of September, 1938, will provide the historian
of the future, or even of next year, with a supremely
illuminating insight into sense and statesmanship and
the status quo. But if, as has been the custom in the
past, the historian accepts as statements of fact the
numerous published assertions as to what the public of
England are thinking about it all, he will, as so often
before, be a typically lousy historian.

Alone of the declarations by politicians during this period stands the Hon. Harold Nicolson, M.P. for West Leicester, with a near objective judgment:

"I quite recognise that the danger of war was such that we were all filled with justified emotions.

When these anxieties were removed, the whole country felt an immediate emotion of relief; and I regret to state that this emotion manifested itself in the House on Wednesday in one of the most lamentable exhibitions of mass hysteria that great institution has ever witnessed."

This called forth bitter comment from several Press sources, caused the West Leicester Conservative Association to issue a widely-published statement in support of Nicolson, who is National Labour. In keeping with the current Press sentiments, the *Daily Express* then carried a leader headed, "Let Him Resign":

"West Leicester Conservative Association issues a statement which is, in effect, support for Mr. Harold Nicolson, National Socialist member for the division, who has taken up an anti-Chamberlain line on the Czech issue.

This association plainly does not represent Conservative opinion in the division.

Does Mr. Nicolson doubt it?

Very well. Let him resign his seat and put the issue to the test in a by-election. Then we'll see."

It need hardly be pointed out that such a proposal would be impracticable and absurd; and while all the results of Mass-Observation confirm the statement that the West Leicester Conservative Association quite probably does not represent Conservative opinion in the West Leicester division, this would of course be true of all other Associations. By this time (October 4) the Press (probably influenced by advertisers, who had suffered severely from the marked trade-slump during the crisis) was shouting that the country was solid pro-Chamberlain and that everything was back to normal, with permanent peace in immediate prospect. We venture to suggest that by the time this book is published any reasonable person looking up the papers of the post-Munich week-end will be not only surprised but amazed. "Have you given your peace gift?" asked Monday's *Daily Express*, heavy type on front page; gay centre-page pictures informed us "Everybody's happy and everybody's spending" in Tuesday's *Sketch* . . . Previous marked falls on the Stock Exchange in the past five years had been:

Hitler arrives in Power (January, 1933)
Assassination of Dolfuss (July, 1934)
Italian Mobilisation (October, 1935)
Militarisation of Rhineland (March, 1936)
Hitler rejects Versailles River clauses (November, 1936)
Mussolini's anti-French speech (May, 1938)
Sudeten negotiations suspended (August, 1938)

Every big paper, including the *Herald*, filled pages with praises of Chamberlain, and not to be outdone, the Premier gave the people a pat on the back, told how the deliberations of the four politicians at Munich had been influenced, apparently in some mystic way, "by the peoples of the different countries". During one whole week, no outsider reading an English news-paper could have guessed that an increasing proportion of the population were feeling once more increasingly bewildered, fearful and ashamed. The readers them-selves didn't guess it in many cases. That is a very important point. The fact that the papers hang back has a delaying effect on public opinion, because news-papers are so much looked to for social and talk sanction. People's sense of shame about Britain has to be backed up collectively, in order to be positive and recognised, just as much as smoking, football pools, etc. (see MO's *First Year's Work* 1938, Lindsay Drummond, 2*s*., on these social factors). By representing pro-Chamberlain as the universally felt sentiment, (when in fact even at its top point he never scored more than 54%), individuals in their homes were temporarily made to feel that being anti-Chamberlain was old, anti-social, or Socialist—until, at work and in the streets, by the third day each had gradually found hundreds of others agreeing in this secret shame.

And the evidence so far to hand suggests that for the first few days many people *were* secretive about their sentiment, which was often of acute personal discomfort at the whole Czech scheme. Gradually they found that a large number of other individuals shared this point of view, and then felt relief. In its simple form, as expressed by most working-class people, this attitude amounted to the assertion that we had let down the whole tradition of England's pledges for honesty, fair play and resistance to threats.

The B.B.C. lent its influential support to this repressing of public opinion by broadcasting in numerous news bulletins information about the tremendous fan-mail received by the Premier at No. 10 and Chequers. It was stated that he would do his best, in time, to acknowledge every one of these. The impression given and stated by the Premier himself was that these were all letters of tribute and praise. Yet from one public meeting alone, in a provincial town where an observer happened to be present, 800 letters of protest to the Premier were actually written, paid for and posted by members of the audience.

We have already seen that in ordinary times a large proportion of readers of newspapers do not believe what they read. We think that whenever public opinion—what ordinary people say to one another—finds itself unrepresented through public channels, this tendency increases. Indeed, that is the one factor which forces the Press back into line with the public, and is largely responsible for the notable cyclic fluctuations in mispresentation. But it's easy for the *leaders themselves*, without research channels into everyman to get from these media this aimed-at impression that the nation is solid behind them. Undoubtedly this misunderstanding influenced the Conservative Party in planning a snap General Election for November. Yet through agents in the constituencies, and straws in the wind like West Leicester, came a slightly better indication of popular sentiment. Though there are many other factors inevitably involved in an election liable to beat all records for confusion of feeling and fact, we can at least safely say that factual observation and real analysis would not show the nation "behind Munich." On the other hand, a sufficient proportion may well favour Conservatism to any alternative at this time, when many people think that Chamberlain is no more than "playing for time", and that we must and should fight "Hitler" in the end. At the moment there are indications that Conservative leaders themselves may become aware of this especial gap between Press and public opinion before an election is finally decided on.

How little the Press can fix people's attitudes over a period of weeks was shown by the failure of Empire Free Trade and the tremendous failure of the American Press to oust Roosevelt.

But if, as one is bound to conclude, the written word in Britain is sometimes inconsistent, there is no reason to accuse Herr Hitler of similar slovenliness. Steadily he works through the points of his four-million-selling *Mein Kampf*. He has now reached Point 3. In speeches, however, he permits himself some latitude:

"May 17, 1933. "The German people have no thought of invading any country."

March 13, 1934. "The German Government have never questioned the validity of the Treaty of Locarno."

May 21, 1935. "The German Government will scrupulously observe every treaty voluntarily concluded . . . in particular they will hold to the Treaty of Locarno. . . . Germany neither intends nor wishes to interfere in the internal affairs of Austria, to annex Austria or to conclude an Anschluss."

March 8, 1936. "Germany will never break the Peace of Europe. . . . I regard the struggle for German equality as concluded to-day. We have no territorial demands to make in Europe."

September 26, 1938. "Now the last problem confronts us. It (the Sudeten question) is the last territorial claim which I have to make in Europe."

Point 4 of his Party Programme is to get colonies; after that, conquer France.

Against Hitler, is ranged, privately and publicly, the hatred (often bitter hatred) of most working-class Britishers. A Worktown vandriver, age 30, represents the rare pro-Hitler. On September 24 he said:

"No, I don't think there will be a war, because it looks like Hitler against all the world. You can't talk to some fellows and say you like Hitler, but somehow I have a sneaky regard for him. There must be some good in it, 'cause I've never heard any good word about him in any paper."

3

DEMOCRACY AND FACTS

PERHAPS we have adduced enough evidence to show that many of the public decisions and nearly all the news in the recent series of international crises have been based often on inaccurate or inadequate reports of fact, and always on inadequate representation or too adequate misrepresentation of public opinion.

In a totalitarian country the only facts that really matter in a crisis are the ones which the leaders admit. At certain points they have to be influenced by the facts as they look to the men and women in the streets, by public opinion, but only if this opinion becomes so marked as to threaten the régime itself. But in a democratic country the facts as they look to each individual are implicity admitted as valid, for on this view, and on this view alone, are the politicians elected by each person's right to vote. The existence of alternative parties and secret ballot leaves no question but that in Britain the opinion of each adult is entitled to play a part in determining how and by whom the country is run. The democratic system of elections, on which Britain's government is based, has grown and expanded rapidly in the past century. Far more rapidly than a similar wide distribution of, say, higher education or wages. Therefore, while on polling day the professor's vote is as good as the miner's, all the rest of the time the professor has numerous opportunities to express his point of view publicly, and in print; the miner has not. Obviously there are many factors complicating this, but the cardinal fact is that a functioning democracy

must be based firmly on the opinions, wishes and
hopes of at least a third of the community. And that in
national and international affairs, especially, the only
opportunity which the ordinary person has to make his
attitude felt is about once every four years at the parliamentary elections. Between these periods the national
and international position may change almost beyond
recognition. The leaders must take the drastic decisions.
That does not mean that they must ignore the opinions
of the mass of the people, even though that mass may be
"ill-informed" (ill-informed by the leaders). In practice,
though, the leaders are still running government in the
same sort of way as a hundred years ago, before the
general franchise. When Chamberlain makes his three
visits to Hitler, he alone represents England. England has
not been asked about it. And Chamberlain does whatever
he and his immediate circle (the Inner Cabinet as it
became called in the crisis) decide. But if public opinion
becomes so strong that even the professors and politicians
can't miss it, if people are seething in 'buses and pubs
and shops, then the political party to which the Prime
Minister belongs gets seriously alarmed. Because sooner
or later it must come before the country again, and ask
all these private individuals who have been ignored in
making the decisions, to vote and enable the same party
to carry on for another four years. In the middle of the
last week in September, public feeling was so strong
that if Chamberlain had then given in to Hitler, the
Conservatives would have lost an enormous number
of supporters, including many of their own Members of
Parliament; that feeling got through even to the top of
the political pinnacle, though the police refused entry
to Downing Street.

Our evidence suggests that if Chamberlain had
then insisted on giving in to Hitler, there might well
have been serious riots in London and elsewhere, while
the pro-Chamberlain Press showed every sign of assisting

in an anti-Chamberlain uproar on this one issue. Now brought into the position where he had to make a stand, an enormous body of public opinion crystallised again in his favour and projected itself onto Hitler but not onto the Germans as a whole—as we have seen, this process was already marked by March of this year. The consequent mobilisation and intense strain over the whole country reached a climax when Parliament was recalled on Wednesday, September 28. His almost-crying radio speech the night before had prepared the whole country for inevitable war by the week-end. Now, with Parliament packed out and all those responsible for expressing the country's condition through the medium of Press, radio and film in attendance, Chamberlain rose to speak. His procedure was described by the *Daily Telegraph* thus:

"All that the Prime Minister had been saying for an hour in a speech of stern unflinching candour portended the grim decision, the last arbitrament of war, for which members had come prepared. They listened sombrely intent, indignation plainly burning hotter, determination hardening.

Then without a change of key or tone, save that the quiet precise voice had suddenly something of eagerness, Mr. Chamberlain in a few sentences told of his 'one more last, last appeal' to Herr Hitler, his message to Signor Mussolini, and the swift consequences, the new chance opening that peace may yet be saved.

Sudden was the shock, immense the change. Set, tense faces were transformed. Members leapt to their feet and cheered and cheered again, waving their order papers aloft.

The surge of relief, of pride in the strenuous effort, of confidence in the Prime Minister's strong leadership. . . . Not Gladstone in his most compelling hour had ever won a triumph like that."

The triumph was another invitation to go and listen to Hitler. Coming in that place and at that moment, it worked perfectly. Even the Prime Minister's most severe critics, ace journalists like Jordan of the *News Chronical*, lost all objectivity, filled the newspapers with reportage of this sort:

"Since the people of this country first earned the right to govern themselves by an elective Parliament, there have been no scenes at Westminster comparable to those which passed yesterday into history; and there probably never will be again. . . .

When he (Chamberlain) came into the House—after prayers were over and the special Collect had been said— he was as quiet and lonely as a ghost; and as pallid. I never saw a more solitary man than that thin figure in black who moved so quietly and then, on the way to his seat, was stopped, suddenly, by a wave of cheering. . . .

Parliament cheers like no other mob; if its approval is as primitive as that of a football crowd, it is usually as harsh and unechoing as the roar of a beast. . . ."

So that Chamberlain went off again with an almost unanimous press-film-radio mandate to negotiate. This time, without any delay for the public to get going again, he had signed within a few hours the terms which the day before had aroused England to a condition where a large proportion of the population were not only ready but even eager to "have a go at Hitler", "it's now or never to stop the bastard". Telephone and aeroplane made Chamberlain's action possible.

Once more the man in the street could do nothing about it, but this time the Conservative Party had less to fear for the future, because in between Chamberlain's second and third meetings on the same subject with Hitler, the tension of war had been provided and released, obscuring other issues. But each crisis dissatisfies more and more men and women with a situation in which they find themselves upset for weeks by sheer lack of information, though they do not necessarily of course connect it with those responsible, at this end, for upsetting them.

All through the crisis fantasy and fact had become entangled, as the *Manchester Guardian* noticed: "This crisis has never for long escaped a touch of unreality. A world war for the difference between the Anglo-French plan and the Hitler memorandum has always carried gleams from the larger lunacy about it, and there was something about the atmosphere of the House to-day which did not quite match the momentous issues of peace or war."

Let us now examine the same sort of hiatus as occurred at so many stages in the crisis, the same sort of hit-and-miss relationship between leader and led, old habit and new, in several other aspects of 1938 England. For we find constantly that the pattern of society is changing in a way which is seldom noticed as significant, and even less often recognised officially by the leaders, but which is nevertheless storing up new tangles and conflicts for the not distant future; bearing in mind that, roughly speaking, Fascism thrives on fantasy, while democracy has grown up with science and recognition of newly noticed facts.

We will therefore next consider two new, one fairly new, and one exceedingly old social habit; and subject them to mass-observational reportage and analysis in several ways. This may illuminate other, more "normal", aspects of this Britain.

4

ALL-IN, ALL-OUT

(a) The Programme reads:

JIMMY B——   *v.*   HUMPHREY P——

Place, Worktown Stadium. An old building in a poor area. Passing a small yard and getting a ticket (four price categories: 6*d.*, 1*s.*, 2*s.*, and 2*s.* 6*d.*) one enters the crowded hall. Shabby elegance is the first impression, but very clean. The hall is of rectangular shape, each sidewall divided by buttresses. Between the buttresses the wall is whitewashed. The windows are curtained by red and blue crêped paper, a little worn and bleached by incoming rain. The wall four feet to the ground is painted red with a green band around the top. The 2*s.* and 2*s.* 6*d.* seats are red plush and evidently originated from very different sources; the plush is rather worn and holes are common. Shilling seats are plain wood with red crêpe coating, and five feet away, separated by a four-feet-high fence, are the 6*d.* stands. The whole place slightly sloping.

In the centre is the ring. Eight o'clock, the lights are switched off, only the ring remains illuminated by a red light. The promoter climbs into the ring, a very militant-looking man, with waxed moustache and evening suit. He announces the fight. In the meanwhile the referee comes in the ring, a wrestler himself, who took on this job for this evening. Jimmy B—— and Humphrey P—— arrive. A Worktown coal bagger watches the

114

fight while skilled observer takes down as he sees and
says. Thus B—— looks tough and tanned, P—— is
tough but not so tanned. The names of both are announced and the referee examines them rather cursorily
to detect any concealed object such as nails in the shoes
or grease on the body, long fingernails, etc. Then he
reads out the rules very quickly:

A MAN IS DEFEATED WHEN—

1. His shoulders are held flat on the mat for three consecutive seconds.
2. He calls "ENOUGH" (Submission fall).
3. He fails to rise when knocked down by a blow or
fails to return to the ring when thrown out, before a count
of 10 seconds.
4. He is disqualified for a Foul under Group "A".
Note.—When a man is felled by a blow, his opponent may:
1. Continue wrestling to obtain a fall or submission.
2. Retire to a neutral corner while his man is counted out.

and enumerates fouls:

> Abdomen below belt punching
> Direct Knuckle Punch in face.
> Breaking a limb deliberately
> Kicking, except to get free from holds
> Gouging, scratching, biting
> Butting in face
> Strangling
> Striking an opponent when he is on the mat, felled
> from a blow.

Then both fighters shake hands, P—— very grudgingly.

"The first round opened in a slow but tense atmosphere.
P—— secured a full Nelson on B—— and pushed him
well over the ropes. B—— managed to get free, returned
to hold on P—— but was crashed to the canvas heavily
by P—— with a flying move, there was very little excitement
in this round except when B—— had a leg scissor on P——'s

head, crossing his legs and pressing him between them.
P—— was shouting in Agony, Gong saved him. Second
round P—— opened this round in a most unexpected
manner, without waiting for the Gong, he rushed to B——'s
corner grabbed him by the hair and kneed him fiercely three
times in quick succession in the lower part of the groin,
B—— screamed in agony, doubles up holding his pelvis.
P—— grabs him and lifts B—— over head. Jack the referee
springs on P——'s back pulling his head backwards tearing
at his hair but has no success and over the ropes and into
the ringside seats goes B——, there is another big scuffle
by the ringside spectators for Jack the referee is thrown
over too—P——runs round the ring beating chest—meanwhile the din is terrific—crowds shouting—dirty rat, swine,
bastard, lousy pig, then missiles hurtle through the air
lighted cigarettes, a key, a piece of Billiard chalk and observer
had to dodge a small iron bolt thrown at B—— from the
other side of the ring; P—— won't let either B—— or Referee
back into the ring, spectators shaking their fists at him.
The hall is in an uproar. B—— manages to get back but
P—— seizes him by the head—and forces him on the ropes,
gouges his eyes, then knees him again, B—— drops on
the canvas close to observer, he is a pitiable object eyes
almost shut doubles up holding testicles shouting he has
hurt me. Bell goes but P—— rushes at B——'s stomach.
P——'s second runs to him and just manages to get him
to the corner, Referee picks up stool and challenges P——
—a comical sight—Jack 7 stone and P—— 17 stone.

Third round P—— again beats gong, rushes at B——
puts B——'s head over the rope and then lifts middle rope
over part of his neck. B—— cannot get loose and seems
to be choking and the crowd are on their feet yelling and
waving their hands—the Referee helped by both seconds
manages to extricate B—— but P—— grabs him a quick
aeroplane spin, gets him with his left hand round the shoulder,
right hand through his left, swings him three times round
in the air and pins him with his shoulders on the floor for
the count of three. Boos and Boos and one or three cheering
in the 6d. stands.

M.C. announces first fall to P—— in 2 minutes 50 secs.
of the third round.

B—— can scarcely rise, the referee is in a fit of temper, attacks P—— with stool, P—— chases him round ring—gong goes for the 4th round—P—— still has stool so B—— picks up the water bowl and with a terrific bang lands it on P——'s head. P—— drops almost unconscious. B—— jumps at him, Jack the referee drops on stomach to count but is fast between wrestlers and can't be seen and he manages to free himself, and counts 1 2 3 very quickly. Second fall to B——.

The positions are now reversed B—— is aggressor P—— is complaining to second about someone who has burned him with a cigarette, observer who is close to him can see an unmistakable burn on his thigh.

Fifth round starts P—— can scarcely stand, his left leg is weak from Indian Deathlock in last round. B—— slams P—— to canvas on his stomach—then secures Deathlock P—— pulls most agonising expressions and offers his hands to someone to pull him out of the ring. B—— drags him back. B—— kneels over P—— and forces Deathlock—P—— shouts—sweat is rolling off both of them—P—— suddenly goes silent then knocks with his hand three times on the floor, he has submitted, so B—— is the winner.

The crowd cheers.

The M.C. declares B—— to be the winner, he goes to shake hands with P——. P—— refuses and tries to hit B——. B—— kicks P—— three times on his weakened leg, the crowd cheers. P—— limps across ring and threatens man in crowd who has burned him. All one section raise their fists few cheer him, but are hushed.

At last both men are coaxed to dressing tent."

Observer asks his neighbour how he enjoyed it. "I can't tell you proper—I can't believe my own bloody eyes." This was a typical fight of so-called dirty wrestling; the next fight described is a clean one. As a matter of fact it is considered as the titbit of the evening by those who like clean good wrestling and plenty of action.

Lew Falkner   *v.*   Jack Atherton

The general atmosphere is pretty tense, as these are
both old rivals. A worker takes over the commentary,
observer scribbling.

"The first round opens in a very quick and exciting manner.
Lew opens the round with the monkey climb on Atherton,
this is one of the most spectacular throws in Free Style
Wrestling, Lew grasps Atherton round his neck with his
hands, pushes him against the ropes still holding Atherton's
neck he springs quickly and buries both feet in Atherton's
stomach, Lew falls to the canvas bringing Atherton with
him, releases Atherton's neck, simultaneously shooting out
both his feet with tremendous force until both legs are straight
Atherton shoots in the air about 8 feet, what a helpless figure
he looks when crashes to the canvas with a sickening thud.
With an amazing speed for a man of that weight, about 14
stone, he is on his feet. Lew seems to allow him a second or
two to regain his senses but Jack does not want any of this,
he advances quickly to Lew with a characteristic gesture he
wets his finger tips. The crowd roar, they expect some
fireworks and Jack does not disappoint them. Atherton
makes as though to grasp Lew's shoulder with a quick
feint he grasps his ankles pulls them up and Lew drops
heavily on his back. Lew is now on his back and Atherton
has Lew's ankles under his arm pits. The crowd is shouting
and Lew is gazing rather fearfully at Atherton. 'Look out
Lew he is after the Boston Grab', shouts one fellow and
he speaks what is in the mind of most of the audience, but
Lew don't need telling, that body of his is twisting and
twirling in every direction, no use Lew, Jack is not going
to let you, with a quick twist Atherton turns Lew face
downwards still pulling up Lew's feet he drops heavily on
his victim's back, he has got the Boston Grab. Lew turns
an agonised face to the crowd tears the mat with his hand,
while groaning in a kind of animal voice, meanwhile his
opponent sits on his back and gives a friendly smile to the
crowd, but that is your own undoing Jack, maybe he loosened
his pressure for a moment while he smiled, with amazing
strength born of agony Lew succeeds in straightening his
back and crush against the ropes goes Atherton, cheers
from the crowd, but Lew cannot rise and the ref counts

up to eight before he manages to regain his feet Atherton rushes at him but Lew lands a right swing to Jack's head, looks like Lew was only foxing and there is Jack almost among the sweet peas only the gong saves him that time.

Immediately the gong goes for the second round, Lew attacks Atherton with both elbows to the head, his speed is terrific and he punches Atherton hopeless against the rope, Atherton sags helplessly over the rope he appears to be all out, but he has a trick up his sleeves, quickly he raises both feet and grabs Lew in the stomach, with a bound he is on top of Lew, quickly secures an armlock and Lew is bound for the count of three. Atherton gains first fall in 1 minute 50 seconds of the second round with an armlock and body press.

Third round Lew starts this round in a determined manner, secures a full Nelson on Jack, approaches Atherton from behind, pushes his arms below Atherton's shoulders and brings his hands round to the nape of his neck, he forces Atherton against the rope and then drops on all fours as Atherton falls back, he trips over Lew and Lew secures a back press he easily holds Atherton on the count of three gaining the second fall in 1 minute 3 seconds.

Fourth round. Both are in deadly earnest this round for the deciding fall. Atherton seems to be more of the aggressor and is lucky to get Lew's head in an arm lock, he takes him round the ring with it and smile his back is to the ref he lowers his arms and it becomes a strangle hold. Lew's head is very red and it seems to be choking, the ref warns Atherton but he refuses to let go, both seconds jump in the ring try to strangle him somehow or other Lew manages to free himself, the crowd now on their feet and there is dangerous glint in Lew's eyes as it advances at his opponent Jack crouches up in the corner and Lew bombards him with punches to the stomach. The crowd is cheering as Lew with a terrific punch sends Atherton clean over the rope. He drops beside observer and with deliberation seats himself in a seat just vacated by a nervous fan. He allows the ref to count up to 8 then slowly climbs in the ring, the ref stops at 9 to give him chance to go in. Lew is quickly at him again this time secures a full Nelson. Jack manages to put Lew on the back, Lew immediately lets go, as he

thinks it is the ref, warning him to let go. Immediately
Atherton puts off the ropes with the flying tackle, sends
Lew to the mat. Lew seems too dazed to know what is
happening and is counted out."

At each Free Style Wrestling night are six fights. A
typical programme (and typical misprints):

PROGRAMME
Commencing at 8 P.M.

**No. 1.   Great Return Heavy-weight Contest 12 5-Minute
Rounds:**

BOBBY   *v.*   JACK PYE

London. The 15 stone Champion of the South. Formerly of Huddersfield where he was a pupil of Douglas Clark. He has defeated King Curtis, Chick Knight, Harry Pye and many other front-rank wrestlers.

Doncaster. The Doncaster Panther and Film Star. The greatest terror of them all: fears no man. Has beaten Carver Doone and King Kong, also fought the world's ex-champion, Jim Londos, the perfect exponent of All-in-Wrestling. Y— challenges the world.

No. 2.   Special Thriller 10 5-Minute Rounds:

AL FULLER   *v.*   JOE ROBINSON

Canada. One of Canada's premier welter-weights who is a fighter from gong to gong.

Springfield. Referee and Wrestler. Regarded by many as the best light heavy-weight in England. Knows the game from A to Z.

No. 3.   Extra Special Contest 10 5-Minute Rounds:

JIM REID   *v.*   JACK ALKER

Leigh. Brother of the famous Joe Reid.

Wigan. British Lightweight Championship winner, 1934.

1 Washday, Bolton 1938, © Humphrey Spender

2 Overheard conversations, bus top, Bolton 1938,
© Humphrey Spender

3   Blackpool, 1937, © Humphrey Spender

4   On Blackpool Pier, summer 1937, © Humphrey Spender

5   George Tomlinson Electioneering, Bolton 1938 (George Tomlinson became Minister of Education in the postwar Labour government), © Humphrey Spender

6   Electioneering, Bolton 1937 (children were encouraged to join in by the candidates who distributed paper hats etc.), © Humphrey Spender

7 Religious gathering, Bolton 1937, © Humphrey Spender

8 Women canvassing for by-election, Bolton 1938,
© Humphrey Spender

9 The picturesque side of Bolton, 1937, © Humphrey
Spender

10 Wasteland, Bolton 1937, © Humphrey Spender

11 Life in the Lambeth Walk, 1938, by Humphrey
Spender, © BBC Hulton Picture Library

12 Doing the Lambeth Walk, 1938, by Humphrey
Spender, © BBC Hulton Picture Library

No. 4.   Sixty-minute Contest 6 10-Minute Rounds.

LEW FAULKNER   *v.*   JACK ATHERTON

Bolton. The Lancashire Coast Express. Atherton says he will put a stop Lew's popularity !	London. One of the most feaned men in the game. Can be clean; but if the other man asks for trouble Jack will sure be there.

There are usually two heavy-weight fights and two light-weight fights. All observers report the same, light-weight fights don't arouse very much enthusiasm, even if the wrestlers are very skilful. Asking for the explanation, we got two. It is essential for the crowd that the two men in the ring can stand more than they themselves; and only a few of the crowd are really able to understand the science of wrestling.

The quality of the fighters varies very much. Some make special use of costumes, the "Golden Phantom", for example, appears with a golden mask and in golden tights; though he aroused in the first place excitement, the crowd soon got bored when they found that he was pushing about "like a schoolboy". Usually wrestlers wear black or blue trunks, the upper part of the body naked. Beneath the trunks they have to wear very close fitting rubber tights; this prevents them from being seriously hurt.

(b) The Stadium and Boss

Until recently there was no sport in Worktown which people used to watch without being vitally interested in betting or gambling on it. Free Style Wrestling is rather a young acquisition to Worktown. In 1933 the Stadium was opened. It happened that Mr. R., its promoter, who was an old amateur wrestler and owner of a pub, noticed in his daily newspapers that Free Style wrestling had in

the U.S. become a great thrill and a big financial success.
Slowly he developed the idea of introducing the sport
in Worktown. Talks with his customers confirmed his
conviction that this idea was a good one, and, as at the
same time in other towns here and there Free Style
Wrestling was taken up, he risked an experiment.

An old mill was hired and converted. This was the
easier part of the job. Much more difficult it was to
find the type of wrestler whom the crowd wanted. Mr.
R. is a scientifically-minded man and he studied very
carefully the reaction of his audience. He wanted to
satisfy their taste and his pocket. Starting with the seats
he tried all different kinds of arrangements, and many
times he had all seats out and in again until he found the
best arrangement. Now he knows in which proportion
he has to provide his 6*d*. and 2*s*. 6*d*. seats, as experience
told him that the number of booked 2*s*. 6*d*. seats remains
always in a certain proportion to the 6*d*. stands. He
bought his seats from the Grand Variety Theatre when
this was newly decorated. He is convinced that his
real competition is from this same theatre. He has a
greater ambition than to run this stadium; he would
like to build a brand new one; on his own plans, with
a very big ring which could be taken out and the place
converted into a circus or a skating stage. He is waiting
until he has enough money of his own, he does not
want to be dependent on big capital. He likes to carry
out ideas which he gets himself, and hates parley with
50 people before anything can be done. "There is no
big business in All-In Wrestling, and this is the reason
why the newspapers give it no publicity," he says. There
is no union of proprietors, but they are on friendly terms
and help each other in discovering new wrestlers. There
is an unwritten but accepted rule that in a town where
there is one stadium no proprietor will come and open
another one. Experience had taught them this lesson;
because always when two stadiums were opened it ended

with both closing down, not so much because the number of customers was too small, as because the number of good wrestlers was too small.

He has his place open once a week in summer and twice a week in winter. Two-thirds of the customers are regular comers. He gets his new customers mainly through his old ones. Newspapers give him no publicity. But he founded a club of the friends of Free Style Wrestling where they meet every Sunday night. Usually they have a concert, sometimes women wrestlers or mud wrestling. The club room is attached to the Stadium and painted with the same red and green. It has a little stage, and the Sunday concerts are in fact variety numbers on a small scale. The walls are decorated with the most sentimental pictures: "Mother's Darling", a little boy caressed by his mother; "Mother's Kiss", a little girl kissing her mother; "The Hunter's Friend", a hunter with a big gun caressing a young deer, and so on.

In connexion with the club he runs Keep Fit classes, but only those for the women are a success.

Asked what he thinks the main reasons for his crowded audiences, Mr. R. says: "Thrill, and to see men who can stand more than themselves. Free Style Wrestling is no good if the crowd thinks they could stand it themselves. This is a reason why Free Style Wrestling in Wigan is always a failure. There the coal miners are used to rough stuff themselves and can't be impressed by a fight."

The necessity to provide thrill makes it difficult to find the right type of wrestlers. He gets them by writing to the more famous ones and fixing up a date and by trying out men who come to him for a job. If a man comes he gives him a chance. But very often he is a failure. To be a successful wrestler the man must be clever. It is not enough that he is master of the science of wrestling, he has to be a clever actor too. He has seen

so many good wrestlers who had to give up because they
lacked this ability and could not arouse any enthusiasm
among the audience. The crowd is really tricky, first
thing to give them is a favourite, so long as they can
cheer him and boo the opponent everything is all right
and they enjoy themselves thoroughly. "The crowd is
really most unfair." Though the rules were made up in
accordance with the taste for rough stuff of the Work-
towners and leave quite a wide scope for everything,
they can't bear their favourite to be counted out. If
the referee disqualifies the favourite, they immediately
shout for a fresh referee, and very often he has to fulfil
the wish. They don't like any disqualifying for a foul,
because they come here to amuse themselves for an evening and don't want the fight stopped after the second
round. They want a dirty wrestler, and though they
shout "foul" and boo a lot it is dirty wrestling which
gives them a thrill, makes the excitement and brings
them back. As a matter of fact, in his experience a
crowd is more satisfied the more they boo. The referee
must be chosen very carefully, but a heavy-weight won't
do. The crowd likes the referee thrown out of the ring;
it is fun for them, and a heavy-weight referee can't ever
make a comical figure, which a light referee very often
does. He himself gets a sure laugh if a small 9 stone
man is crawling on the back of a 17 stone man, or tries
to separate two heavy men. It looks like a fly crawling
on the back of an elephant. The crowd would not like
to miss this comical aspect of the evening.

As for fake; there is no fake, or very seldom, swears
R. Quite naturally the men are good friends before and
after the fight; it's just the same as in the war, you had
to fight your enemy soldier, before you did fight him
you had no grievance against him, and afterwards if
you are captured you make good friends; but during
the fight there is a real fight for life and death. And
exactly he same happens with wrestling. How often

has it happened that a man came in the ring and said he can fight anybody, but after five minutes he had to give up, he was finished. He remembers one man particularly who had such an experience. He comes now every Monday night, but you should see him getting in a fury shouting all over the place "son of a bitch, try you" when it happened, as it did last Monday, with Brookes on the mat downwards, and Pye sitting on his back pulling Brookes' arms up his back, Brookes helpless in agony. A voice shouted "ignore him".

"Some people call it a fake, but it is necessary for a wrestler, if the opponent gets a hold on him, to go with this hold and not to push him away," says Boss R.

(c) The Wrestler

The wrestler is paid £1 10*s*. to £5 per performance. There is no betting inducement, and so the urge to *win* is not so vital as the urge to please. The wrestler is an actor as much as a victor. Ace wrestler is George Gregory who lives near Worktown. Here is part of an observer's write up of him for a local newspaper:

"It was not till he had left school and started work as a nurseryman that young George Gregory first tried his arm at wrestling. In those grand old days of Lancashire wrestling there was a regular Sunday gang of 'Sherwin's gang' who swam and fought beside the banks of Rumworth Lodge, on the good green stretches of turf, only a few minutes from the Gregory home. George joined in with them, and very soon showed an exceptional wrestling pep and dynamite. But he was not to stay with that crowd long, for his pep made him want to get out into the greater world, and soon he took his luck in both of his powerful hands. He shipped for Australia.

In Australia he wrestled wherever and whenever he could, including in booths and in sideshows. From this experience he learned much, as well as from lessons under the king of clean wrestlers, Billy Riley, of Wigan. Back in England after three years, he got down to serious scrapping, and during the last four years has risen to the very front rank. He is now one of the biggest draws in the country.

I asked Gregory who was the all-in champion for Britain. Sitting on a hard chair, his fine red setter dog at his feet, the picture of fitness, as mild and pleasant-looking an eye as I have ever seen, he told me about that. He said it was probably between himself and Clarke. 'It's very hard to say who is the champ. There's no sort of control board or central body to decide these things or official organisation or anything of that sort.' He was very dissatisfied with this arrangement.

Three times he has tried, with friends, to set up a board to control the number, rules, fees, weights, of the wrestlers. He had lost a lot of his own money in the attempt. The first attempt was going nicely when the treasurer did a flit with the funds. The second had too many people on the committee and petered out from too much talk. The third was the best, and the promoters had to take notice of it. They said they would have nothing to do with it unless they had representatives on it. This was agreed to, and their representatives then set to work very effectively to sabotage the whole scheme, which therefore failed like all the others.

'The hardest thing is to get the wrestlers together,' said George. And so this attempt to organise the roughest worked workers on earth failed, and thousands of them, all over the country are at the mercy of the many promoters. It is common for many to fight for a mere pittance, to suffer the agony of 'scissors' or 'squeeze', and get paid less than twenty people pay to come in and watch them do it. And this lack of organisation has damaged the interests of good wrestling; anyone who can put on an act can get into the ring now. As Gregory put it, 'lots of fellows come into this game, they're just like flies, they give a kick and bite exhibition and cause a certain amount of excitement. That makes it bad for the fellers that are good wrestlers. These other fellows will wrestle for next to nothing. It's a great pity it isn't properly organised—because it is a fine sport—there's no kidding.'

I asked George what he thought of the articles that *John Bull* had been publishing, which said the fights were fake. He smiled. He agreed some were 'joey', but no real wrestler found it worthwhile to do that sort of thing. He said, 'It's very plain to see that the man who wrote those articles didn't know anything about it. There's only men in the game who could understand that part of it. Why, he did not even say who he was.' He explained that no one could go on with wrestling unless they had enthusiasm and will-to-win; because all-in is not money for jam: it's money for getting jammed about. I asked what it felt like when a bout got tough. He told me that 'No one can say they enjoy it when they are kicking and punching. Well, when all's said and done, that's too much isn't it? Those are not the real fights. The real fights are the ones you get with real fellows, like Douglas Clarke, and then it's a pleasure to fight and fight clean.'

I asked if the wrestler notices the yells, jeers and cheers that a crowd scream at the fighters all the time. He said he never noticed. 'You see, you have too much to look after without listening to that stuff.'

He lit a cigarette, and I asked him how he kept fit. He does not do any walks, skipping, running, but concentrates entirely on wrestling itself: on practising grips, balance, muscle-control. The most important thing, he says, is 'to be any good wrestling you have got to have that little bit of fire that makes you feel you can squeeze your man in two. You almost feel as if you really want to do that. That you want to tear the other man into little pieces.'

And he says that to get that feeling you have got to eat meat and plenty of it. He buys a whole joint at a time. He eats whenever he feels like it, not at any fixed times. Once he tried a vegetarian diet for six months. He wanted to try it and see if it was good for him. He found that it made him feel fitter than ever before in his life, but, as he puts it, 'I didn't seem to have that little bit of fire.' So he came back to meat in the end.

He has had lots of breaks and dislocations in fighting, including three shoulders, one knee, two ankles, one elbow. The toughest fight he ever had was at the Belle Vue Stadium with De Groot for the European Championship. They fought for one hundred minutes, before a vast audience. Gregory had the cartilage torn from between his ribs in the first round. After that he was in agony, could hardly breathe, but fought on right through. Afterwards he was able to look at himself in that fight on the news reels. He could not see anything wrong with the way he had carried on, it was just as usual.

(d) Public Opinion

Public opinion in Worktown is predominantly against All-In. The newspapers give it no space, the churches register it among those things which are not done, and a woman is considered to belong to the lowest type if she likes to go there.

Among 300 men of all age groups and professions (interviews made where men could be found and easily approached, in the park, the pub, football match, bible-classes, unemployment centre, etc.) asked whether they had heard about All-In and whether they had an opinion about it, there was not one who had not made up his mind about it, though only a third had been to a fight.

The third which had been liked it, or simply stated their dislike without any reference to some moral or other standard, saying simply that they don't find anything interesting in it.

"Have been once. I was not very interested, neither disgusting nor exciting for me."

Quite a different matter with those who never have been; they dislike it very often intensely and measure it always by other standards. First the spiritual type, who would like to suppress the animal in mankind wherever it appears:

"Although I have never seen a match of this type, I have heard many people describe what takes place. . . . This has turned my ideals in the opposite direction. The free style wrestling develops the lower side of the human nature. I have a desire to develop the divine or spiritual side of my being and I would like to see men trying to do the same. I would rather see a football or cricket match or a tennis tournament because the games are good for the mind and the fresh air and exercise good for the body."

Some of the enemies of Free Style Wrestling on moral grounds are so aggressive that they seem to have the fire (as George Gregory describes it) necessary for a good wrestler:

"The game has the same reaction on me, when I think about it as have games, long out of legal permission, such as Bear Baiting, or cock fighting. Several nights ago I listened 'On the air' to a wrestling match, and the people and fighters alike reduced themselves by the noise they were making to absolute cannibals, the sooner they blacken their faces and leave the country for Afrika the better."

The biggest group criticises it from the point of view that it is not a proper sport, because it is staged, faked, and in their opinion not a "play the game" affair.
The objection of a keen footballer:

1. ". . . I have not attended any show but my brother and friends have witnessed several ones and they tell me that it is plain to be seen that some of the contests are faked. Incidents occur during the fight which are specially staged, put up affairs for the enjoyment of the spectator. I dislike it specially because it is useless as a national sport, it does not develop the sporting play the game spirit."

2. "All-in wrestling is not a sport as it is carried on to-day, not as we understand sport, to be for the building up and strengthening of our bodies not the tearing of each other to pieces, it is not human or civilized nor barbarian, words cannot be found to describe it."

3. (Unemployed.) "You ask me for my opinion in all-in wrestling. Well I have been asked to go and watch them many times and they would pay for me, but when they have told me the tricks they do some are children tricks

E

and some are mad men tricks and all the match are faked.
Men use false names. I think it is a waste of good time
to go and watch them."

Many of these attacks are good descriptions of Free
Style Wrestling. They are sometimes so good, indeed,
that the investigator could not help the feeling that
these men must have been to one or more fights; though
they don't want to admit it. It remains to ask why they
don't want to admit their presence at a fight? Because:

"My friends tell me that the spectators are mainly of
the lower uneducated class, who are always seeking some
new kind of thrill, and are not interested in true clean sport."

And there is no Worktowner who would like to admit
that he is not a lover of true clean sport.

"I don't like it myself but it seems a very popular sport
with certain classes of the public, but they appear to me of
a low class."

The same reason prevents this man going to see a fight:

"I always want to go and see it but I can't find anybody
to come with me. I am sure it would be very exciting"
(Civil Servant).

(e) The Crowd Roars

Sixteen reports about different nights by different
observers show the same. The hall, which has room for
two thousand, is full up to the last seat. Talks with the
"regulars" confirm that it is every night the same.
There are usually not many women in the hall, the
average is between fifty and eighty.

Sample questioning made it clear that every class
of trade was represented, including a police sergeant,
a coroner's officer and a priest. As one "regular"
puts it, "everybody who is interested in sport turns

up in time, at least once". Observer could not notice anything specially cruel or rough in the faces of the audience. To check this impression of normality in Free Style Wrestling customers, we gave to all those "regulars" a questionnaire asking them to vote on ten given items they considered most important for human happiness. The result:

1. Knowledge
2. Security
3. Equality
4. Humour
5. Pleasure
6. Action
7. Religion
8. Leadership
9. Beauty
10. Politics

In giving the items this order, the wrestling fans don't differ in any way from a wide sample of other males of whom we asked the same question in four other and detailed investigations.

One hundred and fifty people answered the question: "Why do you like Free Style Wrestling?" Their answers can be divided into six different groups. They come to Free Style Wrestling because it is: thrilling, humorous, cheap, clever, real strength is displayed, and rough stuff can be seen.

The numerical distribution of those motives is shown in the next table.

For 100 "patrons" who mention THRILL as an important motive

58	,,	HUMOUR
38	,,	STRENGTH
38	,,	SKILL OR CLEVERNESS.
36	,,	CHEAPNESS
21	,,	ROUGH STUFF

In their own words they talk like this:

1. "Firstly I like the way which it is put across and secondly the thrills you get out of it, and finally the laughs and enjoyment· you get by paying a visit to the Stadiums which then'd do you more good than all the doctors and medicine put together."

2. "It gives sport humour and thrills in one entertainment, it is worth while to hear the crowd one minute they are in hysterics with laughter and the next shouting their heads off with excitement, why it beats any tonic a doctor can prescribe."

Humour has an important function for the Free Style fights, if the fight is too slow and gets a bit boring, the spirit is aroused by songs, "Let me call you sweetheart", if the wrestlers are doing plenty of hugging; "Marry the girl", "Kiss me sergeant", "What blue eyes you got", are often heard. Laughter and the possibility of expressing oneself saves the situation. On the other hand when the tension becomes too strong "so that one has the feeling one's head will burst in the next minute", a witty remark and a roar of laughter releases the tension.

"Two very thin, tall wrestlers were buttling, they look all arms and legs. Suddenly one voice shouted 'come on spider'. Immediately a loud authoritative voice replies, 'Don't be a fool spiders have bodies.'"

"The last round of an even contest, one of the wrestlers has his opponent doubled up, legs twisted round his neck, arms up his back, the crowd very quiet in tension, when a voice from the tanners shouts 'do you want a skewer'. The tension broke, the crowd broke out in releasing laughter."

Again, a "regular" wrote:

"Almost every wrestler is an individualist. They are not encumbered by lots of rules and fine points such as is the case in boxing and catch as can wrestling, therefore each wrestler develops a style and many tricks and gestures that are essentially his own. Secondly I like those unusual incidents that are absent in other sports. Such as german wrestler giving the Nazi salute and getting the rasberry in return. Ali Baba taking out his mat and praying to Allah. Wrestlers refusing to fight until their opponents nails have been cut or grease wiped off his back, this latter act causing intense excitement before the fight has commenced. Smashing the bowl on each others head, breaking the stool, challenging and spitting on the audience, dancing shouting and running across the ring in a temper tearing the referee's shirt off, jumping on it and then throwing the referee out of the ring."

Another factor is that wrestlers are well built and He-men.

"All in Wrestling can be enjoyed by every one without exception. It is a thrill a minute exhibition of skill and strength by men who must be tip top as no weaklings could enter into the sometimes almost ferocious bouts which take place between the men of the mot world. Unlike boxing which gives us a repetition of things in every round, wrestling gives us a variation of skill in wrestling, brute strength and boxing."

A woman:

"Wrestling at first disgusted me, but now I like it very much. No other sport has such fine husky specimens of manhood as wrestling. I find it such a change to see real he men after the spineless and insipid men one meets ordinarily."

A man:

"I love it because it brings back to me, I am 67 years of age, my young days when men were men and not the namby pamby, simpering, artificial, hair curling variety that is most prevalent in the present days generation."

The inhabitants of Worktown are on the average not strongly built. Work in the cotton mill is not the route to strength and health. What one observer felt, many feel at times:

"Went home by car, very crowded with people coming from the performance. Suddenly felt very depressed. Wondering about this change in my mood and searching for the possible cause, I found myself thinking, how terribly degenerated are those men round me, small, narrow shouldered, how different were those in the ring. What a poor thing is our civilisation."

The possibility of identifying oneself with those who are what all want to be, strong, healthy and powerful, must give excitement: and sadism; is this not the main attraction in Free Style? Some of the patrons belong to this class of people, who get pleasure out of seeing others suffering pain, writing thus:

"We like the rough stuff whats more we get it. After that the patrons that know all say get a fresh Referee well if we get a bigger one he would probably stop the rough stuff and that would stop what we all want the Thrills.

One even puts this wish for brutality in the form of rhyme:

" What the public wants is some tough guy
Only who can let his both fists fly.
Right into the opponents chin and chest.
Then get him down and have a rest.
If you think he is a real Hell cat
Just get his shoulder pinned on the mat."

or shouts like this: a wrestler tugging his opponent's arm, "break it off, throw me a piece."

These seem, judging from their answers, to be a small minority. To be sure at this point, we asked, after people had answered us, a leading question: "Don't you think it is interesting to see how they hurt each other in the ring?" The big majority answered: "No, it is not the hurting, but the strength to stand some roughness that makes it interesting." Most overlook or repress the fact that hurting is to a big extent involved in Free Style, and go so far as to say that they don't hurt each other. Here is the impression of a person who went for the first time in his life to the stadium:

"At first the whole affair seemed boring to me and I wondered what pleasure people find in hurting each other or to look at it. That T. was wrong in saying that they don't hurt each other. It was obvious from their distorted faces and the sounds of pain, which came from their mouths. Really I had a feeling of disgust . . . after the interval . . . suddenly found myself absolutely in favour of Hercules, so much that I found myself holding my breath back for fear Hercules may loose. By this time I had completely forgotten that half an hour ago I was bored and disgusted, but all tension when Hercules won the upper hand and furious with Rough House if he was stronger. . . . The next fight was even more exciting, the crowd rose in sympathy with its hero. . . ."

Others, interested in the sport as a sport:

"I like the sport because—I am constantly looking for the unexpected to happen—new holds—new tricks—hoping that the referee may escape punishment—laughing but indignant when he gets it anticipating the defeat of a prominent wrestler in fact thoroughly enjoying to see one who gets just outside the rules, become the receiver of rough stuff—and further enjoy it for its effects on the crowds."

Wrestling is not only practised in Worktown in the Free Style fashion. There is also a Catch as Can Club, where wrestling is done after fixed strict rules, like any other sport. This is dying out. The advertised annual competition of the Catch as Can Club could not attract more than fifty onlookers. The reason, as one Catch as Can wrestler puts it, "If you go to a Free Style fight you have both, the art and science of wrestling and the thrill of the unforeseen and exciting." Whereas in Catch as Can you have only the art, which is difficult to understand in all its details.

The last though not least advantage of Free Style is its cheapness:

"I think all in Wrestling is the best money worth in any sport. I think it is clever and exciting, a real evening sport. Glad that there is some thrilling entertainment different than pictures. We patrons receive as cheap an evening excitement as it is possible to produce."

Though our sample is not perfect in this respect, the proportion of unemployed "patrons" is specially high.

To get a fair understanding of the "patrons'" attitude it is necessary not only to know what they like but also what they dislike about the show. Asked this question, very many answered "nothing", if we leave out complaints like bad ventilation or the lack of a microphone. Those who could mention a dislike centred it always round the question of bad treatment of the referee and certain fouls or unfairness:

1. "There is one thing I would like to have stopped and that is lifting the knee up in the abdomen I think it spoils the sport altogether and have heard plenty remarks about it with others."

2. "The things I don't like is gorging the eyes and kneeing in the testicles. The one that does it should be disqualified."

3. "I don't like these uneven fights when there is a difference of a couple of stone in the wrestlers. I hate to see too many dirty wrestlers on one bill. Women should not be allowed in at half price. They take much of the enjoyment out of the bouts with their cat calls. The practice of hitting or assuming to hit each other in the privates ought to be stopped it prevents a lot of good patrons from bringing their lady friends."

Reading carefully through all dislikes, one finds they are mentioned in connection with the bad reputation of Free Style and at the same time express the wish to do something to change this bad reputation. Some of the suggestions meant as remedy for this evil are amusing:

"What I don't like about this sport is this, whether the management can do anything to stop it or not I do not know, I daresay it is a thrill for some people, but not me, it is the striking of the referee by the contestants, which I think is quite objectionable and childish, let me suggest a way out of the difficulty. I say keep the referee out of the ring altogether, yes I can hear someone saying, who is going to part the contestants when there is any fouling, well now look here, now look here what a chance has a referee about 10 to 12 stone, against these big heavyweights, many a time they don't take the slightest notice of him so why have him in the ring at all."

In reading those dislikes one should never forget that they are felt by people who at the same time say that they go to Free Style because it is so exciting. We have seen before that the excitement is produced to a high degree just by those events they don't like, but at the same time want, because they want to be excited. The explanation of this contradiction is not very difficult. Though they like Free Style, they dislike what public opinion has against it. This is embarrassing and they would like to change it if possible. That they are not very rational in their suggestion and don't know very much about what they like and dislike is another matter, typical of mankind.

Free Style Wrestling is so successful because it meets certain needs of the people. It is very similar in this and in other respects to the football pools, with which it has three important features in common: it is thrilling, allows dream-wish fulfilment, and gives the feeling of being a member of a group by talking about it. Free Style Wrestling gives excitement, satisfies the sense of adventure; betting does the same. Identification with the wrestler in the ring makes it possible to think one is strong and vigorous and not afraid of an opponent; daydreams about big prizes can make one believe that one is rich and secure. Both things can't happen in reality, neither will the weaver with the weak lung be ever strong and powerful, nor will the Littlewood better be ever rich, never can those things be achieved in reality; but as they are so situated, the easy way out is identification and daydreaming, and as those two opportunities provide both, they are used by the "crowd". The same is true of the thrill; probably all those who want to be thrilled would not mind indulging their sense of adventure in another way, where more effort and activity is needed, but as there is no chance for it in the ordinary life of a working-class man, what remains is again betting and entertainments like Free Style Wrestling. And about the third common feature, the social common bond; we have shown elsewhere how it is fading out in all spheres of life, the churches losing influence, the political parties with no ideology; what wonder, as human beings are herd animals, that this common bond is taken up wherever it is found in tune with contemporary need and industrial presentation.

Without doubt the actions in the ring are thrilling because it is possible there, for once, to deal with the opponent without authority interfering.

This entertainment costs only sixpence, and is therefore one that everybody can see and about which everybody can talk. This is, for one evening, a way out into the unknown adventurous, taking away the dull life of routine, boredom and boss. With no press help, no big business, All-In has become the only all-the-year-round popular sport in Worktown and over the whole country. A new, and "astonishing", habit.[1]

[1] Fieldwork for this section was supervised and arranged by Dr. G. Wagner, previously of the Pilgrim Trust's "Men Without Work" survey, one of the best of its kind so far; she is now working with the Worktown survey.

5

DOING THE LAMBETH WALK

> Any time you're Lambeth way
> Any evening, any day
> You'll find us all doin' the Lambeth walk.

THIS is the song that half the world started singing in 1938. To the song a dance was added, a dance that was half a walk, and it caught on as no new dance has done for years. You could, and can, find them doing the Lambeth Walk in Mayfair ball-rooms, suburban dance-halls, cockney parties and village hops. Scotland and the industrial north took it up as keenly as the south. From all sorts of out-of-the-way places came news of its penetration. An observer who visited the far-away isle of Arran reported that the "natives" were doing it there. It spread to New York and thence right across America; to Paris and thence to Prague— Geoffrey Cox reported in the *Daily Express*, September 6, 1938: "Czechoslovakia's Little Man is keeping his head. . . . Over the week-end his thoughts turned to . . . a strange new English dance, the Lambeth Walk, which has just hit the dance-halls of Prague." While a leader-page in the same paper, crisis-day, September 19, said:

"Paris was herself last night, the restaurants were filled, and they were all doing the Lambeth Walk, and when a Frenchman does it, it looks like drill in a gymnasium.

They love the song, and think it is a sort of national anthem. When everyone toasted 'M. Shamberlaing' in the café last night, they sang the 'Lambeth Walk' at attention."

If you are prepared to be scientific about society, you must be prepared for surprises and forget your pre-conceived ideas. What people feel about the war danger is an obviously serious subject, but it is less obvious why the popularity of a dance is of anything more than a frivolous interest. But if we can get at the reason for the fashion, and see it in its setting, it may help us to understand the way in which the mass is tending. We may learn something about the future of democracy if we take a closer look at the Lambeth Walk.

What is it, and how did it originate? When we have answered these questions, we shall be better able to answer the basic question: what was the reason for its wide appeal?

The song was part of a musical show, "Me and My Girl", which started its very successful run at the Victoria Palace at Christmas-time, 1937. Lupino Lane, comedian, took the part of Bill Snibson, native of Lambeth (Cockney area, south of the river), who inherits an earldom but cannot unlearn his cockney ways. At a grand dinner party he starts "doin' the Lambeth Walk" with such effect that duchesses and all join in with him and his Lambeth pals. He sings Douglas Furber's words:

> " Lambeth you've never seen,
> The skies ain't blue and the grass ain't green.
> It hasn't got the Mayfair touch,
> But that don't matter very much.
> We play the Lambeth way,
> Not like you but a bit more gay,
> And when we have a bit of fun,
> Oh, Boy——
>
> Any time you're Lambeth way
> Any evening, any day,
> You'll find us all doin' the Lambeth walk.
> Ev'ry little Lambeth gal
> With her little Lambeth pal,
> You'll find 'em all doin' the Lambeth walk.

Ev'rything free and easy,
Do as you darn well pleasey,
Why don't you make your way there,
Go there, stay there,
Once you get down Lambeth way,
Ev'ry evening, ev'ry day,
You'll find yourself doin' the Lambeth walk."

While he sings, Lupino Lane walks up and down the stage with a swagger and roll of the shoulders which represents the typical cockney walk. When the show had already been running for some months, Mr. C. L. Heimann, managing director of the Locarno Dance Halls (and therefore one of the cultural directors of the country), saw Lupino do his walk, and was sufficiently impressed to get his ace dancing instructress, Miss Adele England, to elaborate the walk into a dance. Starting from the Locarno Dance Hall, Streatham, the dance-version of the Lambeth Walk swept the country.

Thus, baldly, the story. Clearly the Lambeth Walk, as now established, owes its origin to several sets of people:

1. The cockneys of Lambeth and elsewhere whose walk Lane imitated.

2. Lane—and with him Noel Gay who wrote the tune and Douglas Furber who wrote the words of the song.

3. Mr. Heimann and Miss England who invented and put over the dance.

To these we should add, as formative factors:

4. The B.B.C. and the newspapers which gave the Lambeth Walk publicity.

5. The mass of people, without whose enthusiasm the Lambeth Walk would have been stillborn, and who in many cases used it in their own way and added their own spontaneous variations.

Of these five factors, 2, 3 and 4 represent the Few who cater for the Many—in this case successfully.   Factors

1 and 5 represent the influence of the Many. The cockney world of Lambeth—its humour, its singing and dancing, the way it walks—is a mass-product with a special local character. But this character is strong enough to appeal to a much wider mass of people as soon as it is made known on a wide scale.

"Lambeth you've never seen" say the words of the song, and thus emphasise the basic argument of this book—the ignorance of one section of society about how other sections live and what they say and think. "Why don't you make your way there?" asks the song, and that is just the question which this book sets out to ask. Why not? If the song had been a rumba and the words had been "Cuba you've never seen", there would be reasons of distance to explain why only a few people have seen Cuba or know what it is like. But Lambeth is not so far away, and there is the equivalent of Lambeth round every corner. Tyrolean or Hungarian songs and dances can be, and are, exploited by tourist agencies: as a result of the picture they suggest, people do make their way to Hungary and the Tyrol. But to invite people to go to Lambeth is a new kind of tourism. Blackpool, Southend and Margate have followed suit and produced a Blackpool Walk and a Southend Walk and a Margate Walk, but these too are good publicity for holiday centres, they don't ask you to go to a place where "The skies ain't blue and the grass ain't green". None of them have caught on fully.

Lambeth Walk is a working-class shopping street, just off the arterial Lambeth Road and the Kennington Road with tributaries of Lollard Street, Jaxon Street, Old Paradise Street, much condemned housing; street market; a cinema also used as chapel. It continues into Tyers Street, flanked on both sides by huge blocks of working-class flats. The people who live in these flats have mainly come from other parts of London and this is changing the character of the district.   There are many factors which are tending to destroy the native cockney culture, but you don't have to look far to find it still vigorously existing.   Here is an observer's report:

"At the —— —— at 2.15, drinking Best Ale (3*d*. the half pint) with six members of the —— —— Darts Club. One of the functions of this club is to hold parties on Sunday night after closing time (10.30) in the house of one or other of the members. Wives and married daughters are present, beer is drunk and the local dances danced to piano and accordion.

These include the Bull Fight, the Cake Walk and the Lambeth Walk. But they are always inventing new ones:

'For instance Timmy here came round with two new steps.'

Obs.: 'Did you have to think them out beforehand?'

Timmy: 'No. . . . Well, it came natural.'

Another: 'We go to a party you see. Then we go out and do a dress, I mean we put on knickers, perhaps we put on Fanny's knickers. (Fanny is nickname for landlord's wife.) We paint ourselves up with a bit of rouge. . . . Of course we're always half drunk.'

Obs.: 'What happens when you want to arrange a party?'

A.: 'Well we have parties nearly every Sunday. We sort of get together, have a whip, a few bob. It's at one fellow's house one Sunday, another fellow's another Sunday, anywhere there's a piano.'

Obs.: 'How much room do you need to dance in?'

A.: 'Oh we can dance in any room, we need just that (pointing out a space about 8 ft. square). For the Bull Fight we need about 10 yards. We've broken many a table. . . .'

Obs.: 'Are there some people who're specially keen on dancing?'

A.: 'Well it's the club. Just a bunch of us. In this bar we all cling together. . . . There are about 24 in the club. . . .'

Obs.: 'What happens in the Bull Fight?'

A.: 'Oh it's just sort of mad. One man's the bull and the two others are matadors. Then we do the Three Stooges. It all comes out unintentionally. . . . Once the party gets going, you never know what they're going to do. Strip tease as well.'

Obs.: 'What are some of the other dances called?'

A.: 'We've never known the names. We just do 'em ourselves. For instance, the chap who's just gone out to sign on, he wants to be a dog. If he's half drunk, he wants to be a dog. He wants to bark. . . . Then we has bloomers and blouses, we dresses up in them. . . . The other night we had the woman on the floor, fighting over her like two dogs. We don't do it very legal you know. I come home with a black eye.'

Obs.: 'What's the average age in the club?'

A.: 'Thirty-six to forty-eight. The oldest is 70 years old, Tommy G—. But the younger generation is just as keen. It'll never die out.'

Landlady: 'Aren't they a scream? They think the world of themselves here coz they're Lambethians. . . . We had old Hinks the murderer in here you know. That was his chair (pointing). That was more than two years ago.' She then asked an old lady in another bar:

'How long do you remember them doing the Lambeth Walk, dear?'

Old lady, after some hesitation, not understanding what is meant, suddenly with emphasis: 'Oh years ago when we were little shirt buttons. Fifty years ago. We used to call it the jig.'

Obs.: 'What kind of jobs have most of the men got that are in the club?'

A.: 'Most of us was in the war. I was a sergeant, staff instructor in physical training. I'm in my uncle's business, fish-shop. This chap here is a bookmaker's clerk. Then there's Timmy. He has a natural turn. He comes out wif fings you never fort of, he don't care a damn who comes in here. He's an inoffensive sort of feller. He come in here and give a joke, but you can't take offence. There's one chap you always find him asleep on the pavement. He's not drunk. He just likes to sleep. . . .'

Observers talked to many other Lambethians and attended some of the private parties where the dancing takes place. They confirmed the information given

in this report. A spontaneous talent for dancing and
song is a Lambeth tradition, having its connection
with music-hall tradition but also having a life of its
own. It has many features in common with primitive
dancing. Men dress up as women or pretend to be
animals. Beer plays its part, but observation showed
that those who take part may be *half* drunk, but are
certainly not whole drunk. It certainly is true of Lambethians having a bit of fun that:

> " Everything's free and easy,
>   Do as you darn well pleasey. . . ."

On August Bank Holiday night, an observer was asked
along to one of the parties. It was the end of the holiday, most of them had "been to Hampstead and got
all boozed up". On the Sunday there had been a
big wedding party which some of them attended and at
which the bride had broken her arm. Most would have
to be starting work at 6 or 7 next morning. After
closing time the whole party proceeded from the ——
—— to a house nearby, carrying crates of beer, each
holding four quart-bottles. Already at the —— ——
they had started swaying into the dance, and on the
pavement outside two of the women were dancing with
linked arms.

The party was held in an upstairs sitting-room, about
14 by 12 feet, with a piano, two settees and chairs round
the wall, and an elegant blue-tiled fireplace—the tiles
came unstuck later in the evening. Men and women
were there in equal numbers, and including one or two
who came in and went out, there were 24 all told—and
28 quart bottles of beer. The party lasted from 11.30
to 1.30 a.m. Four performers took turns at the piano;
they all played by ear, and they all played very well.
Three others took turns with the accordion. Dances
alternated with songs—there were solos by a woman,

a young man, and an old man of 83. He was the best singer and his age didn't in the least prevent him from having a good time with the rest. His songs included "Up Goes the Price of Meat, Ta Ra Ra" and "My Bradshaw Guide". All joined in the choruses of these and others, such as "Lily of Laguna", "The Lambeth Walk", and "What does it Feel Like to be Poor?". The songs they enjoyed most were the ones that were nearest to their own lives, with economics well to the fore. (But the people who go to the Dorchester don't listen to songs about dividends.)

The first time the observer's glass was filled he emptied it. Then he noticed that the others after taking a swig from theirs, handed it on. Perhaps on the same analogy, when one man's nice-looking wife came in half way through, another man, friend of the first, gave her a good kiss. It was all free and easy and went with a terrific swing, but order was kept and there were certain rules, like keeping silence during the solos. Mostly the women asked the men to dance. Everyone danced, old, middle-aged and young.

The striking feature of the dancing was the rolling tempo, less nerve-taut than American swing and hot rhythm, somewhat less martial than the tune Noel Gay wrote for the "Lambeth Walk" (he also wrote "Round the Marble Arch" and "The King's Horses and the King's Men"). This tempo the pianists and dancers managed to introduce into waltzes and fox-trots, but it was most obvious when they danced their "own" dances, with improvised steps. The dancers faced each other, by two and two, or by three and three, with linked arms. They did jigging steps with their feet, plus some high kicking, then the two lines crossed over, turned and re-formed. As they crossed, they walked in the half-lilting, half-swaggering way that Lupino Lane used in his Lambeth Walk. For the men it is a swagger, arms out from the sides, like a

boxer playing for position; for the women it is more
of a lilt, with hips swaying. The two get mixed, though,
when the men dress as women and behave like them—
which is part of the tradition. Also, men dance with
men and women with women quite freely.

Two of the toughest men came in, some time after
midnight, made up with red eyebrows and white cheeks,
each wearing a woman's hat and dress, and also (under
the dress) pyjama trousers. One had false breasts,
the other a pregnant belly. A woman came up and
kicked the belly, and the man with the false breasts
made his wife hold them. One of the men made
an appropriately lewd remark and there was some
pantomiming of the kind that is usually classed as
"obscene" and which is familiar to anthropologists in
many kinds of primitive dance. Later another pair of
men dressed as women and behaved in much the same
way. Finally the party broke up in the best of good
temper, singing:

> "We play the Lambeth way,
>   Not like you but a bit more gay,
>   And when we have a bit of fun
>   Oh, Boy——"

The eldest son of the G.O.M. of the party, a fish-shop
owner, mid-aged, told the observer how a song called "The
Lambeth Walk" suddenly became the rage in 1903. He
was 11 years old then, and danced it outside the Lyceum
with his sister. Then it faded out, but in various forms,
always changing, still went on at the Lambeth Walk
parties, along with the Cake Walk. Observer: "Did
you dance the Lambeth Walk before Lupino Lane
took it up?" He: "Well we had our own show, it
hadn't any name. But we always used to say 'Oi!'"
The words of the old song as he remembered them
were:

" Come along my honey
Bring all your money
Put on your Sunday clothes
And come along with me.
I know a nice walk
Just like the cake walk,
Come along my honey
Honey do".

The Cake Walk came to England in 1898. It was a "coon" dance, and its tradition blended with the cockney and coster tradition of the Music halls. The first coons to dance and sing in London were the Virginia Minstrels, 55 years earlier. On the Cake Walk the *Daily Telegraph* commented (March 14, 1898):

"After an interval of more than fifty years since the appearance of Sweeney (early coon banjoist) there came to the Alhambra 'Miss Willie' and Mr. 'Billy' Farrell, who are described as the 'original champion cake-walking coons'. The science of 'cake-walking' does not appear to be a particularly abstruse one. Indeed, it may be said to have been anticipated by the English minuet. Cake-walking is, in fact, a graceful motion, conducted upon the toes and ball of the foot."

It is said to have originated among the French negroes of Florida, who in turn copied it from the ceremonial dances of the Seminole Indians. It caught on in England anyhow, and the first (1903) version of the Lambeth Walk was clearly a popular link between the American importation and the native cockney dancing. In his book, *From Theatre to Music Hall* (1912), W. R. Titterton makes a curious attack:

"With the passing of the old, healthy sensual (but not sensuous) English dances came the rushing in of alien elements; chiefest and most deadly, the cake-walk, a marvellous, fascinating measure of tremendous significance. The cake-walk tells us why the negro and the white can never lie down together. It is a grotesque, savage and lustful heathen dance, quite proper in Ashanti but shocking on the boards of a London hall."

A chap of 55 standing on one of the corners of Lambeth Walk told an observer:

"What they used to do was called the twist, they kept on humming or singing the old time songs. As they did it when they kept on turning round, sometimes they'd put their hand up to their heads.

The women used to get hold of the bottom of their skirts, and lift them up, sometimes if they'd had a bit of a booze they'd cock it up proper and make a noise, like they do the Oi in that bleeding Lambeth Walk, but not Oi if yer follow what I mean, it was when they were coming forward they made the noise. They used to be at both sides of the street, some at one side, some at the other, then they'd go across to the other, passing the other blokes."

A woman said:

"We used to have lots of dancing, sometimes in the street, sometimes when the old barrel organ came round, especially on Saturdays after we had a beer or two. . . . It was the jigs they did that's all, like the Irish jig, lifted up their arms under their armpits and then jigged, nearly always to one tune. . . . Sometimes if there were a lot, then they'd be arm in arm and some at this side and some on that of the road, then they'd cross to where the others had been, it was jigging all the time, not like they do to-day."

Most of those to whom observers talked said that things weren't what they used to be. A man of 60 at the "Jolly Gardeners":

"This place is not what it was, it's all different now, there used to be dancing round here, but it all changed, oh long before the war, I should say it was about 1900 when it began to change. They used to do the jig sort of dancing, that's what it was, they used to do the 'Knees up Mother Brown', that's what it was."

The words of "Knees up Mother Brown" vary in different versions but the song is an important element in cockney culture, and it connects up with men dressing as women and the associated pantomimes:

> " Knees up Mother Brown,
> Knees up Mother Brown,
> Under the table you must go,
> EE Aye, ee aye, ee aye, oh,
> If we catch you bending
> We'll turn you upside down
>   (*or* We'll saw your legs right off)
> Knees up, knees up, don't get the breeze up,
> Knees up Mother Brown."

Lambethians said that their characteristic roll of the shoulders was connected with the tradition of the bare-knuckle fighters. It was semi-aggressive and meant "Keep off!" just as the cocked thumb (featured in Lupino Lane's Lambeth Walk) was originally a signal to "Hop it!" Said one man:

"If there's any of that (roll of the shoulders) it's when them as 'as been boxers have had a bit of a drink, nobody else. . . . The old women used to lift up their skirts a bit when they danced, you remember that song they used to sing,

> Chase me Charlie, chase me Charlie,
> Chase me Charlie do,
> For I'm the Cock o' the North me lads,
> For I'm the Cock o' the North, wo-up!"

"Wo-µp!" and not "Oi!" seems to have been the original exclamation at the end of the dance. Another man said of the shoulder roll: "It's the liberty takers see wot does it, when they've had a drop."

An observer talked to Jock ——, 70-year-old prize fighter, about the days of bare-knuckle fighting in

Lambeth, of which he was a leading exponent. Jock has done all sorts of jobs in his time, all round about Lambeth. In the old days he was a worker in a big brick-yard, and he worked in the Lambeth Walk as well. Now he is a pensioner, and about 11 stone, light grey hair, full face and healthy-looking. He spends most of the day out, has breakfast late, then about 11 goes out down the Walk. He stands about the outside of a pub at the bottom of the Walk, and looks straight up it. For meals he goes into the dining-rooms and coffee-houses. Here he meets the men of similar age and fortune—they are all old-timers. He goes into the pubs when they open, then back on to the corner and about the Walk; then may go home towards midnight. The woman in whose tenement he lives told the observer: "You never know when he'll be in, he might be off to his widow . . . we don't know where she lives . . . somewhere about . . . he was there on Saturday night . . . they had a party till nearly 4 on Sunday morning, came home . . . no not drunk . . . he's a funny chap . . . not particular what he says sometimes . . . no offence though. He likes talking about the old times, if you can get him talking." Here is the observer's report on his interview:

"'You should be seeing Jock soon 'cause it's opening time.' Within 2 minutes he appeared on the opposite side of the street, he made his way to the dining-rooms opposite the Queen's Head. This place is run by a man and his wife, he is an old soldier, looks the type, 7 inch moustache, white apron in front of him. The tables are flanked with the high backs between them and the next, the seating by scrubbed forms, the table top of scrubbed deal.

In here is Jock, there are 2 others of the 60 to 70 ages, one of them is in his best blue suit, a bowler hat laid beside him as he eats, white collar and black tie, moustache. As I make to sit down, noticing the Bowler, the old man makes a dive at the Bowler, grabs it and doing so knocks his large cup of tea over on to the Bowler, and his suit. This caused him to glare at me, there never had been any chance of my sitting on it, it was just fear for the Hat. 'I've had it 20 odd years', the woman then brought a dish cloth, this was used to wipe the hat and then the trousers, then the table top.

Jock was eating 2 sausages and bread and a large pot of tea, they all glared at me, then after a while of small talk they began to ease up, although Jock would not say much about the days of the bare-knuckle prize-fighting. 'It was kept secret' he would say.

He talked of the old days. All talk round here among the old men is of Jack Jones of the Jolly Gardeners, 40 years ago, he used to give a pig to the winner of the climb up the greasy pole. This was organised for the men who worked on the water, and those who worked at Doultons. There were two or three of these Fetes held every year. The flagpole was covered with grease, and anybody who would climb to the top and get the flag could then have the pig presented to him. Once or twice the pig escaped into the water and they said that it cut its own throat. The idea seems to be that if a pig gets into a river, then it cuts its throat by means of its feet.

They used to have rowing matches, held on the river; entrants were the Watermen who lived in this part of Lambeth. The prize was usually two or three hundred pots of beer, each pot a quart. These were for all the people in the pub. If the winners usually drank at the Jolly Gardeners, then they drank the whole lot with the people who made that their port of call. Hilarity and beer were the high spots of these events. Another event was that of rowing a race in the river, the boats being washing tubs, the oars the old woman's mop.

'Now the bleeding rowing is up above', that is, up the river.

'In 1888 in July they had one of the biggest of the regattas, these being held under the auspices of Doultons; that time they had a misfortune. Of the three racing boats, two were upset. There was Millar, Bob Adeen, and Tom Bettison, they was all our pals, they was drowned, after that they dropped off.

'All the kiln workers used to be in on it, there was real fun then in those days. They had the Greasy Pole too. This was sticking out from one of the barges, and you had to walk it. They wore women's clothes, bonnets and feathers in their hats. They used to shake the bloody barge till you couldn't hold on, then you fell in the river.

'Although we were landsmen we used to go round the shops to beg for stuff to be given as prizes, we used to all muck in together. Thousands used to come from round Lambeth, Camberwell, Westminster and Vauxhall. This stopped 37 years ago, there was none after that.

'I've heard tell that the old folks used to go dancing in the Vauxhall Gardens, that's where they used to dance a lot.

'We all went cadging in those days for the prizes, and they had to bleedin' give or they lost their customers.

'The flagpole was forty feet high, they had to climb that for the pig. There was no scrambling, everybody had a chance.

'We had the barrow races, they used to have prizes for them as pushed the barrow fastest to Crystal Palace and back. They had the celebrations of the Barrow Race in the old Queen's Head. The prize was a new coster's barrow. They never had the pearley kings down this way, they wore the ordinary clothes of that time. There was none of this 'ere Oi what they sing out now. They made that sort of Wo-up !

'Them funerals used to be big things rawnd here, they used to have 'em all on Sundays, they used to go rawnd to all the folks and get a subscription for the wreaths, everybody had to give something. When they had the funerals of the blokes who belonged to the Sons of Phoenix Temperance Soc, they all used to come out in their sashes, there was all colours, depended on what they was. Then they had their banners, they was all silk they was. Crawds used to watch 'em, when it was anybody else they used to stop half way there and pull up for a drink. Now they don't have any funerals on Sundays, it was the only time they all could go then. It all stopped abawt 1900, it was more convenient for the working class on Sundays.

'At one time they used to start opening the pubs at

5 o'clock in the morning and keep open till a half-past
twelve at night, now it's all like a bleedin' coffin.

'Beer was a penny a pint then, half a quartern of rum was
2½d. Porter was three pence a quart, mild was fourpence a
quart, and it was beer then. They used to have ½d. worth of
coffee and a penny worth of rum or gin in it, that was when
they went out early in the morning, everybody went out of
the pubs half boozed of a night.

'They used to have lots of beer races on Saturday after-
noons, and lots watch and bet on it. Naw . . . there's no
dancing and singing now, only when they have a party in
the house. Last week we had one, 20 handed of beer (20
crates). We were at it till 4 o'clock in the Sunday morning,
a doin' all the old dances and songs. None o' this 'ere
Lambeth Walk. There's nothing in it like the old dances.
We do the old jigs and old fashioned waltzes. It was high
tide up to your leg wif beer. . . .

'We did the "Charlie are you coming out to-night lad"
    "Three Pots a shilling"
    "Seventh Royal Fusileers"
    "Fighting for the Queen and Country too".
Them's the songs of the days of Dan Leno. The old folks
still do 'em. We were enjoying our little selves.

'Drinkin' in the old days was a sight. They used to take
their coats and waist coats off, shoot the whole bloody lot
off when they was havin' a regatta. There used to be lots of
barrel organs in the streets, all day long it was, they used
to play tunes we wanted then. They was all fellows of the
district who took the organs out, hurdy gurdies. They used
to pay a shilling a day for the organ. They used to jig from
one side of the street to the other. They was mostly Irish
and Scotch in them days living here.

'I used to go fightin' in them days, up at Ascot, for the
gentry. They would come and take you out of bed sometimes.
They used to keep it all secret when it was a knuckle fight.
I used to fight at Sergeant Green's in Fleet Street them days
and the Blue Anchor in Shoreditch. For the knuckle fights
we used to take boats up to the Fields at Putney, or Hammersmith, or dawn the river to Barking Creek.

'Fourteen, twenty or thirty-five rounds was common. We
used to dodge the police. There used to be private gymnasiums

in the West End where the gents used to watch us. Everything was comfortable like there. We had to take on anybody at any weight. If you did well yer got a collection from them.

'We used to meet secretly at the foot of Westminster Bridge, then move off in ones and twos, sometimes to a boozer in the West End. Took us out of bed they did to fight. Free beer after for it.

'Now there's nothing like that these days, everybody's for his bloody self'.

The other man said 'Like bleeding hell they are.'"

"Ou sont les neiges d'antan?" The oldtimers lament the old Lambeth.   Here is a working man of 65:

"They used to have the dancing and singing in the Vauxhall Gardens, that's when I was a nipper. . . . They used to have wot's called 'Harmonic Meetings' in the Pubs, you paid a penny to go to them and they had music and sometimes dancing.

It was all ding dong sort of thing. They started at eight o'clock and went on till the pubs shut. They used to be at the Black Dog. There was old Sam Sharp, he wouldn't sing if anybody talked while he was singing.

I remember Liza and Annie, Humbry and lale, and Marie, she was a lovely singer thirty years ago, they used to have them on the Saturday nights in the pubs. They used to drink their beer while they listened. We used to take the old woman to the Harmonics. Popular they was then.

They won't let you have anything like that these days now. Sometimes in the pubs there's a bit of singing like when they get near to closing time in one or two of the pubs, cops don't like it though."

No, the cops don't like it.   Here's the evidence of a lad of 25:

"I used to live round here. Now I live out at Tooting. I've got a job at Boots in Soho, they're a good firm to work for. I'd sooner be at Lambeth Walk among the old lads, used to have fun here, they all stuck to each other, it was proper Labour here. I was 16 when I left here, but I come in the Walk when I'm anywhere about the district, can't keep away.

We used to play dice in the backs, the Police would chase us for it, this was at the back of the Cock and Bottle wot's pulled down now, play cards as well. The cops used to make a round up every now and then, that's all stopped now. There always was a bookie in the old houses, a tout was watching all the time for the cops. There's Mr. Brock and Johnny Curly and a chap called Duggie Stuart.

The cops caught one of the pals once, he was singing 'Don't tell the news to mother, Just tell her how I love her', when up comes the cop and pinches him. The cop said 'I'll tell her all right'. He was only an orphan so the cop let him go, they was decent abawt it.

They used to have fun on Sundays after the pubs closed, you'd see them come out of the Cock and Bottle and start singing when they'd had a bit to drink, then go home. They used to sing:

> 'Knees up Mother Brown'
> 'I'm forever blowing bubbles'
> 'By the blue lagoon she's waiting'
> 'Daisy, Daisy, give me your answer do'.

I've heard them say that there was passwords to get through the houses when the cops was about. Only the lads used to roll the shoulders, when they used to think 'I'm it', these who would fight, they'd go to the Hercules Arches so the cops couldn't see them scrap."

Something of this kind of background is conveyed by Lupino Lane's creation, Bill Snibson. Bill first appeared in "Twenty to One", musical show at the Coliseum. In this show he already had his characteristic "Lambeth" walk, but it didn't play the same important part. In "Me and my Girl" he becomes a Lord, but can't fit in with the smart people at Hareford Hall. He has lessons in deportment from the Duchess. She tells him: "Don't wear your hat in the house"; "You must aspirate your aitches"; and "You must alter your walk". The last is too much for Bill Snibson who protests (in the rhyming slang): "You'll never alter my ball of chalk."

A letter arrives from Lambeth, marked private, which says:

"We have a lovely home now but it's near the soapworks and I'm sorry to say there's a horrid smell from Bob Martin.
PS. We thank you for your invite which we can none of us accept because we're not your class."

But Sally and the other Lambethians arrive all the same to the grand dinner party in the evening. Their behaviour shocks the upstage people, but when Bill starts to do his walk and sing his song, there is a terrific effect of social breakdown, everyone joins in and shouts "Oi !" and the Duchess finally goes into dinner on Bill's arm, wearing his bowler on her head. (This was what happened when observers saw the show, but there is no "book" and the gags change from one performance to another.)

The point of the show is essentially the contrast between the *natural* behaviour of the Lambethians and the affectation of the upper class. In a difficultly academic book of criticism called *Some Versions of Pastoral*, William Empson has pointed out how important this sort of contrast has been in literature, and it is worth quoting what he has to say at this stage, because it is this contrast which gives its basic appeal to the "Lambeth Walk" song and dance. "The essential trick of the old pastoral, which was felt to imply a beautiful relation between rich and poor, was to make simple people express strong feelings. . . . It was much parodied, especially to make the poor man worthy but ridiculous, as often in Shakespeare; nor is this merely snobbish when in its full form. The simple man becomes a clumsy fool who yet has better 'sense' than his betters and can say things more fundamentally true; he is 'in contact with nature', which the complex man needs to be, so that Bottom is not afraid of the fairies; he is contact with the mysterious forces of our own

nature, so that the clown has the wit of the Unconscious;
he can speak the truth because he has nothing to lose."
In Shakespeare, the final laugh is usually at the poor
man, even when he is made a sympathetic character.
Shakespeare's audience was composed of both rich and
poor, and he had to please both, but it was more important to please the rich. In the show at the Victoria
Palace the situation is rather different—there are plenty
of West End people in the audience, but the laugh is
really on them. There is an amazing scene in which
Lane comes on in his full peer's robes and coronet
and pokes unmistakable and uproarious fun at the
solemnity of the Coronation; he even at one point
lies on the floor wrapped in his robes, with his coronet
on his stomach, in such a way as to suggest a com-
parison with the Lying in State of dead royalty. To
some extent the reverse happens, and fun is made of
the working-class girl who is given a five-pound note
and doesn't know what it is. But the point comes out
quite clearly that the working-class characters are
"nearer to nature" than the upper-class ones: George
Graves, who takes the part of a whisky-drinking but
benevolent member of the aristocracy, says to Sally
the Lambeth girl: "I like you and I like your Bill.
You're two little simple children of nature." Later
he says to Bill: "Your modesty, your simplicity, proves
you one of nature's gentlemen." But Lambeth, where
"The skies ain't blue and the grass ain't green", is a
far cry from "nature" in the ordinary sense. It is
the cockney character which is more "natural" than
the upper-class character. Observers' reports show, as we
shall see, that people who like the Lambeth Walk like
it because it is natural; those who dislike it think it is
"common". An observer's mother was one of many
who lodged protests against 2 a.m. Lambeth Walk
parties in Hill Street, Mayfair.

An observer waiting at the stage door of the Victoria

Palace for Lupino Lane saw him drive up in a huge
Rolls Royce. The little man got out on the pavement,
did a huge stretch and yawn and started to talk to some
stage hands hanging round the door. He is an alert
little cockney, on his toes the whole time like a boxer,
and with the same suggestion of popular prestige and
sportiness. While he was changing and making up in
his dressing-room, the observer asked him how he
came by the idea of the Lambeth Walk. "Well, I just
did some Mass-Observation, if you like," he said; and
went on:

"I got the idea from my personal experience and from
having worked among cockneys. I'm a cockney born and
bred myself. The Lambeth Walk is just an exaggerated idea
of how the cockney struts.

The cockney is well known for his wit, grit, guts and
humour, and these are expressed in his walk. If you'll go
deeper in the matter, the walk will tell you the nature of any
man or woman. If it hadn't been for me, there would have
been a dance and no walk. The walk came entirely from
myself. . . . No, there's no cockney dancing.

Twenty years ago I had a famous song, the 'Different
Walks', it was written by Harry Lupino. It showed the
different ways in which different people, different kinds
of people, walk."

Lane was out to show that he was responsible for the
Lambeth Walk idea. And he certainly deserves the
credit of having put it over. When asked why Lambeth was chosen, he said it was pure chance—might
have been Hoxton or Stepney—but "in the previous
show, 'Twenty to One', this little fellow Bill Snibson
that we invented, he came from Lambeth. We had no
special reason then." He explained also:

"The cockney has no social distinctions. He'll go in and
say how d'ye do to the King. He calls 'em—good old Teddy,
good old George.

The last show was about a racing tout who converted anti-gamblers to betting. In 'Me and my Girl' you get the cockney breaking down the prejudice of a narrow-minded outlook.

My next show is still secret but it will take a similar line. It will be dealing with Peace and War.

Lupino Lane has to pass everything. It's my judgment that puts it in the show and puts it in front of the public. In any play that I do, I shall always do the Lambeth Walk. What I call *my* Lambeth Walk."

We'll have more to say later about these comments of cockney culture-hero Lupino Lane. First let us see what soft-spoken Miss Adele England said about her share in the creation of the Lambeth Walk.

An observer went to see her at the brand-new-looking, glass-and-chromium Locarno Dance Hall in Streatham, and found her smart-costumed, full of efficient vitality, more like Mae West than Ginger Rogers, but more in the English, Edwardian, tradition than either. Said she:

"Now I'll tell you the whole story. Before I saw the Lambeth Walk, I had arranged a cockney dance to try out here, but it was never shown to the public.

One day the Manager of the Locarno, Mr. Heimann, phoned me up and said: 'Go to see the show at the Victoria Palace—there's something there that will interest you.' I went, and saw the Lambeth Walk. 'There's one thing that interests me,' I told Mr. Heimann 'and that's the man's walk.' Something could happen, I thought. I started to walk. . . .

I worked out the turns and put in the knee-slapping instead of the slight back jump and hat touching. Putting in 'Oi !' instead of 'Hi !' was Mr. Heimann's idea, to end each movement and start the next.

One night we did it as a novelty dance in the Locarno here. The very first night there were thousands on the floor. They kept on wanting and wanting it. . . ."

The observer asked if she had ever watched cockneys dancing. Her reply:

"Oh no. The walk has been something for years and years which we wouldn't know about. I just had sixteen bars of music and I had to fit in something easy. This dancing is getting so serious, the people won't be bothered to learn. . . .

But really and truly I had no idea it would be like this. The cockney dance I arranged before was nothing like this. No, I never knew the Cake Walk or the old Lambeth Walk. The Walk idea was just Lupino Lane.

Of course people will do it their own way. In the real version you don't hold arms to start with. That's wrong until the swing-round. Whole rows of people link up together too but that's wrong. Ours was done for couples, just for couples. You get the lines in the Palais Glide.

It's cocky. Everyone can do it, they don't have to learn it. There's never been an *English* dance success like it before. We have so many halls we can push it. I started in the Locarno, then I went round to the Ritz, Manchester; the Grand Casino, Birmingham; Sherries, Brighton; the Locarno, Glasgow and the Piccadilly Club, Glasgow; the Palais, Edinburgh; and the Royal, Tottenham. I did it all in a month. By the end it had really caught on.

Mr. Heimann hopes every so often we shall present a new dance to the public. We want to keep them all English now and they'll be simple.

I saw them pull up their skirts at the Victoria Palace. I thought, that won't do for the ball-room. It wouldn't do for the Dorchester—they'd like to do it of course, but it'd be too much for their dignity. It might be all right for the Locarno on a licensed night, So I put in the slapping of the knees instead.

The funniest thing was when I had to go to the Victoria Palace to teach Mr. Lane the ball-room steps. He had been asked to dance the Lambeth Walk at a big private do at Carlton House Terrace, and he didn't know the ball-room version. So I taught him, and we did it together.

We want something different in dancing. The steps of the Lambeth Walk have nothing to do with anything I've seen on the Halls. I thought them out for myself."

F

Unlike Lupino Lane, Adele England did not claim that her conception of the Lambeth Walk was based on "Mass-Observation" of Cockney life; but she did imply that it was based on her experience of the sort of dances people want. That is the point on which she and Mr. Heimann have expert knowledge. So they form an essential link in the chain between Lambeth and the mass public. She herself had never been to Lambeth, but was enthusiastic to go when the observer suggested taking her to see the people there one Saturday night. The version of the dance which she created was in terms of the big dance-hall, and she tended to complain about "unauthorised" variations which the public themselves invented. We shall see later what the Lambeth Walk can become when the mass gets hold of it.

Another essential link in the chain was short, broad-faced and constantly laughing Cambridge graduate Noel Gay, No. 1 English jazz-writer. He told an observer (at an ordinary friendly meeting), speaking even faster than Victor Gollancz, that he did five versions of the Lambeth Walk, each one increasingly simple. He aims always at simplicity, "in plugging it's absolutely necessary to stick to one or two ideas and keep on repeating them"; that's why he had: any evening, any day, every little Lambeth Gal, everything free and easy, all. He believes—and all our evidence entirely supports him—that ordinary working folk are not satisfied with the endless American heaven in your arms and moonlight on silent waters; he deliberately goes for everyday, homely symbols, with simple repetitions, or otherwise new angles on old situations. He attributes much of his success in this respect to his boyhood in Yorkshire where the singing of the mill-girls coming home from work stays strong in his memory. That success can be measured by the 350,000 sales of the "Lambeth Walk" in Britain so far, more than "Yes, We Have No Bananas".

The music and dance has spread all over the world. An observer recently in Hungary reported that she had heard nothing else but the "Lambeth Walk" for a fortnight. In Germany it boomed after the Nazis had officially inquired into Noel Gay's pedigree. In Scotland, instead of "Oi !" they're shouting "Och Aye !" The Blackpool version says: "EE! By Gum, it's cham-pi-on!"

A special brunette went from London to teach Mussolini (October). To America it was brought by Mayfair's socialite sportsman Russian Prince Serge Obolensky, who introduced it to U.S. café society on July 29. Commented *Life*: "At once stately and silly, the Lambeth Walk is better designed for hot weather than the violent, obsolescent Big Apple. Its evolutions include an arrogant shoulder-swinging strut, a leisurely arm-in-arm turn; a good deal of 'business' with elbow and thumb." While by September 12, *Time*, reviewing a Duke Ellington recording of the tune, had got snooty and said:

"Theme song of the 1938 summer dance madness, doubtless played more interestingly than it ever was at its point of origin, London."

We have studied the first three factors in the growth of the Lambeth Walk. Next comes the question of publicity. Four hundred people were asked if they knew what it was and how (in July) they first heard of it. Of those asked, only 17% did not know what it was. Those who did know what it was, first heard of it from the following sources:

	%
Wireless	41
Friends	18
Saw it danced	16
Newspapers	15
Other sources (including news reels, Victoria Palace, etc.)	10

That wireless publicity was the most important is borne out by other evidence. Observers listening in report that it has sometimes been played as many as eight times a day. When the dance-bands play it, listeners can hear the dancers singing the words and shouting Oi ! They are thus made conscious that it is something different from the ordinary dance tune, something with mass-participation behind it.

Of those who remembered the date they first heard it, 30% heard it before May, 1938, 20% heard it in May, 25% in June, rest in July. (The answers were sent in at the beginning of August.) This suggests that during the summer the rise in its popularity was continuous and steady.

Here are some typical accounts of how people first heard of it:

1. "It is exceedingly difficult to say how and when I first heard the Lambeth Walk. It seemed to have dropped out of the sky, for, on the one day, I heard the milk boy and the butcher boy whistling it, heard it played on the roundabouts at the local fairground, heard it on the wireless, again during the interval at the cinema, and at the end of the day was humming it myself—it is a very catchy tune."

2. "I first became associated with it at a dance, and was greatly surprised at the way people took to it, for without knowing how to do it, they watched the few who could, and before the evening was out, everybody was having a try at it. I was one of those who had a try, and I must confess that the carelessness and half lazy swagger of the thing appealed to me very much."

3. "I heard it at work. Our compositors are always first with new dance tunes and they whistle and sing them until everyone else in the works knows them too. There was no escaping the Lambeth Walk."

4. "I first discovered it was a dance on the 16th July. This was our factory sports day. In the evening there was a band and dancing in the field. About 10 o'clock the canteen was

running dry and we were all in a merry mood. I was with my family and relations from Glasgow, we discovered the Lambeth Walk was on, everybody dancing and singing. We didn't do the dance properly as we didn't know it, we sang with the rest and danced about as we wished, walking round, grabbing each other, and swinging. It was very lively and everybody seemed to thoroughly enjoy it. The field was not lighted in any way. A car was run up near the band and they played by the aid of the headlights. Dark forms moved into the light and out again, mingled with flickering shadows, and the scene was rather enchanting. A summer evening, the mood of the people and the liveliness of the song and dance made it an unusual occasion to first make acquaintance with the Lambeth Walk.

I liked it fine as it seemed to be just the thing to fit a lively mood. . . . The outstanding feature to my mind is the combination of the song and dance. Doing what you are singing."

Observers tell stories which show the sort of way in which the Lambeth Walk has become a national catchword:

1. "One day in the middle of July, when I was cycling with a friend a few miles from home, we were passing a few isolated houses when a girl of the mill-hand type, apparently having made some remark about us to her friend called out to us, 'Can you do the Lambeth Walk?' We made no reply, and, in any case, neither of us knew what the Lambeth Walk was."

2. "When I got home for the holidays I was walking up the lane, occasionally doing little skips because it was a beautiful morning, and a yokel on a bike came up behind me. 'Doing the Lambeth Walk?' he remarked cheerily and departed.

On the boat as I came across there were two drunks down below rolling about. The chief engineer remarked to me: 'Funny, they think they're doing the Lambeth Walk.'"

3. "My niece has just begun to walk, her pace is very faltering and flat-footed. My mother calls this the 'Lambeth Walk'."

People were asked how they thought the dance originated. Of those who answered, 23% did not know, the rest thought as follows:

	%
Lambeth, costers or cockneys . . .	24
"Me and My Girl"	19
Composer's own idea	12
Some stage show or film	5
America	4
Other sources	13

One observer says:

"I understand the Lambeth Walk is a coster dance, and I imagine it originated with the costers and girls promenading. When I first heard of it I connected it with a dance which I remember some of the cockney lads used to dance in our Batt. at Salonika. Suddenly one of them would shout —Come on let's have a 'Riley', and a dozen would form in two rows facing each other, and off they would go, to the tune of 'Knees up Mother Brown'—advance and retire, and turn around, with much shouting and Oi ! They always seemed to enjoy it."

A good many thought the dance was based on the behaviour of courting couples. Special theories included:

1. "I have an idea that it originated from a simple sort of country dance, modified by the crowded state of Lambeth Walk on a Saturday night. . . . One friend was of the opinion that it took its form through the passing in and out between the costers' barrows. Another had the strange idea that it was based on a game of darts. (Three steps forward, pull the darts out, three steps back, throw. With the winning throw a shout of 'Shot' or 'Oi' and a slap on the back.)"

2. "Shows the pride of the market men, who are proud of their sense of balance brought about by carrying baskets."

Once given the idea of a "free and easy" dance, people invent their own variations, just as they do in Lambeth itself.   This comes out in the following remarks recorded at a dancing class:

"*Girl about* 20: ' I think it's a silly thing.'
Man about 40: 'It's jolly good fun, there's no doubt about it.'
Man: 'It's a really catchy tune.'
Man: 'They dance it differently at every place you go to!'
Woman about 40: 'Nobody seems to do it the same.'
Young man, 21: 'I like it, but nobody seems to do it right.'
Girl, 19: 'I think it's jolly good, but none of the dancers I know do it the same way.'
Man: 'It looks marvellous when you see a whole crowd doing it.'
Girl, 19: 'It's not much good learning it properly. There are ever so many ways of doing it, and in any case you have to follow the pair in front of you.' "

Of those who knew the dance and said whether they liked it or not, two-thirds were in favour of it, the remaining third was hostile.   The words which those who like it use most often to describe it are: fine, jolly, popular, friendly, free and easy.   Those who dislike it call it stupid, daft and silly.   Behind these words seems to be some kind of defence of their own dignity.   Some think it common or vulgar (others think this too but like the dance for just that reason).   Some think the dance is a mockery of the working class, or that it is a false piece of class-fraternization.   Some say (like Titterton on the Cake Walk) that it is suggestive and degrading—though there are more who think it less so than other ballroom dancing.   A school-mistress said:

"I couldn't afford to lose my dignity by dancing that in public."

A maiden lady of 35 :

"It is vulgar and should not be danced by a lady of modesty."

The following from a Glasgow observer:

a. "Miss B. (50), Cashier: had a house on the coast during June, and every evening while on the steamer she heard the band play the Lambeth Walk till she got sick of it. . . . Several times individuals indulged in what she thinks must be the Lambeth Walk step. They walked about swaying their hips in an exaggerated and vulgar manner. It was a kind of wiggle waggle, and definitely not nice.

b. Mr. M. (43), Export Manager.
Obs.: Do you know anything about the Lambeth Walk ?
Mr. M.: It's daft, DAFT, the DAFTEST THING IN THE WORLD.
Obs.: Why, what is it like ?
Mr. M.: Oh, I've never seen it, but I hear it's a cross between the Black Bottom and the Charleston. Someone is doing it in a booth at the Amusement Park at the Exhibition, beside the Giraffe-necked women and the Freaks.
Obs.: But if it is a dance, surely it would be in the ball-room that they would do it ?
Mr. M.: Oh my no ! It wouldn't be allowed there. It is simply a side show. Someone swings himself about, and wriggles and moves his body. It's daft.

c. Miss MacP. (36), Bookkeeper; is a keen patron of the dance halls, but due to family mourning has not been since 1st May. She has heard of the Lambeth Walk but has never seen it. By what she heard it is a shillyshally that shakes you in all your limbs. She does not think much of it, nor indeed of any of the dances nowadays. They get more and more suggestive. She really doesn't know what the world is coming to !"

Another observer:

"I mentioned the subject in the laboratory where I work. One fellow (27) said that the clergyman had mentioned it in his sermon the previous Sunday (Baptist Church). My friend (amongst general amusement) showed us how the parson had demonstrated the dance by slapping his hands on his legs, and then jerking his thumbs over his shoulders. The parson had also said words to the effect that he did not think much of people who spent their time performing such antics."

Here are more complicated anti-attitudes:

1. "I have seen it danced on rambles and at the W.E.A. social and I hate it. Ballroom dancing is nothing more to my mind than an excuse for the commencement of sex relationships. The whole exhibition of the Lambeth Walk shocks me. I can interpret the gestures into something I despise. I resent too the presentation of the personal life of the lower classes as being amusing. It leads to the viewing of slum-life with all its poverty, dirt and misery through the rosy spectacles of the wise-cracking Cockney and the glamorous Pearly King. It is a common dodge to make us laugh at our miseries and put them out of mind that way."[1]

2. "I cannot say how the Lambeth Walk originated but it is popular because it is part of the modern movement to boost the proletariat to keep them quiet rather than with a view to ameliorating their conditions of living. The Lambeth Walk is designed to please the cockney—a mean,

---

[1] He is objecting to the Lambeth Walk because it induces the feelings which Empson calls "pastoral" between rich and poor. Empson says it would annoy a Communist to admit that W. W. Jacobs is a proletarian author: "Probably no one would deny that he writes a version of pastoral. The truth that supports his formula is that such men as his characters keep their souls alive by ironical humour, a subtle mode of thought which among other things makes you willing to be ruled by your betters; and this makes the bourgeois feel safe in Wapping." But as we shall see, the working class has taken up the Lambeth Walk with more enthusiasm than anybody—a fact recognised and made use of by both the Communist Party and the Labour Party. In the latter case, it was partly due to a long discussion between a leader of M-O and the Transport House propaganda experts, who could not see the faintest connection between the Lambeth Walk and politics until the whole history of dancing and jazz had been gone into.

mannerless and socially unfit specimen of English society. That it has been taken up in the West End is a tribute to the obliviousness of our upper classes to stirring dances and the erotic nature of their pleasures."

3. "I think it might possibly have originated as a facet of *almost* deliberate propaganda of the 'See Britain First' variety(and-to-hell-with-all-this-Yankee-stuff-and-why-should-England-be-run-by-America-anyhow) plus a vague kind of patronising attitude *on behalf of* 'Our Betters' towards the ordinary working-class cockney, such cockney being pictured as of the pearly-king coster variety *only* (of 1888 at that!) such picture being the inevitable product of complete class-ignorance."

4. "I have seen it danced only at a London café. Here the dance-floor was crowded. . . . My reaction was one of disgust and anger. It seemed to me that the rich were deriding the poor, or, at best, pretending to share in pleasures that find their natural expression in totally different circumstances. I now see that these objections may be just as applicable to all those dances of to-day derived from those of negroes, creoles, etc., to which I take no exception. It may simply be that Lambeth is nearer home: as danced by the rich and upper classes it seems to me a sign of Fascism."

The reaction of a retired Major, though not typical, is not without interest:

"When first I saw it at a smallish dance of about 150 people, I was astounded that decently brought-up young people could give themselves up publicly to what had all the appearance of the preliminaries to an orgy. The rapt look on the faces of both the boys and the girls could have been interpreted by the blind! It is possible, probable even, that the youngsters did not realise what it was all about. The second time I saw it was in a public dance hall, where probably about 1,200 people were all doing it to a band that knew its business. There was no tune but merely rhythmic percussion, and the effect was the same as that produced in a 'deluka' (native festival) in the Southern Sudan, where anything from about 40 upwards of naked

young men and women get into a circle and jump up and
down, giving ecstatic groans, sweating and stinking, to
the beat of a darabuka, in the flickering light of a fire.
They finish up quite frankly in the way one might expect.
In my view, eroticism is the main attraction of all dancing."

This is quite a different interpretation to that of the
great majority of those who have danced the Lambeth
Walk, who stress its social and friendly character.
For example:

"Saw this danced in 'Me and My Girl' and liked it
immensely. I do not usually care for popular songs, but this
one seems different. Felt I wanted to join in and when
hearing the song I always feel that it draws all classes of
society together. Those singing it seem to have a friendly
feeling towards the listener. The whole thing gives out
friendliness and makes me like the costers better. Compared
with other dances, it seems an out-of-doors dance and one
full of vitality and movement and careless happiness."

Another brings out its social character when he
says:

"In my opinion the Lambeth Walk is rather like wearing
paper hats, a rather silly sort of thing that is enjoyable
when a crowd of people is doing it."

The reverse reaction to this is seen here:

"I haven't danced it, but I really was disgusted at the
idiot way people let themselves go while dancing it. I felt
that it was an intrinsically *bad* thing for adults to behave
in such a childish manner."

Again:

"I have danced the Lambeth Walk several times, and
rather like it. Its main appeal is in its informality. I cannot
do better than quote the words of the lyric, 'Everything's
free and easy'. Whilst actually doing the turns, I sometimes
get the feeling that it's all a bit aimless and slightly childish,

but this is compensated, paradoxically enough, by a pre-dominant feeling that I can be as silly as I like, and no one will criticise my behaviour.

We are all so bound up with ridiculous conventions and rules as to what we must and must not do, that it is a great relief to go as crazy as we like, be it only for the time of a dance. The other two things that I like about the Lambeth Walk are the tune, which really is catchy, and the fact that its unconventionality breaks the ice among a crowd of dancers, and seems to make them all considerably less serious."

This explains very well why the dance is called both "silly" and "jolly". Breaking conventions is "silly" from the point of view of those who are keeping them. Conversely, keeping conventions is "silly" from the point of view of those who are breaking them. It fits in with Lane's remark about "breaking down the prejudice of a narrow-minded outlook". Children are less conventional than adults, therefore those who break conventions are called "childish" by those to whom such behaviour is embarrassing. At the Victoria Palace, George Graves speaks of Bill Snibson and his Sally as "two little simple children of nature", and the words of the song:

> "Every *little* Lambeth gal
> With her *little* Lambeth pal. . . ."

give the impression of treating the Lambethians as children.

Commenting on the Oi! at the end of the dance, an observer asks: "Is this a shout of triumph (Look what we've done!)? Or is there something left over rhythmically in the dancer's mind that seems to call for that 'Oi!' or what?" Another points out "the fact that you speak to your partner (Oi!) as a definite part of the routine—which feature is unique, I should think, in a modern ballroom". An explanation of this is that given by another observer who comments:

"A good dance to 'break the ice', for after shouting 'Oi!'
to a stranger, in some strange way he ceases to be one."

Other relevant comments:

1. "The dance gives a sense of complete unity to the whole
body of dancers and not just individual pairs."
2. "I thought it was a jolly dance, and a lot more friendly
than most of the dances danced nowadays, more like the
old style of dancing. The part that seems to amuse is the
slapping of knees, turning the thumbs up and shouting Oi.
One thing that struck me was the way the dancers seemed
to throw themselves into the part, as though they were
play-acting, especially the men, who seemed to fancy they
were costers, imitating their mannerisms. The outstanding
features, I would say, are the action, friendliness with other
couples, humour, opportunity to act in unison, chance to
express themselves vocally."
3. "I have danced it and liked it, (i) Because it is simple,
the step being a swaggering walk which you can vary according to your feelings; (ii) It is a set dance so that you know
what you should be doing at a given moment and do not
have to read your partner's thought; (iii) It is common,
particularly the 'Oi' bit at the end, and I think it is lovely
to be common and let yourself go in these days of refinement."

A big proportion of observers mentioned as an outstanding feature of the dance that it includes gesture,
speech and action, and is therefore more like acting or
impersonation than other dances. When you do the
Lambeth Walk, you pretend to be a Lambethian. If
you don't want to do that, there is no point in the dance,
as appears from the following story:

"A German dental student who is a beautiful dancer
said that he did not care to do it, it was a senseless dance.
I explained that it was supposed to represent a couple of
costers out together, he said: 'But I do not wish to be these
people—do you?'"

One thing which the huge popularity of the Lambeth Walk indicates quite definitely is a very widespread "wish to be these people", though of course that wish is not a simple or straightforward one, and includes elements of make-believe and ballyhoo. The upper classes wish to masquerade as Lambethians; sixteenth century lords and ladies played, in pastoral make-believe, as shepherds and shepherdesses. The middle classes wish to be Lambethians because it temporarily lets them off a sticky code of manners which they usually feel bound to keep up. The working classes wish to be Lambethians because Lambethians *are* like themselves, plus a reputation for racy wit and musical talent—partly they represent that part of the working class which knows how to have a good time.

All this quite reverses the more usual cultural current which flows from the upper class *down* to the working class. Shopgirls dancing foxtrots and rumbas are impersonating debutantes. With the Lambeth Walk the impersonation is the other way about. The "conventions" which the Lambeth Walk breaks down are the means by which one class apes another which is better off. That sort of "conventionality" goes pretty deep in the working class itself, and is one aspect of the each-for-his-own-self, individualist pattern which dominates the whole of 1938 England. As a symptom of changing social attitudes, the Lambeth Walk points the other way from Football Pools and Daily Horoscope. But included in the simple fact of its popularity are many contradictions. For instance, it is extremely doubtful if the management of the Locarno Dance Hall, which launched the dance, thought of it as having the opposite effect on people to that of astrology. In fact, in August, the Locarno had two special Horoscope Nights, with a "Special Distribution of Free Birthstone Rings and Delineations". (On other nights they have Gift Distributions of "Eve" Shampoos, Meltonian Cream, Pom-

peian Beauty Products, " Nufix ", Brylfoam and
Kolynos.)

Eddie Cantor made an A.1 record (Decca F.6741)
of the Lambeth Walk, finishing with some remarkable
verses of his own:

> " You know, folks, when I get to the U.S.A.
> I'll meet the President and he'll say,
> My friend, what's the big news in England ?
> And I'll answer the Lambeth Walk.
>
> Why the Lambeth Walk will cure the blues,
> You can even go and tell Mr. Howard Hughes
> That he may have flown around the world——
> Ah, but can he do the Lambeth Walk ?
>
> Perhaps I'm just day-dreaming,
> Or maybe it's crazy scheming,
> But if you happen to see my eyes gleaming,
> Why the reason . . . is pleasin' . . .
>
> What a happy old world this could be
> If the leaders of nations would just agree
> To make their people forget about war
> And teach them the Lambeth Walk."

At first glance, this looks like a suggestion to "dope"
the masses with a new kind of dance-tune, but the interesting implication is that the President's ideas about
"big news" (and those of the other "leaders of nations")
are somehow wrong, and that the Lambeth Walk is
somehow right. Possibly Lupino Lane's new show,
which he said was going to deal with "Peace and War,"
will take the same line as the Anti-Fascists who broke
up a Mosleyite demonstration in the East End by "doing
the Lambeth Walk". The feeling of the Lambeth Walk
is unsectarian but not unsocial.

The Meadows Labour Party, Nottingham, led an
agitation against an insanitary rubbish-tip by publicising
a song to the tune of the Lambeth Walk which ran:

"Any time you're Meadows way,
     Any evening, any day——
     Cripes ! What a stink !
     Blowing across the swamp !
     Oy !"

Commenting on this, the *Daily Worker* wrote (August 20, 1938):

"We in Britain have been rather slow to realise the effectiveness of bright, topical songs, but once the idea really catches on, the possibilities should be obvious. It is to be hoped this new 'song-consciousness' will generally improve the Labour movement's singing style."

Following their argument with mass-observer, propagandists of Transport House produced a song (to tune of the Lambeth Walk) for use at Elections:

" Come on out and on your way
     For it's Polling Day to-day,
     Do yourselves good
     Swelling the Labour Vote.

     Every little Worktown pa
     With his little Worktown ma
     Do themselves good
     Swelling the Labour Vote.

     Go out and fetch your neighbour,
     Tell him to vote for Labour,
     Labour's the lot to plump for . . .
     Cheer for . . . jump for . . .

     When we've sent old (Higgins) in,
     Happiness we're sure to win,
     Do yourselves good
     Swelling the Labour Vote."

But it was never used; forgotten in crisis. While the Naval Reserves called up in crisis time swung into Chatham (September 28), singing the Lambeth Walk, recalling Tipperary in its London nostalgia.

More significant, because its effects were observable on a large scale, was the L.C.C. experiment of having Open Air Dancing in the parks. This was in August, 1938, and the parks were in working-class areas: Islington, Wapping, Southwark and Camberwell. The success of the experiment was largely due to the popularity of the Lambeth Walk and its capacity for bringing people onto the floor and making them dance. In each case it was played three or more times in the course of the evening—the band leader announcing it as the "Wapping Walk", "Highbury Shuffle", etc., according to the place. The performance ended with a prolonged Lambeth Walk, the climax in which everybody joined.

At Myatts Fields, Camberwell, on August 8, 1938, there were 3,000 dancers and spectators. The band played from a covered bandstand round which the dancers danced on the asphalt. Then came a dense ring of spectators and outside that a circular concrete path with people walking round it. Most of the dancers were young, though there were many elderly spectators. Few of the girls had hats, though nearly all carried bags. About half the men had open shirts. Sample counts of the couples dancing showed that there were about equal numbers of man-and-girl and girl-and-girl couples; one or two man-and-man couples were observed. This was not due to a lack of young men but to their relative shyness about going onto the floor. According to an observer with dancing training, most of those dancing had had no lessons but danced well all the same—if they didn't know the steps they invented them. The first time the Lambeth Walk was played, the floor crowded at once. There were threes and fours as well as couples. No one worried about the exact stage reached in the dance. Everyone shouted 'Oi!' and sang.

An L.C.C. official made a speech from the bandstand: " . . . We are watching these experiments very closely.

. . . Success depends entirely on you. . . . It largely depends on the way you support them. . . . It's a very fine crowd. . . . Hope you enjoy the rest of the evening." (Cheers.)

The "Big Apple" got a much smaller crowd than the Lambeth Walk. Most of the dancers just walked and two-stepped. A father and mother went round with a small child on the father's shoulder.

Another speech: " . . . How very pleased I am at the way you're behaving. . . . Good night." Old woman in crowd comments: "Did you hear the man say he was pleased the way they had behaved to-night; they can if they get the chance." Man: "He only said that so he could get a clap."

Youth to another: "Bet you there'll be a lot of love affairs to-night." . . . "Blimey, if I was in your place. Crikey. You've got the best chance of any of us."

Quick fox-trot starts off crowded floor and is very popular. There are several men couples and some walk forward hand in hand. Quick dances go better than slow on the asphalt, and there is this tendency to break up the ballroom pattern and dance more freely. Final speech: "Wish we could go on for another hour or two. . . . But one question I want to ask you. Have you all had a good time to-night? Give me a loud yes or no." YES!! "Hope you'll come along next Saturday night. I want to add my thanks to the band. It's a very good band isn't it?" YES!!!

The final Lambeth Walk is a dense march round and round the bandstand, no room for steps. Heads bob up and down as the tempo quickens into a gallop. Everyone is doing it. There is no doubt this is what they like.

Here are snatches of the talk which one observer heard during the evening:

Man : "I'm parched, they should have a bar."
Woman : "There is one, it's grape fruit."
Man : "I'll sup water before that at that price."

.   .   .   .

Man : "You'd think they couldn't walk round there, it's packed."
Man : "See that chap, his job is to keep them back, he's pushing them now, it's about time."
Woman : "You can't see, there's nothing to see."

.   .   .   .

Man : "They ought to open more of these, it's just right for it."
Man : "If this is anything it's a wow as Alice sez."

.   .   .   .

Man : "Hello Ernie, how's tricks, been on there ?"
Man : "Too crowded for me."
Woman : "He won't come on, makes me mad he does."

.   .   .   .

Man : "Eh that's old Joey down there in front of us, see him ?"
Woman : "Who's he with this time, another woman I'll bet."

.   .   .   .

Youth : "Eh look at them two skirts, not so bad, coming ?"
(They move off after the 2 girls and speak to them.)

.   .   .   .

Woman: "He's making a speech, what's he saying, Jack ?"
Man : "Dunno, it sounds like storm or elephant's wind if you ask me."

.   .   .   .

Man : "It's a real wow of a success."
Woman : "It's too crowded here, they should have made more room."

.   .   .   .

Man : "They'll have to get Harry Roy here next week if it's like this."
Man : "It'll need it, then some."

.   .   .   .

Man : "It's a shoe wearer that's what it is, they're in league with the repairers."

There was the same enthusiasm at Highbury Fields, Islington, on August 11, but on a far larger scale. There the crowds totalled some 20,000, and the official arrangements broke down under the strain. The inner ring of asphalt meant for the dancers became lined on both sides with onlookers as well, leaving only a narrow lane for dancing. One had to fight to get in or out of this ring. The bulk of the crowd stood round outside watching and listening to the music. Announcements and speeches were drowned by the voice of the crowd, in spite of powerful loudspeakers. This was the second open-air dancing at Islington, and the crowds were more than double what there had been at the first. Here too the Lambeth Walk was the chief excitement, though the dancers in the end just tramped and bounced round in a solid mass, speeding into a blind scrum. At this stage the greatest goodwill was maintained, but there was little chance of dancing in the usual sense. The park-keepers who had to hold the outer ring were sweating and exhausted. An observer's report:

"Very dense crowd surging outside the small gate in the railings. Three keepers forcibly controlling influx and efflux. Big one forcing a 'Gangway !' through the crowd for people coming out. Entrance in little spurts of 3 or 4, every few minutes. Enormous pressure, usually towards gate, sometimes a reaction as keeper pushes them back. Impossible to avoid treading on other people's feet. Impossible to raise an arm. Crowd rather annoyed on the whole, especially when people are coming out. Keepers pushing, threatening, reviling, reasoning and making jokes by turns. One, small, worried, standing on a seat immediately inside the gate: 'Anybody got a pint ?'—laughter from crowd; girls repeat the words. Without any personal effort, Observer was sucked towards and finally injected through the gate. Immediate contrast: no rows of seats at that point, large empty space between railings and outer ring of onlookers, no pressure at all.

To two consecutive dances there was no dancing at all. They went round in arm-linked groups of 4–7 or so. Later there were many couples as well as various kinds of grouping, but on the whole no real dancing. Band played 'Daisy Bell', 'She was one of the Early Birds' and 'Two Lovely Black Eyes' in quick succession. No dancing proper. Crowd sang the words. . . . Later, conditions for dancing seemed to be rather better—there were fewer people attempting it. Many young children, in pairs or other groups, trying to dance, unsuccessfully, and barging the adults. Many pairs of youths dancing in unorthodox styles. Band plays 'Make a Bonfire of your Troubles'. Everyone livens up; dancing stops; they hop round together in close lines. Some merely walk. Five young men form a close-linked circle and go forward, rotating slowly. Two young men do separate eccentric steps side-by-side, next to outer ring, causing much amusement among spectators. At end of 'Bonfire of your Troubles', pace increases to about double: everyone gives up dancing and runs round. More like a cattle stampede than a dance.

Loud but unintelligible announcement from loudspeakers. One young man to ditto, ironically 'Garron, clap; that was good, wahnit?'

Final dance—'It's 3 o'clock in the morning'. Words sung. Joke made about title. Dance ends. Announcer says, after pause: 'Wait a minute: there's one thing more. Can anyone tell me what it is?' Small boy somewhere: 'Lambeth Walk!' Others take up the cry. Lambeth Walk begins. . . ."

Interestingly, the Lambeth Walk has become *not* the final dance, but a necessary ritual winding-up of the whole affair. And the other dances are reduced to a form as like as possible to the mass-version of the Lambeth Walk. Among other advantages of the varied grouping which supersedes the conventional male-female couple is that it means the boys don't have to ask girls to dance. In the earlier part of the evening when couple-dancing prevailed, an observer counted in two consecutive dances 30 mixed couples and 74 women couples—some indication of the shyness between the sexes. That this is not entirely due to male bashfulness is indicated by several stories like this:

"Three boys held a whispered argument a few feet behind a girl. Finally one went up and asked her for the dance. Although she had obviously been waiting for the request she blushed and shook her head."

That shyness diminished is shown by a later count, when there were 56 mixed couples to 54 women couples. Some scraps of talk:

Man : 'Some of 'em here at six waiting for it to start.'
Short woman : 'I can 'ear 'em going round.'
Woman, at clapping : 'Do they deserve it?'
Man : 'Can you see?'
Young woman to boy she carries : 'Can you see 'em Peter?'
Woman : 'There's a crowd there.'
   Laughs at Oi!
Two middle-aged working-class men :
   1. 'Look as if they're enjoying theirselves, don't they?'
   2. 'It's a damn good idea.'
   1. '. . . Ratepayers pay for it.'
   2. '. . . somebody's payin' it though.'
Elderly man to young : 'Do you want to get through to dance?'
Young man : 'No, had enough of it Saturday. Don't want to wear my boots out . . . get corns.'
Woman : 'You can't see nothing.'
Woman : 'Cahm on, don't go in there—it's too crowded.'
Woman : 'Well, it keeps people off the streets.'
Man : 'They wanta keep it on till ten, nine ain't late enough.'
Young man to elderly woman emerging from the floor : 'Enjoy it mum?'

That this mass-dancing accepts and glorifies the Lambeth Walk is significant of the nature of its social appeal, and makes it much more than a piece of middle-class romanticism about working-class conditions. It

proves that if you give the masses something which
connects on with their own lives and streets, at the
same time breaking down the conventions of shyness
and stranger-feeling, they will take to it with far more
spontaneous feeling than they have ever shown for the
paradise-drug of the American dance-tune.   The dream-
sex of the dance lyric points away from social feeling
and activity and towards a world of personal superstition and magic (see the analysis of the dance by Tom
Harrisson, *New Writing*, Winter, 1938).   It is no more
about reality than Hitler's speeches are.   Ballroom
dancers sleep-walk to its strains with the same surrender
of personal decision as that of uniformed Nazis.   These
Lambeth Walkers are happy because they find they are
free to express *themselves* without the hypnosis of a jazz-
moon or a Führer.

The dance, then, was in the first place an out-door
thing of the seasons and of communal participation,
"a prayer with the legs".   But it lost all earth and
harvest meanings when industrialism submerged the
village green in factory and soot.   Yet the dance-urge
is strong, and stuck.   Through the nineteenth century
dancing stayed largely social, though more exclusive
(big houses) in patterns of Lancers and Waltz, indoors.
Jazz scattered that, and, with the war, made dancing a
couple affair, the boy and girl, in a restaurant or
dancehall.   The words still had the pre-industrial
angles, heaven, rain, moonshine and corn, thanks to
the American Negro and his homeland nostalgias.
Co-operating dances faded away, and for the past fifteen
years we have been doing steps increasingly stereotyped
and repetitive.   Last year Big Apple and Shottisch
attempted to socialise slightly again.   But only the
Lambeth Walk succeeded in a big way, because it makes
everyone do the same thing at the same time, and express
their togetherness with smack and shout.   The effect on
the private tempo of dancing has been great, may be

greater.   Partly because one or two people sensed the
deficiency in Hollywood jazz, more by chance hit and
miss in a situation where many ordinary folk felt that
deficiency, the Lambeth Walk has swept the world, is
the first contemporary dance from this country that
has put the world on its feet, in the same sort of way
(but much more so) as its close relative, the Cake Walk,
did when taken up by Charlie Chaplin who lived in
Lambeth thirty years ago.   And the success of the Lambeth Walk has shattered a whole lot of dancehall
dogmas, about people's inhibitions, the urge to escape,
etc., etc., etc. . . .

Charlie's old Lambeth landlady was positive that's
where he got his cake-walk. But Chaplin himself,
not:

> "Charlie Chaplin Film Corporation,
>   1416 North La Brea Avenue,
>   Hollywood, California.
>   September 19, 1938.

Mass Observer,
6, Grotes Buildings,
Blackheath,
London, S.E.3,
England.

Dear Sir,
This is to acknowledge yours of recent date addressed to
Mr. Chaplin who has been absent from the studio. It has
only just come to his attention.

He wishes to thank you for your courtesy in writing and
express his appreciation of the compliment. However, he
does not think he can really give any assistance in regard to
the subject matter of the 'Lambeth Walk'. It does not have
any connection with his screen character that he is aware of.
That walk would seem to be the logical effect of being compelled by necessity to wear ill-fitting shoes—much too large
for his feet.

> Thanking you again for your interest—"

6

A SLIGHT CASE OF TOTEMISM

ON the road between Bolton and Wigan is the small mining town of Westhoughton. Arriving there on Saturday, August 27, 1938, anthropologists of British culture had a busy day. It was the beginning of the "Wakes" week, the local holiday, and this traditionally falls on Bartlemass, church feast commemorating the flaying alive of St. Bartholomew. Calling in at the Dog and Pheasant, prosperous public house run by Dick Tyldesley, England and Lancashire slow-bowler, observers found announcements of the "Keaw Yed" festival and effigy. In a room upstairs at this pub locals were admiring an elaborate construction. A large canvas was painted with the landscape of the neighbouring hills and through this landscape protruded the stuffed head of a cow. By this stood the effigy of a farmer in the act of sawing off the cow's head which was apparently stuck through the bars of a gate. Laid in front of this scene, as though sacrificial offerings, were a tankard of beer and a pasty on the black-painted stump of a tree. On either side were pots of flowers and strewn below were cabbages, turnips, carrots and pasties. Posted on the wall were some verses with the title "The Legend":

"Long years ago a cow got its head
Fast in a gate, like this, it is said,
And the Farmer, who in a bit of a doubt,
Sawed off its head to get it out.

185

Now while you are viewing this exhibit here
Don't forget, downstairs, we have Magee's noted beer
Which for years, like this legend, has stood the test,
And acclaimed by all to be the BEST."

Clearly the native festival had come in handy for
the local brewer and there was an additional tie-up in
the form of well-displayed collection boxes for the
Westhoughton Sick-Nursing Association.

In four other pubs, the Hart Common Hotel, the Red
Lion, the White Horse and the Commercial, were
exhibited other versions of the farmer and the cow.
This story is the central feature of the Keaw Yed festival
in which this town of 20,000 inhabitants joins with
the utmost enthusiasm.   The other big feature of the
day is the eating and baking of pasties, some of which
are immense affairs costing up to £1 and decorated with
pictures of the cow and gate.   There is also the Fair
with roundabouts, coconut shies and side shows which
draws huge crowds from outlying places.

The cow's head story and the pasties are a Westhoughton speciality.   Nowhere else in Lancashire is
there anything like it.   Other Lancashire towns have
their own specialities—Bury puddings, Bolton trotters
and others—but here the localism is more marked,
the tradition more deeply felt.   In the course of the
day's observation many curious facts about the ceremony
came to light.   This is no mere piece of rustic folk-lore,
since it thrives in an industrial setting.   What are the
factors which make for its strength ?   Would it be
possible for it to become more widespread ?   In what
sense is it an isolated freak and how far does it fit in
with other tendencies in our civilization ?

In Westhoughton you can see the pit-head next door
to the wheat-field.   The ruined arches of derelict factory buildings stand out against the landscape of rolling
grassy hills.   The farmer and the cow are still real enough

figures in this town with its 12 slaughter-houses and 82 dairies, but the whole pattern of the town's life is that of industry, or was, until one pit after another started closing down owing to flooding. Now industry is practically at a standstill in the town; there is 50% unemployment and those who are in work find employment outside Westhoughton. But this has not made the people any less keen on their Keaw Yed festival. Some change in emphasis there has been, but the traders and publicans on one hand and the spontaneous pleasure in their legend of the Westhoughtonians on the other keep the ceremony very much alive.

One elderly shopkeeper told an observer that 30 years ago all the pubs of the town had the cow's head and it was much more of a feature.

Forty years ago, he said, after the head had been on show the people tore it down and ate it and he remembered 20 years ago how they had roasted a bullock in the Market Square and sold sandwiches made of its flesh. He said that the cow's head side of the celebration was going down, but that the pasty eating was going up.

This was borne out by an old man in the Red Lion who said that there used to be two or three times as much of the Keaw Yed, but that the eating of pasties was growing. He also said, "Fifty years ago they used to march along the streets in processions. It was called The Boowin Cloob (Bone Club) I can't remember if they had the cow's head, but I think it would be cooked for them to eat when they came back. They used to stew it up for broth. It was killed on the Friday, they showed it on the Saturday and ate it on the Monday. I remember them roasting a bullock here and at Allerton. They used to lead it round the streets, showing the beast that was going to be killed. About a ton's weight, it was. When they roasted it, the fat dripped off the carcase and it was collected in tins. The meat

was made into sandwiches and everyone ate them."
He said that the pasty feasts had also been a feature
when he was young, and they were connected with
the cow's head. Other informants told us that the
head itself had at one time been cooked in pastry like
a large pie, and the local journal speaks of pies in the
shape of a cow's head being in great demand. There
seems, therefore, to be a direct connection between the
ceremonial eating of pasties and the formerly widespread custom of eating the cow's head itself.[1]

At the Hart Common another elderly drinker said,
"I remember them marching through the streets with
the head on a pole. It was all decorated on the Saturday and eaten on the Monday as broth. The broth
was given out free in the pubs, but this was stopped
because it was against the law for the pubs to give anything away free". The same man said with the deepest
conviction and a smile of what seemed pride on his
face, "It's real, you know. It really happened. I
can show you the place, but I couldn't tell you when,
not the year exactly".

A collier started off by saying that Keaw Yed was only
an excuse for a booze-up, and that the brewers ran it.
He told the story of its legend sceptically, but quite
proudly took the observer down the street to look at
one in a pub. Talked of the drunks there would be
as if he was disgusted with the thought and then added
that he would not say he would not be one himself.
When the observer suggested (from the way he had
been talking) that everyone now regarded Keaw Yed
as a bit of a joke not to be taken very seriously, he disa-
agreed strongly and emphasised several times that over
90% of the population believed it really happened. The

---

[1] "At Westhoughton, Lancashire, a huge pie is made in the
shape of a cow's head, which is eaten on the day of the Wake,
the Sunday after St. Bartholomew's Day. The inhabitants are
sometime called 'cow 'yeds'." P. H. Ditchfield, *Old English
Customs Extant at the Present Time*, 1896, p. 131.

observer adds, "I think he was definitely one of the 90% himself."

That there is at least a minority in Westhoughton which would like to see the Keaw Yed abolished is shown by the following item in the local journal:

"A protest against the periodical references to the Keaw Yed legend which is associated with Westhoughton, was made by Mr. James Tonge, a prominent Westhoughtonian, in his speech at the opening of the Westhoughton Horticultural Society's Show on Saturday.

After referring to the excellent display of bloom and the great work the Society was doing in the town, Mr. Tonge said he wished those people who chronicle the interesting events which take place in the town would remember and emphasize more the record of institutions like the society and forget those other events—real or imaginary—which were also said to be associated with Westhoughton. It was Wakes Saturday, and the Wakes, from being a very old and definite link between the customs and celebrations of the Church, had descended chiefly into 'a ghastly description' of an entirely untrue legend of a farmer, a cow and a gate.

A truer idea of the nature of Westhoughton people, of their occupations, recreations, intelligence, and skill were more likely to be found in other of the town's institutions than in local hostelries where crowds were chiefly from outside Westhoughton's boundaries. The implications of the absurd legend which was a slight on the townspeople's intelligence were not worthy of a town which had contributed its fair share of highly intellectual men and women, and of respected and honoured sportsmen too."

The story of the cow's head is used as a joke against Westhoughtonians by people in other Lancashire towns. It looks as if the joke was resented by certain of the town boosters. The same feeling possibly accounts for the way that local antiquaries, journalists and others whose education and outlook separates them in most respects from the majority culture of Westhoughton, repeatedly claim that the whole performance started quite recently; but with deeper vision a *Manchester Guardian* reporter wrote up the story in 1935:

"For a century or more since, the cow's head . . . has entered into observances that have varied in their exact nature from generation to generation. Recollections are preserved, in the lively gossip which revives at every 'wakes' time, of bands of textile workers and colliers who walked through the town bearing sometimes a cow's head on a pike and more often (being a practical folk) the bones of a head off which they had already feasted.

When two bands met there were running battles in the streets, and the bones were carried off by the stronger. John Coop, an amateur of local history in the latter half of the last century, handed on a circumstantial account of a street battle in 1815, when the people of Westhoughton celebrated the Battle of Waterloo with the public roasting of a cow to feast the poor of the town. Two crowds from Chapel Moor and Daisy Hill, then known as Lower Side, fought for the possession of the head, which the former had carried in procession. The people of Chapel Moor won, and their defeated opponents threw at them, according to Coop, the name of 'keaw-yed' which stuck. . . .

The festival is far older than the 'keaw-yed' story; like so many local feast days, it was a religious observance several hundred years ago. St. Bartholomew is the patron saint of Westhoughton Parish Church, and the 'keaw-yed wakes' always fall about the time of the patronal festival. . . . There are records of rush-bearing ceremonies when the people of Westhoughton took a cart-load of rushes to the mother church at Deane."

Actually there is no evidence either for or against the existence of the cow's-head cult before 1815. The majority of Westhoughtonians think it has just been going on for ever. To an anthropologist the interesting thing must be that here we have a set of beliefs and customs which, if met with among primitive peoples,

would undoubtedly be considered a case of totemism.
The people call themselves Cow-heads. At their annual
festival, a cow is killed, its head exhibited and afterwards
eaten. The festival includes heavy eating and drinking
and the day ends with couples making love in back
lanes all over the town. (An observer who lives there
said that this was more open and on a larger scale than
at any other time.) The correct answer for a Westhoughtonian, when asked why the Farmer of the legend
sawed the cow and not the fence, is "We wanted some
beef"; in other words, that those who eat the totem
animal acquire its qualities.

Frazer, in *Spirits of the Corn and of the Wild* (Vol. 1,
p. 289), says the cow was often used as a form of corn
spirit, as well as other animals, and killed to promote
fecundity. For instance at Pouilly, near Dijon, an ox
is led round the field when the last sheaf is left, then a
man dressed as the devil cuts the last ears of corn and
kills the ox. Part is eaten at the harvest supper, part
kept till spring sowing. Near Bordeaux an ox used
to be killed immediately after the end of threshing. The
last sheaf in many places is called Cow.

Nearer Lancashire, it is recorded that at Loch Maree
in Western Ross in 1656 the minister complained that
people sacrificed bulls to St. Mhaolruth, patron saint
of the island, on August 25 (same date as the Keaw Yed
festival). This happened again in the eighteenth
century. (A.D. Lacaille; "The Bull In Scottish Folklore,"
Folk-lore, 1930, Vol. XLI.)

Finally, "At a village called Valle Pietra near Subiaco,
on a certain day in August the villagers drive a cow
round the village, goading it with thrusts of knives and
other weapons, and singeing it with lighted sticks. After
this the animal is put in a stable for the night: but it
is essential that it should not be fed. The following
day it is again hunted in the same manner, and it is
finally killed and the meat eaten. On the second day,

as it passes the houses, the villagers give money to pay for the cost of the festival, and whatever remains is given to the village priest. The village is twelve miles from any railway or police station, and on enquiry it was found that the festival was unknown to the authorities at Rome". (Communicated by Frazer to H. A. Freeman, "An Italian Cattle Festival", *Folk-lore*, 1919, Vol. XXX.)

Already there is nearly enough evidence to satisfy a "diffusionist" that the Westhoughton ceremony is a relic of a formerly widespread cow or bull cult, which can be traced back to the origins of agriculture in the Nile Valley. Without accepting or denying such a possibility, it is still surprising that at Westhoughton the *whole* system of totemic ideas should have survived, in spite of industrialism, Methodism, primary education. Alternatively, it may not be a survival but a spontaneous product of the people and the place. Why, then, has it taken a form which can be paralleled from Australia to the Arctic? The Freudian answer might be that there is a deep-seated tendency in human nature for people to identify themselves with some animal, and at certain times to kill and eat it, for the reasons which Freud sets out in his *Totem and Taboo*. Professor Malinowski might point also to the way in which the ceremony consolidates the Westhoughtonians as a group, and gives them a special kind of local patriotism, and he would attach importance to the reunions of families and friends which are a feature of the Wakes. At this time, people return to their native town from all parts of the country. "An excuse and justification for such reunions is the eating of a special kind of pasty which housewives and bakers make in great numbers at this season."

An outstanding attraction of the present-day Keaw Yed festival is the Fair on the Market Square, thus announced on rainbow-coloured posters:

WESTHOUGHTON
ANNUAL
W A K E S

will open on the usual ground

OPPOSITE WHITE LION HOTEL

Friday, August 26th

with the

Swirl of Life
Noah's Ark
Wall of Death with monkey
Boxing Booth
and all the latest and up-to-date side-shows.

GLAD TO MEET OLD AND NEW FRIENDS—AND
DON'T FORGET THE PASTY FEAST

The Market Square was the site, more than a hundred
years ago, of a mill, the first to use steam-driven
machines. Workers from another mill, resenting the
use of steam, sent a lad in through a window to set fire
to it and it was burnt to the ground. The lad, aged
16, was hung for it at Lancaster. The ground has
been thought unlucky ever since and nothing has been
built there. Each year the swings and roundabouts at
Wakes time make it bright with lights and loud with
music; in the evening it is packed tight with people, and
at 9 p.m. it was like this:

"Raining hard but the Fair doing a roaring trade. Two
roundabouts for adults and older children and two for tots.
People queuing up for the faster one on the street, young
boys and girls holding onto each other shrieking as their
carriages get flung round. All the usual sideshows and one
with pin tables patronized by the more sober.

3d. to see a girl handling reptiles. About half-a-dozen
slow moving pythons. The girl hangs them around her neck

G

and gives a little talk on the way they are fed, when they change their skin, how they are bathed and kept warm with hot water bottles. They attack tigers and lions in Africa and crush them to death, but any bit of twisting they do around her body she has to encourage. She finishes with a 'Kiss of Death', and holds the largest python's mouth in hers. With an offer to any lady to do the same, she closes the performance without waiting for reply.

6d. to see the 'Wall of Death'. Two monkeys tied to a minute motor-car. While the performer is encouraging the crowd to come in, one monkey tries to have a sleep. Then they begin to get restless. The one with the longer rope looks among the rubbish and spanners in the middle for food. The other tries to move the car but his lead is so short it keeps pulling on him. Ridicule from the men, women and children who have come to see the fun. Not a word of sympathy. The voice suddenly is silent outside, the monkeys are immediately alert, standing motionless peering at the trap door. Two or three minutes before their owner comes. The monkeys hardly move but seem to be straining everything to hear and see him. They dash to the car when he comes. The one with the short lead is tied to the pole in the centre. He claws at the man who playfully slaps the monkey's face. The other monkey careering about while the man does his little introductory talk. At a signal he jumps in. The chain is untied from the car but placed in the back carefully while the monkey is not looking. The car is pushed off with the monkey at the wheel and makes a hideous noise as it speeds around the top of the wall. Each time around the man shouts and brings his hand down as near as he can to the monkey's face to prevent him making a leap. A dozen times around and the engine stops. The audience applauds."

Data about the attitude of Westhoughton to animals, parallel to the grim jest of sawing off the cow's head. Curiously, that myth has a way of re-making itself, as seen from these local press-cuttings:

"Two versions of the 'Keaw Yed' legend as seen in Westhoughton last week-end.

On Friday evening, at a local hotel, a stuffed cow's head complete with electric lamps for eyes and a miniature gate, were hung outside over the doorway to attract patrons.

Suddenly something went wrong ! Owing to the heat of the lamps the cow's head burst into flames, and within a few minutes all that was left was a mass of wreckage. This was placed in an upper room and proved more of an attraction than the whole head had been when it was hanging outside.

On Monday, in Westhoughton, a goat tried to emulate the legendary cow. It got its head through the railings bounding the field in which it was kept. Fortunately it was able to free itself before a saw was needed !" (*Westhoughton Journal*, August 30, 1935.)

"A few days ago members of the Westhoughton police force had a shock when a cow strolled into the police station. Whilst one would not like to suggest that the animal knew that 'Howfen' Wakes was at hand and had come to give itself up in order that its head should form one of the many 'Keaw Yed' tableaux which will be found in different parts of the town, the incident was particularly appropriate at this season of the year." (ibid, August 26, 1938.)

There is also the peculiar tale of the time when the Keaw Yed legend was staged with a real cow and a real five-barred gate :

"The cow's head was thrust through the gate, and a man stood by, saw in hand, in the act of cutting off the animal's head. A photograph was taken of this little enactment, and copies became widely distributed. When the incident had almost been forgotten there arrived in Westhoughton an official of the R.S.P.C.A. to make definitely sure the barbarian had not actually cut off the cow's head." (ibid., August 24).

The Keaw Yed tableau at the Dog and Pheasant made use of a stuffed cow's head, but at two other pubs the head was a real one. At the White Horse, one of the barmen explained that the cow had been killed on

Thursday night. "The head has four pounds of beef on it. We'll eat it on Monday. The butcher takes the meat off the jawbones, and we make it into potato pies. The tongue has been taken out and is on the table now. I had some for my dinner."

This evidence is clear enough. Yet the intelligent young journalist at the office of the *Westhoughton Journal*, for whose help we owe thanks, was sceptical when it was suggested to him that the Westhoughtonians still eat their totem. Even in small Westhoughton there is clearly a gap between official views and mass facts.

Opposite the Market Square is the butcher's shop that supplied the White Horse with its cow's head. The butcher, Mr. Morris, short, thick-set, white-overalled, has been killing the Keaw Yed cow for forty years. Twenty-six years ago, he told an observer, he patented a new technique: "I was the first man to treat the head this way. It was my suggestion to cut the head right off, skin and all. Then I treat it with this white powder, which preserves it. It makes it much more natural like. In olden times they used to skin the head and bake it with pastry; it just looked like a pie-crust. On the Monday they used to make a feast of it. . . . I first had it my way 26 years ago, and it caught on and I've done one every year since, for different houses, and the other butchers copy me now." He opened a large white-enamelled frigidaire safe and pointed out a great blood-red, bone-hard object—a skinned cow's head—to show the old method. Then went on to demonstrate the slaughtering: "First we knock the beast down, and then we stick him. At least I shoot 'un; I've a gun." He produced his gun, loaded it and fired into the cow's skull. A loud report, and a neat deep hole in the skull.

Talking to Mr. Morris, one had the strong impression that one was talking to the priest of a cult that persists and even creates new forms for itself. Two factors may

have helped to make the Keaw Yed so strong. One is
that Westhoughton, though industrial, is isolated from
many of the influences which make the big towns uniform in culture and outlook. Second is the close-
knit, vigorous character of the smaller industrial community, making it a sort of tribal unit.

Lambeth culture, we have seen, has also this character. Its strong individuality helped to make the
"Lambeth Walk" a national institution, even an international one. The Keaw Yed has remained a purely
local institution, and probably in many other small
industrial towns and villages there are equally vigorous
but localized institutions. In finding out about them
and trying to understand them in relation to the whole
perspective of our industrial society, we can perhaps
hit on means for making life less "boring". If Lupino
Lane, the B.B.C., the newspapers and Oxo, wanted to
make the Keaw Yed a national Saturday, it is probable
they could succeed. John Bull, Roast Beef of Old
England, and the Mustard Club's Baron de Beef. Or,
as King's Medallist poet Auden once wrote:

> "John Bull, John Bull, I understand well;
> I know, Bull, I know what you want me to tell.
> Calm, Bull, calm, news coming in time;
> News coming, Bull; calm, Bull.
> Fight it down, fight it down,
> That terrible hunger; calm, Bull; first
> We must have a look round, we must know the worst.
>
> England our cow
> Once was a lady—is she now?"

A topical question, asked in another way by Jerry Doyle,
cartoonist of the New York *Post*: he saw it pictorially in
mid-September, 1938:

7

TWO-MINUTE STOREY

THE Two Minutes' Silence on Armistice Day is the only occasion in the year when the whole mass of the people is supposed to be doing the same thing at the same time. Or rather they are not supposed to be doing anything; for those two minutes they are expected to do *nothing*, to stop work, to stand still and keep quiet. They are supposed to think certain thoughts and to feel certain emotions which are related to events in the past (which every year mean less to more people) but which also have a bearing on the future. The central ceremony at the Cenotaph, attended by the King, has a religious character and thousands of secondary ceremonies take place all over the country at churches, or round consecrated war memorials. Yet the Silence itself is not confined to people with religious beliefs; it also has a national and social significance, and amounts in a sense to a reaffirming of confidence in the motives which led to this country joining in the Great War. Of course it is possible for anyone to treat the Silence as a personal experience, connected with personal memories, but these almost inevitably join on to wider, less purely individual feelings. To some extent, at any rate, the vast majority are compelled by the circumstances of the Silence to stop in the middle of their individual lives and think in terms of their own country and other countries, of war and peace, life and death. From the religious point of view, the Silence is a kind of link between living and dead—like other ceremonies the world over at which the

199

spirits of the dead members of the tribe are thought to return to their former home on earth. But from the secular, non-religious point of view, the Silence is an act of social solidarity, with implications connecting it with this life rather than the life to come. It is on this side that the institution of the Silence is suffering a certain strain. The general attitude towards the Great War has changed. A new generation has grown up. Since 1918 the League of Nations has come into existence and then practically faded out again. The Versailles Treaty has been made and broken. The Great War is less in people's minds than the possibility of the next war. So it is not surprising that on November 11, 1937, a very large number of people felt uneasy about the whole performance. Repeating the same ritual year after year is a way of *stopping* time, of keeping it fixed at some point in the past. This is possible when the point in the past is mythological, like the death of a corn god, but it is trickier when the events are recent enough to have implications in the present, yet long enough past for other events to have changed people's ideas about the first events. When Hitler makes Germany stop work and listen while he talks, there is no easy means of telling whether Germans do so with good will, we don't know if they are pleased, annoyed or bored. But in this country we can find out comparatively easily what people are saying and thinking and doing at a certain time on a certain day.

When M-O decided to make a survey of the Silence, it was without any preconceived ideas about it. 1,000 observers were simply asked to describe exactly what happened to them between 10.30 and 11.30 on the morning of November 11, 1937. They sent in the reports, which are analysed in this section.

The survey, as it turned out, revealed the widespread feeling that the ceremony was already out-of-date and should be stopped. But this feeling would have remained voiceless without the intervention of ex-serviceman Stanley Storey. His shouts broke the silence. They were heard by millions who were listening-in to the Cenotaph service. Next day this entitled Hannen Swaffer in the *Daily Herald* to write: "Armistice Day's formal Empire service at the Cenotaph, with its Two Minutes' Silence, should never be held again! Yesterday's happenings made this even more obvious."

Five observers were near the Cenotaph, but only two of them knew that anything had happened. Of 56 who were listening in, 44 heard the interruption. The story was well told by the *Manchester Guardian* :

". . . An instant after the last wreath was in place, Big Ben struck the first note of eleven, the maroons sounded, and the silence fell like a curtain.

For a few seconds the air was empty of every sound except the rustling of the plane leaves. And then suddenly there was a commotion on the pavement outside the Home Office and behind the line of Cabinet Ministers. The rigid line of sailors at the edge of the crowd was abruptly broken, and a thick-set, fair-haired man, bare-headed, and wearing a mackintosh, rushed out into the roadway, shouting in a high tormented voice, 'All this hypocrisy!' and after it another phrase which sounded like 'Preparing for war'.

He ran forward in a direction which would have taken him past the Prime Minister, but half a dozen policemen burst through the gap after him and brought him down in a struggling heap about two yards away from Mr. Chamberlain. They piled themselves on top of him until he was invisible, and tried to muffle his shouts. But again one heard faintly from beneath the heap his cry of 'All this hypocrisy', and another incoherent sound in which one could only distinguish the word 'war'.

The Silence still held everybody else rigid and dumb. Mr. Chamberlain never moved, though all this was happening just behind him. The King turned his head slightly towards the disturbance for an instant, then looked to his front again and stood motionless. The sailors whose rank had been broken re-formed it silently. A police officer cantered up to see that everything necessary was being done, and the policemen on the ground got to their feet and dragged the interrupter back into the crowd, where they laid him down and kept him quiet. Not another sound or movement came from all those thousands of people; the Silence still held them.

When at last it came to an end the police could be seen escorting the man away through the crowd towards Downing Street, where he was taken to an ambulance station. They were supporting rather than escorting him, for he seemed almost unconscious by this time and made no more noise.

The crowd through which he passed remained orderly, so far as one could distinguish from a roof on the other side of the street, though there was a certain amount of shouting which was drowned by the roll of drums that followed the end of the Silence. A few excitable people are said to have shouted 'Kill him !' but so far as one could judge there were not many people who made any noisy protest.

Afterwards one learned that the man was one Stanley Storey who had been confined to an asylum last February and had escaped in September. At the time, of course, this was not known, and his shout seemed rather the agonized cry of one who had found the strain of the moment and of his own convictions too much to be borne. As such it heightened one's own feelings almost intolerably. There must be few people who can attend the celebrations of Armistice Day without having to thrust into the background of their minds the fear that all the suffering of twenty years ago has not prevented more sufferings to come. . . ."

The fact that Storey had been in an asylum would have tended to make people dismiss the incident, if his words had not expressed what was in so many of their minds. "The rulers are mad, the people suffer." The symbolism was obvious. Many were saying next day that Storey was not so mad as the people who shut him up.

Of those who reported on how they spent the Silence, 80% kept it, the remaining 20% went on with their work.

Taking only those who were by themselves at the time of the Silence, 30% did not keep it, as compared with 10% of those who were in the company of others. This suggests that a good many of those who kept the Silence did so because others were doing so. But observers reported a number of cases where offices and factories did not observe the Silence.

In this factory, the Silence was observed, but no one mentioned the Armistice or the Great War:

"Having placed a notice on the works clock to the effect that the signal would be given for the commencement of the two minutes silence by the blowing of the Works hooter, I felt that this would have the desired effect of all the Works joining in the silence together with an impressive result.

I have during previous years made a rule of going down into the workshop and observing the silence with the men, and to this end I had endeavoured to arrange my morning's work. A certain amount of tension was evident towards 11.0 and I felt we had the correct atmosphere.

At 10.55 I levelled my tie, straightened my collar and overall and endeavoured to look what I thought was grave, and made for the shop. But here my plan went astray. I'll be hanged if the phone didn't blare out its nerve-wracking call for attention. No time to go down the shop now, I had just time to place myself by a lorry underneath which one of my men was working when the hooter went, but so low was it, it seemed as if it were afraid to make itself heard. I removed my hat, and tried to realize how far and how near the whole thing was to the hypocritical, for I felt that some of the very persons, who at that moment were praying for peace, probably depended for dividends on the sale of armaments to enhance their financial position. I am afraid my thoughts were not in keeping with the intentions of the founders of the ceremony, to be honest they were a little bitter.

The man under the lorry was evidently more concentrated on his job than on the silence for he went on hammering until I requested him to observe the silence.

At 11.1 a train went roaring over the near-by bridge, no silence for the driver and fireman.

Those 2 minutes seem a long 2 minutes and it is somewhat of a relief when the buzzer or hooter again gave us the signal to recommence.

Now from 7.0 a.m. when the notice was posted until 11.0 I never heard anyone even mention the Great War or the Armistice and after the Silence ended, work was resumed and everyone carried on in the same manner that can be observed on any normal day, and 11.30 found everything sailing along as usual. Phone ringing, buses hastening to make up for lost time and people hurrying about their business."

That report was from an assistant manager in the Potteries. This one, from a factory in Staines, gives a rather similar picture:

"At 10.30 I am working in section of the paintshop. I am, or learning to be, a trimmer which covers the work in a car better known perhaps as upholstery.

I have been given a job of padding some wheel arches. On this particular car it is unusual for this to be done, but this is a special order. I am working by myself and do not notice anything unusual except that one of the chaps, a cabinet maker is whistling at his job a few yards away. He is a fellow from the Midlands, and has a most profuse supply of wit, and is generally whistling or 'singing'. I noticed that this time he gave us 'When the Poppies Bloom Again', but after trying it over a time or two he found nobody taking any interest in it, so he switched over to his usual selection of popular tunes. When the hooter blows at 11, I am on my feet outside the car, so I 'down tools' and assume a more or less upright position, and watch the others. There is a painter who has been on his back blocking a chassis. He is an old man, and he wriggles his way out and lays there, propped on one elbow, with his brush in his hand. In crawling out, his cap was pushed over one side. He goes to put it straight—seems to wonder whether to leave it on or not—leaves it on, and lies there—in an uncomfortable position, and therefore what I suppose he thinks—a good enough one. He is less comfortable than if he was to attention, so I suppose he thought that much about it.

A few seconds after our hooter go the whistles and sirens of near-by factories and then the gun. Our works is quiet by this time, and there is only the noise of the self-stoking heating plant. I looked round me. There were only about 5 men in sight, and two of these had taken off their caps and were standing stiffly to attention. One of these is a proper 'old soldier', and is looking forward to a trench supper to which he has been invited. The other was a very old man—70 or more, and for the first time I have seen him bareheaded. His hair was white and he stood there—thinking perhaps of a son or relation killed, and the other, by his side must have been remembering his mates. These two were the only ones that I saw who seemed to treat the silence for what it was—remembrance. The others seemed bored, or uneasy, waiting—for perhaps the first time—for the second hooter to blow and the work resume. There is a terrible lot of things that can pass through ones mind in two minutes, and I wandered away from our shop, to think that everybody else was still, and thinking of the other observers who were turning these two minutes of inactivity into two minutes of keen observation or were some of them thinking of comrades lost? I 'came back to earth' again to notice the hiss of the air—the compressor starts automatically when the pressure falls below a certain level, and I wondered if it would start up and shatter the silence. I was prepared for it, and I wondered how much it would startle the others if it started. I was thinking of this— watching for the two 'old soldiers' to jump, when the second hooter went. There was instant movement and relaxation, the compressor started as the hooter shut off, and together with this came the noise of the overhead shafting starting up, and the din of the panelbeaters. I started work again.

The general impression of the chaps was I think that it was a bit of a nuisance, and to some an embarrassment to stand still—silent for two minutes, but the only comment came from the men who had memories of the war—'If you'd seen so and so, and been through what we did some of you young chaps would feel different about it."

For some, the effect of the Silence was to give added dignity to the men when they stopped work:

1. "There are two of us in the coal-wagon and another holding the bags. My pal swings the first spadeful and me the second, so on alternately and almost invariably the bag 'draws' on the fifth spadeful, seldom a nut too many or one short. . . .

There has been no mention of the 'Armistice' and I was completely unconscious of it until I heard a long 'buzzer'. Suddenly I remembered the 'two minutes silence'. We put down our spades and removed our caps. A deep and pleasant silence was everywhere. I looked round the sidings. Every man, cap in hand, a thoughtful expression on the face, and a kind of dignity I had never noticed before. . . .

I notice one or two of the men growing a bit fidgety. The silence is broken by the barking of a dog, then, with a feeling of relief, the buzzer goes again. In a second or two the traffic moves in a nearby street, Church bells start to ring, yet the men stay in their positions a moment or two longer —none wishing to be the first to move. Then everyone seems to start just where he had left off. Both my mates reached for their 'Woodbines' and I noticed how everyone else in the vicinity had commenced to smoke. 'It's funny how everything goes silent,' my mate said. That being the only comment."

2. "Every man was still in the positions in which they had been working. Some men were standing caps in hands. There was one man bending down, his head bowed. There was another man standing on the machine where he had been loosening or tightening some bolts holding the job on the machine. For myself I was standing cap in hand, head slightly bowed. No one seemed to have their eyes closed so I did not close mine. Anyhow I wanted to see what impressions I could gather. A feeling of reverence swept the building and filled the atmosphere. For two short minutes human beings, who were literally parts of their machines they worked, had brought themselves back to men again. . . ."

For these two working-class observers the ceremony is moving for reasons which do not seem to be connected with ideas of War and Armistice.

Several observers mention grins and laughter as a form of relief after the Silence is ended. Another reaction: "Sam has just told me that we ought to have gone right into Germany and wiped them all out."

Here are some extracts from reports showing the tendency to oppose the ceremony or not to take it seriously:

1. "10.30. No mention of Armistice.
10.40. One of the older chemists was getting ready a box to stand on so that he would be able to switch off an electric motor which was making a noise. I do not know whether he had been told to do so by the Boss or not but heard afterwards that the Boss had said he did not want any noisy machines running.

While he was doing this the head brewer came in and said 'Silence' laughing at his own joke.

10.50. I am working with a young man of 26. We start discussing Armistice Day. He says that we cannot go on indefinitely observing it to which I agree saying that we may soon have another war and that so far as I can see this is not helping to prevent it.

10.56. I am talking to another workmate age 26. He has forgotten about the silence until I pass some remark. Another workmate, age 22, comes in, we hear the sirens and stand silent leaning on the benches for the two minutes. Immediately it finishes the older one remarks that he does not see the point in it.

11.5. I go out to do a job outside and although I see and speak with a few people there is no mention of armistice up till 11.30. Neither is there any sign except the wearing of poppies."

2. "I am alone in the staff room quietly processing books. The janitor comes in. I ask him: 'You're an ex-serviceman, aren't you?' He says Yes. 'What do you think about the

Armistice business? Don't you think it ought to be stopped?
It means nothing to people like me. Does it mean anything
to you who were in the War?' 'It ought to be stopped' he
says. 'It's only the people who weren't in the war who want
to keep it going. The average fellow who was in the thick
of it wants to forget all about it.'

The gun. I stand still thinking vaguely of war and
peace. Become aware of a tap noisily dripping water,
disturbing the silence. A dog breaks the silence with a
terrific yelp.

Nobody mentioned Armistice or silence."

3. "At 11 o'clock, vacuum cleaner upstairs promptly
begins to work and loud singing accompanies it. I have
asked maid whether she would like to hear service on wireless but she has refused, saying that she doesn't hold with
that kind of thing as it only opens old wounds."

Another observer was having a permanent wave.
The girl who was giving it her did not stop for the
Silence, but said quietly: "I haven't any use for this."
In an office, a man said: "I think it ought to be stopped.
It's only a bleeding nuisance, messin' up the traffic
the way it does." Another observer remarked to her
milkman it was a cold day: "He replied, 'It is nice for
the Cenotaph Service'. I said I wondered how many
more services there would be, and he answered, 'It
is time it was washed out. We want to forget, not
remember.'" Another observer records that after a
service at the local War Memorial: "A middle-aged
artisan said 'I'd like to see a bloody bomb drop on the
whole bloody——' (I'm not certain what the last word
was.)"

It was in this frame of mind that a large part of the
nation heard Storey's outburst on the wireless, or heard
about it afterwards. Feeling that another war was not
distant, many people resented as an imposition and
mockery the version of history which the Armistice

ceremony seemed to convey. While a year ago Colonel
Blimp found the lunatic's protest a sacrilege on the
"War to End War", six weeks before November 11,
1938, he was boiling to start another one, the War to
End Hitler.

In 1938 sale of white poppies trebled, though still
nowhere near reds' forty million sold by 360,000
voluntary sellers, and made by 364 ex-servicemen in a
Richmond factory (gasmask centre in the crisis) at 1/2
an hour. They use 3,454 miles of wire, $5\frac{1}{2}$ tons paste,
a year. As a big Irish ex-sergeant poppy-maker said:
"This is the place, mate, where the poppies don't
bloom again."

Late in October 1938, 69% of men passing the
Cenotaph did not doff-hat; on November 13th only
5%; October 29th in London 43% persons interviewed
were against continuing the silence for two of the year's
half-million minutes. But on November 11th itself, this
has fallen to 20%, with 11% doubtful, 69% pro.
Such feeling swiftly ebb and flow.

And, after 20 years of a simple flat stone for the
Unknown Warrior's Tomb, where Mrs. Chamberlain's
detective didn't pray, it is to be "elevated" because
people walk heedlessly over it. . . .

8

CASTLES IN THE AIR?

THROUGH this welter of public opinions and percentages, local traditions and mass habits, it must not be forgotten that each and every person is automatically an individual, conforming outwardly, covering his or her private parts like anyone else, but underneath with repressions and furies which are partly "personal". Storey broke through the social barrier, the rigid line of troops, the conventional silence, but he was mad—his repressions had been too much for sanity. His madness was accepted by millions as more sane than the official ritual attitude.

Ordinarily there is no chance for such breaking through of the ordinary past the official—it must take the form of shouted protest or signed petition or cross on a ballot paper. But the document that follows, from an engineering worker, describes a day in his life at random, unmarked by politic, not exceptional, typical of a vast section of the population which has no public voice, expressing everything in "personal" attitudes and relationships. Despite crises, despite out-of-touchness, regardless of press and radio, he lives on :

"'Quarter to seven.' 'Right.' I stretch and pile out, go to the bathroom and swill, the cold water breezes me up and I feel properly awake, scrub with my towel, pull my vest off and put a sleeveless shirt on, the weather is hot and humid and I sweat like hell in the red-hot machine shop— so a lighter kit's the ticket. Part my hair, transfer money, keys, cigarettes and matches from my best suit to my overalls, check my money, have spent 18*s*. since Friday night,

210

slap my side pocket to see if my rules are there, O.K., now I can hear the hurrying crunches of the 7 o'clockers, so downstairs.

'Mornin',' 'Good morning,' my landlady fetches my breakfast, eggs, bacon, dry bread and tea, she fumbles the tea and some goes over the cloth. 'Oh dear,' she says, and sits abruptly down by the window, as I eat I watch her profile against the outside light, she stares out, but her eyes flick up, down, up, down and blink, she moistens her lips and nervously rubs her wrists, now and then the dog whines outside and she gives a little jump. I say to her, 'Think it's going to be warm again?' and she gazes dazedly at me for a bit and then says, 'Yes, I think it will be'—I know what's biting her, the man next door, a Mr. D., inspector on the G.W.R. cut his throat yesterday and she saw him do it, and so she's kind of shocked. I say, 'How'd he get on?' and she knows who I'm referring to and says 'He died at 12 last night.' I say 'I'm very sorry,' and add, 'If he hadn't made a job of it he'd have been stuck away in a nut house.' She says 'That's right.' I ask 'how's the old lady taking it?' My landlady smiles a little and says, 'Oh, wonderfully! She's a little brick.' 'Good!' I say, and finish my breakfast—a clatter, the kitchen door bursts open and in comes A., he stands and screws his eyes on the clock, then grunts in satisfaction and flops on his chair, he hangs his head and sighs hard, I say 'Hello, pal,' and he wobbles his head and says, 'Oh hell, my head'—he got tanked up last night and has a hangover, he starts on his breakfast, I sit and smoke, he catches my eye and flicks his towards next door, I hold my hand in front of me and thumbed down, A. grimaced and nodded, he then looked towards the clock and back at me and I made two fives and two with my fingers, he shook his head and got on with the eats. I went and got my jacket, clipped my trousers and picking my lunch off the table went outside and stowed it in my bike-bag. Sun was well up and getting warm already, the dog pulled his chain taut and got up on his back legs yawning. I gave him a thump in the ribs and rolled him over, I looked up the next garden and saw a bunch of iris and other stuff broken and flattened near the gate. 'Uh, uh,' I thought, 'that's where he dropped.' The dog shook his chain and started to bark for more play, so

I told him 'Quiet,' and went in, 7.40, said 'Good morning' to the landlady, and 'So long, sucker,' to A. and got off. I join the stream of cyclists heading for the great Estate here. Road packed, riders 3 and 4 abreast, girls and men about 50/50, lots of girls with wee cane baskets on the handlebars, never seen them before I came South, some of the local guys carry women's shopping bags on their bikes, 'B—— pansies' I think, just the way I was brought up and the place I come from, I suppose, because I *still* reckon it's a pansy business, I ride fast and weave in and out, ride into the works, stick the bike into the rack, get my lunch out, walk over to the clock. Ding ! 7.51, go to my machine, hang my coat up, get my keys out, unlock my chest, get my most-used tools out.

'Brang-g-g !' the shop gong rings and the men in blue troop in and move to their jobs, I reach for my starter, down, the motor stirs to life, with a low hum, second ! The fly increases its speed, 'boop-boop-bo-o-op' she says on a rising scale. Top ! away she goes in a crescendo of howls which fade to a steady high whine, the big belt starts flapping and cracking as she gains her top, the performance is being repeated all over the shop, I reach over and start up my mate's motor, he says 'ta, cullie.' I have a job on from Sat. and get away on it, and soon I am engrossed, 1⅝, 1¾, race fit, recess, screw ⅝″W., part, turn about, face and chamfer. The metal is chrome-mobyldeum and takes a swagger finish, after about 10 mins. I begin to take glances about, the shop is beginning to warm up and is filling with a blue acrid haze, I can taste its smoky bitterness in my throat. It comes from the forges, furnaces and welders, I put a roughing cut on and watch a welder, he squats in front of a girder frame, pulls his gauntlets on, levels his electrode with one hand and holds his face-shield with the other and peers through the blue-window—then spit, spit-spit, an intense bluey light and the shower of white and red metal as the flame cuts the girder, the quiver of the electrode hurts my eyes and I look away and blink them back to normal. I look at my mate, his face has a dreamy look as he pores over his job, I grin because of his expression, the riveters suddenly make a thundering clatter and his lips move as he curses them to himself, I grin some more at it, he looks my way and winks and shouts 'Hi,.hi, Wullie !' I shout 'Hi, hi, Jock !' . . . I finish my job, report to foreman, 'a special here, Bill,' he gets the blueprint and we lean over the machine and discuss ways and means, 'good job, this, take a bit longer and make sure it's a snip, got to pass A.I.D.' 'Right, I've got it'—I study the print, sure *is* a hot job, three sizes scale 1/10/1/1000, a 14″ bore with $5 \sqrt{10'}/1000$ parallel tolerance, what is it, look at the bottom of the sheet. 'Undercarriage-compression tubes, 2 off, anodic finish, Sea-gull V, Super-marine Aviation.'

We kick off again—finish my job and signal the foreman, he comes over and looks at the job, is pleased, 'shinin' like a dollar on a nigger's a——, that's the ticket, how's she for size ?' 'O.K.' I reply. 'Right, give you a toffee job now,' he says, I get the 'toffee' job, turning a 5 ft. drive spindle, takes about ¼ hr. a cut, that's the 'toffee' part, set the job up, put a cut on, and sit on the bench smoking. I feel pleased with myself so I start to sing 'We'll rant and we'll roar !' very loud, Dasher puts his fingers to his nose and pulls an imaginary chain as a sign of disapproval. Syd smiles and winks while Jock bawls 'gerrwa in the next bludy street !' I shout 'Rudy Vallee' and Jock shouts back 'Who's that ?' Dasher joins in, 'Knocking-shop between two marntains, mite !' We all laugh, I get off the bench and strike the writhing swarf with a big file to break it in case it jams the ways and then drag it clear with a stout wire hook, I watch my hands as I do so, as this stuff one long razor blade and will cut to the bone in a second, I've had some, so I am careful, I sit up again and watch it snaking and twinkling off the job, my mind goes back to Mick P. I met coming to work, I remember the good times we had on W.'s night-shift in Liverpool when we were 16 or 17, I think how different things are in the South, good money and conditions, no 55 hr. night shifts at 24*s*. a week *here*, and yet I had more fun at W.'s, 50 or more of us . . . I think 'night's drawing on,' signal the foreman and get a screw-cutting job, big Whitworth belt, have to concentrate on this, my eyes feel tired, I feel oily, dirty, the heat of the cut turns the cutting oil into stinging smoke and I swear at my burning eyes, I blow the smoke away so as I can follow the screwing cut, the saw-man has cut the bar too fine and I haven't got much to hold it on so if I hit the shoulder I'll have the job out on me, so I force myself into concentration. I'm too young to get bumped off, ses I, I finish it at 7.30 and then I see the foreman. 'O.K., Bill, that's your whack, scram now if you like.' I reply 'Watch me, cheerio, Jake.' 'Cheerio, mate.' Gather my tools quickly and lock up, clean my hands. . . .

Upstairs, strip my vest off and have a dam good scrub, change into clean gear, stick some Brycleen on my nut, shave, put my best suit on, downstairs, 'My word, what quick work !' Have my dinner, pork chop, french beans and potatoes and black-berry tart and custard, tea and a smoke, feel good once more, a new guy, getting twilighty, sit quiet, smoke and rest my back, eyes still smart a bit, but R.I.P. for ¼ hour. Look at my watch, right we're off. 'Give her my love !' 'Night'—'Night' out.

I met her at the top of the road, it was already dusk and she was standing under the yellowy glow of the corner lamp. I identified her tall figure and blonde head 40 yards or so away. I walked with a longer stride and 'snuffled' at the cool night breeze, scented by the surrounding gardens. 'This is great,' I thought, 'after the oily, fumy, sweaty atmosphere of the shops.' I felt alive, I was clean and cool, clean vest, shirt and best suit, polished shoes and a cool breeze through my hair as I walked quickly along. 'Lo, Do,' 'Lo, Bill.' She had two letters to post and was shy of a stamp for one, so we went down the road to a P.O. and got one from a machine, posted the letter and retraced our steps down the Stoke Road towards Stoke Poges, down the lane, now quite dark, the tall firs and pines stretching blackly into the night sky, we talked of the rotten heat of the day, what we had done, she said she had made six red flags and I was surprised. 'You turning Communist, cherie ?' She laughed and said it was a Council order, the flags were for road repairs. We cut off into a narrow lane leading to Stoke Poges Church, the lane is like a black tunnel and quiet as the grave, not a light or sound, I feel an eerie feeling and so does D. She clutched my arm. 'Boo, it's queer here !' 'Good pull-up for spooks *this* joint !' I say, she shakes me and says 'Be quiet !' I laugh at her and ask how loud she can scream, she says, 'I'll deafen you if I *do* see anything.' I laugh some more, we find a break in the trees and enter

a field, we walk carefully picking our way through long grass
and sit near a hay stack. I lay on my back and dig my heels
into the ground and stare at the stars, the hay smells fine.
Away across the dark fields is a red glow, that's a cinema in
Slough, Adelphi. I look at Do, she's sitting with her knees
under her looking intently into the woods. 'What's up?'
She doesn't answer. 'What's to do, kid?' Then she says,
'It's a queer place.' I laugh and say, 'Frightened of a bit
of dark.' She says, 'No, I thought I heard something.'
I say, 'Guess it's birds.' We are silent for a bit and then
I get a queer feeling, I think, 'Are we being watched?' I
look up and see a whitish patch in the trees. I stare, it moved
but I could hear nothing, the skin of my face seemed to
tighten and the hair rose on my neck. I thought, 'What the
h—, a ghost?' I'm not, I think, superstitious, but I couldn't
make up my mind about this, I tensed all over, I felt my
feet under me, Do stared in the dim light, I whispered 'Don't
move, someone here.' 'It' came closer, out of the shelter of
the trees, and I saw a light coloured figure bend forward
in our d'.ection, something said in my mind, 'Up! quick,
at him,' and I sprang forward, leaping through the swishing
grass, I was all set to fight, but I sure was hoping it wasn't
a ghost, the figure stayed still a few seconds as I came flying
at him, then turned and dashed into the wood, but I had him,
I was going like a kangaroo and he didn't get but a few
yards. I jumped on him and brought him down face first,
and I think I was mighty glad to grab flesh and blood, he
rolled and I put one hand on the ground and butted him
square in the pan, he shouted and done another roll, I
jumped again, knees in the pit of his belly, he croodled up.
I got up and hauled him up, he was falling all over the place,
into trees and bushes as if he was drunk, I could see him
plain, he had flannels and a whitey sports coat, so I followed
up and upper cut him, I tried to crack him again but he went
down and I fell over him, my face bumped his and I got what
I thought was spit on my face but it was blood after, he
grabbed my arms so I gave him my knees again, he let go
and I cracked him again and he either went out or pretended
to be out, I stood up and started to strike a match to see
what he looked like, but I heard Do, she'd got the wind
up so I dashed out to her, I told her it was O.K., just a

snooper and he'd got a pocketful, she wanted to go across the fields but I made her come and see this guy. I told her he was flat out but when we got there he was up again leaning against a tree and snoring through his mouth and nose. I felt angry and thought, 'I'll lay you out this trip,' so I went over again and hit him sideways away from the tree in case he ducked and dropped him with my other hand and if he wasn't out the first do he was out the second. I felt the old 'clunk' up my arm, 'one of Nellers' I thought as he keeled over (Nel Tarleton, L'pool scrapper), next thing I heard someone running down the road nearby. I beat it out onto the road and ran down, I think I thought at the time the snooper had a pal but it was Do, I stopped her, I was feeling kind of pleased with myself, but I soon got the starch taken out of me for Do played hell with me over the do, I was pretty indignant as I reckoned I would have been a right bum to let him get away with it, she reckoned I should have let him be the first time, maybe I should or shouldn't, we argued and chewed the fat all the way to Elliman Avenue, when we got there she saw some blood on my face and thought I'd stopped one and was nice as apple-pie until she found I wasn't, then the barney started all over again, and lasted until we got to her house, her brother Syd was outside, and I stopped and had a chat with him, he'd got a new job in my line and I gave him a few tips on the graft, we also talked about football coupons and about a mutual pal, while we were chatting the girl friend got hot and bothered and beat it inside, about 10 minutes later, I called 'Good night' *and* got no answer, so I said good night to Syd. 'Been havin' a row?' 'Yeh, she's moaning about nix, cheerio, Syd.' 'Good night, Bill,' and I walked off. I was feeling a bit ratty at first but I was grinning before long. 'Women! they're nutty, all of 'em—and they're all female, too!' I cracked to myself into the digs, all in bed, 'like hens round here', have my supper, bread and cheese and cold tea. Bath a scratch under my eye and my hand, thumbs swollen and my ring which is loose had cut a knuckle, got a dull pain in the top of my head, think, 'must have near butted his head off.' Sponged my face and stuck my head under the tap, felt lot better, get a clothes brush and brush my coat and trousers, had to sponge my coat, all serene, put the light out and go to bed, 11.15. put my best gear away, see my working clobber handy and put keys and money in my overalls, open the window, opened the curtains, yawn, into bed, 'O.K. this——.' I go asleep.

That is a vital working-class (August) day. Though not a very "average" one, its situations are expressed typically enough in the direct outlook and language which predominates in the millions of words of this sort of material now in Mass-Observation's files.

Through all our research results the interest in oneself and one's own home has predominated far and away, over international and general political concerns, except in the upper middle class. Until the last week in September, 1938, the great mass of working people were never observably affected in any marked degree by any crisis within the eighteen months during which we have been making observations, and it was only when the international situation threatened to enter their own homes, as gas, that a real mass response was apparent. In this world of rearmament and fortifications, an Englishman's home is still his castle, although well under half are their own landlords.

Within his own home a man may do more or less what he likes, provided his wife likes it too; even so, certain persons, the gas man, the sanitary inspector, the overcrowding surveyor, may have rights of entry. Broadly speaking, and apart from such inhibitions, within his home a man can live his own life in so far as his income and upbringing permit.

But to-day the leaders, politicians, are taking an increasing part in determining how people shall live. Most obviously, they are breaking up the pattern of living in streets, each home on its own plot of earth, and rearranging people, not side by side but one on top of each other. Basic in this and the elaborate legislation which enforces it, is the assumption that ordinary people want better homes than the ones they live in.

There is no objective data or analytical material either to prove or disprove this, which is therefore simply a hypothesis on the part of the leaders, a characteristic attitude towards the working class, and a mix up of what ordinary people are supposed to want to have and what the leaders of "public opinion" think they ought to want to have. So that here again we may expect to find new frictions set up, yet another hiatus between the law and the fact, the institution and the individual, what people are said to do and what they actually do, what leaders think people want and what people do want.

There are many possible techniques—many we have already experimented with—for discovering people's individual wants and home feelings, and we can only suggest some aspects and start some hares at this stage. For instance, 500 children, mostly from elementary schools, wrote (for us) unprepared essays on "My Home and Who Lives There", which give a simple and illuminating child's-eye-view of home environment, personalities and problems.

The children's essays were from twenty schools in various districts, including a small country town, a mining village and a London area where many of the children are tenement-dwellers. Analysis of the whole collection showed the most frequent mention to be of parents, brothers and sisters (68%); second, number of rooms (57%); third, situation (45%); fourth, furniture (42%). Some significant differences between the younger and older children included:

Mention of	Older (11 and over)	Younger (7 to 11)
	%	%
Animals . .	22	55
Toys and games	12	39
Garden . .	32	41
Situation . .	58	30
Wireless . .	20	8
No. of rooms .	66	36

Differences between the various districts were marked. Animals are all-important to the younger country children (mentioned by 93%). Of the mining-village children, 75% mention the number of rooms. The tenement children are clearly more conscious than the others of their neighbours—mentioned by only 16% of the total but by 67% of the tenement-dwellers (61% of whom mention father, 37% mother). There is frequent mention of "happy home" in all types of essays. Only the tenement essays mention noise.

Here is an essay by a boy of 13 who, not yet having been re-housed, still lives in a row:

"The people who live in my house is my father my mother and all my family down stairs is an old lady and an old man my father works in a coffee stall and my mum helps him I think we are all comfotable and quite well we ought to because we was all born in the same house and my mum has been in that house 36 years and never caused any trouble or any rows and my dog is eight years old and I dont think we would like to move now and I think Id never get used to it living in a new house besides I would get used to a sissy boys street I am rough and ready and tough and the people who live in my hous are very and clean and clean in body and clean in mind and she is 82 years old and when my mum goes out she leaves the doors open and when she comes back every think is allright and she tit tots about and do all she can but my mum says go in and rest your self granny I do what you want done and does all her work and gives granny about a shillin for her dinner and I think she tries very hard to do her work and her husband earns about a shilling day and tries very hard indeed we oun foour rooms and 8 room in the house so half the house is my own and it is a lot of work to keep the house clean and tidy."

He says he is comfortable and doesn't want to move. Another boy, same age, is living in a tenement and finds restrictions heavy but gets on well with the neighbours (unlike others we quote):

"The people who live in my house are very good. Their names are Nora the girl, William the boy, and Mrs. & Mr. Brown. My house is not very long been built up it was built three years ago. My house is name is —— House, and it is modely built. We have hot water already for use. But we have very strict laws to obey. We must not have cats and dogs, and we must not buy second hand good before they are fumigated because of fetching dirt in our new houses and we can't say out side the house. We can't play criket out side the house or inside. I play with Bill Brown who live next door he is forty the first of September. We go over the little scrubbs to play criket. Sometimes I play criket with some big boy age sixteen I go and play sometime whick Bill Brown up Kensington Garden. I like fishing up Kensington Gardin which my mate Bill Brown who live next door. I like Mr. & Mrs. Brown. They take me to Picture. I like going to picture which the Browns family and Stokes family we go to South End for days. In the summing holiday, I go to the picture every Saturday afternoon." (Age 13.)

There is less harmony in the next one; he starts off by saying "My house is very nice", then goes on:

"We have three rooms, and a bath room, scullery verander, and lavatory.

We have hot and cold water if we want hot water, we have to make a big fire.

That heats the water pipes and that makes hot water.

The rent is 12/6 for three rooms, that is very cheap.

The people overhead kick up a row, and are very noisie.

When they get up in the morning, they knock chairs over the baby starts screaming, altogether there is a jolly fine row. The people above us are Irish. The father gets up about six o'clock in the morning makes some tea has something to eat and drink, then goes off to work. Just as he shuts the front door, the two girls get up and start fighting.

One pulls the other ones hair, and then they both start to scream. Altogether it is realy worth living rent free.

But the mother is very good to them, but she lets them have their own way, and play her up.

We have one day quite that is Sunday. Sometimes he takes them to the pictures or if its raining the stay indoors and make a row."

Some disadvantages are felt by the next flat-dweller, but he says:

"My house is not a bad one. The People who live in the house are nice especially, the lady in the first floor she is very nice. The lady in the top floor is nice as well she went to the seaside for a beno. When she came home she give me a big rock. The only thing that is wrong in our house is that the flat roof lets water and when it pours of rain it all comes through our ceiling, and the next is that we got mice in the house. The old lady down stairs her gran sons come down in the yard and dig it all up and make mud pies or stuff our wirerless up with dirt they make a swing out of some rope and fix it to the tree and swing on it they got shovels and toys out in the yard and play with them. they dig up a lot of dirt mold and make a sort of a fort. so that they can put there soldiers in it and there horse and carts. there is a welshman in the Backroom and he is a naviey he is quite as a mouse he dont speak hardly when down stairs One day I lost my glasses and I could not find them and I had to come to scool without them but when I came home my mother found them in a Jug. I was having game on the drain I was in the yard and I was climbing up the drain pipe I got about ten yards up and I slipped and I went down into the yard and cut my head."

But relations with neighbours in tenements are often more strained, to judge from the number of essays which tell stories like this:

"The people who lives at the top of our house is a Irishman and he has some pigeon he let them out most of his pigeon are racing pigeon and he put rings around thier feet so he cannot loose them and he pigeones food comes every monday and the people who lives under them are Iris she has no husbude but she has a son 11 year old and we play cherters and we stay out till about ten o coalk at night. We are Elish and we live in the plor floor we have got a cat the basment is comden and nobody lives in it it is dark down there are mouce and we go down there to the lavatree and there are spidder and colbwebs down there my dad is out of work and I have only two sister in work and one of em are working at Davies Dary and Clarner and the other workes down Chidren Wellfare and I have a bike it is a nice race and I left it in the hall and the Irisman told me to take it out or put it in my bedroom and I said to him you dont own the house and that cause a row so my mother hear my and so she asked what at happen and so my mother said lieve it there and he got old of me bike and was goan to threw it out of the door but my farther came in just in time and my farther took the bike away from him and they start a fight and they were stopped by two Policman and they askey what was they fighing over and so my dad told him all the story and they put the Irisman in jail of brake the peace."

Opposite in point of method is the house-to-house questioning of the commercial research organisations. The research department of the I.B.C. (International Broadcasting Corporation) kindly agreed to add to one of their inquiries the additional question, "If you had to economise, what would go first?" Housewives were canvassed, mainly in London, also in Reading, Brighton and Sutton. They belonged to four "classes", arbitrarily standardised by Market Researchers, as follows:

Class A have at least one maid; telephone; medium-priced car; detached or semi-detached house of more expensive kind in suburbs, with 8–10 rooms, bought on mortgage arrangement: or comfortable central flat in "good district". Children at private or good secondary or grammar school. Typical occupations: Owner of small factory or large retail shop: minor executive in business; managers and assistant managers:

owners of small commercial concerns: medium-grade professional men, e.g. members of small architectural firms, medical general practitioners with smaller practices: upper-grade civil servants.

Class B. Regular maid rare and usually no telephone: occasional domestic help: secondhand or cheap car: detached or semi-detached house, 5–8 rooms with garden—on repayments: flat in inner suburbs: or cottage dwelling in less congested parts of town. Children usually at secondary school. Typical occupations: Owner of small to medium-sized shop: owner of small workshop: younger members of professions: technical and managerial staff of business concerns: executive and higher clerical civil servants: bulk of middle-aged and older bank and insurance officials: key workers in certain trades.

Class C. No maid or telephone: occasional domestic help: house reasonably well kept: house and street definitely superior in character to D: 4–5 room house: 3–5 room flat: house semi-detached in suburbs or more commonly, in row: small garden in less congested areas: occasional motor cycle and very rarely, secondhand car: good push bicycle: children usually at elementary school. Typical occupations: Foremen in most trades: skilled workmen, e.g. printers, typesetters, and semi-skilled workmen in sheltered industries (L.P.T.B. employees, building trade and distributive trade workmen): bank clerks: draughtsmen: secretaries and non-junior typists: lower-grade blackcoated workers generally, except for juniors: higher-grade shop assistants: managers and assistant managers of small concerns: owners of very small retail shops: lower-grade civil servants: office and works superintendents.

Class D. No telephone or maid. No paid domestic help. Cheaper council houses or older houses in rows, or tenements: 2–4 rooms. No garden as a rule. Poorer working-class areas, excluding only the worst slum quarters. Typical occupations. Lowest grade office and warehouse clerical staff: semi-skilled and unskilled in most employments, e.g. cotton, coal mining, building: semi-skilled in seasonal trades.

PERCENTAGES

WOULD GIVE UP	CLASS				TOTAL
	A	B	C	D	
Car . . .	27	15	2	1	13
Pleasure (general) .	7	10	7	5	8
Cinema . . .	2	6	10	15	9
Wireless, gramophone	5	7	10	12	9
Smoking . .	5	2	8	10	7
Drink . . .	1	2	2	3	2
Sweets . . .	1	2	2	2	2
Smaller house . .	3	6	3	2	4
Food . . .	1	4	8	15	8
Clothes . . .	4	8	6	5	7
General economy .	5	14	13	6	11
Holidays . .	2	2	6	2	3
Other items . .	14	22	23	22	17
TOTAL PERSONS INTERVIEWED . .	232	248	294	183	957

Outstanding points to be seen from this table: in Classes A and B, the question "Can we afford a car?" in crucial, but it doesn't affect Classes C and D. The latter would economise on cinema and wireless, while the two better-off classes take these more or less in their stride. The poorer classes have to think carefully about what they spend on tobacco and on food, but in Classes A and B these do not involve important economies. The other important items, size of house, clothes and holidays, are of much the same consequence for all the classes. Less than 1% of the total think of economising on newspapers, as compared with 9% who would economise on wireless and gramophone—a conclusion which, if correct, makes the newspaper still more important than radio in opinion forming.

Everything points to a position where we know as little about personal needs and individual ideals as we do about wider social feelings and mass responses. Everywhere we turn in the British scene, we are faced with no data, or data utterly inadequate for any scientific or long-term judgments about our society and culture. While science goes blinding on in every other direction, and some scientists pause to form committees about their social relationships, the science of ourselves is left in the hands of a few independent bodies, supported inadequately by private persons and by what they can earn. It is easy to get money to alleviate something that is very, very obviously wrong, or to patch up some drastic social or personal ill. But when you want to study human health in a context of normalcy, with results which are likely to be more far-reaching than all the day-to-day ameliorations imaginable, you have to beg and struggle, as does the Pioneer Health Centre at Peckham. Unique in another field is P.E.P. (Political and Economic Planning), whose surveys of the economic and documentary aspects of institutions are in a class by themselves. No other organisation is carrying out any impartial and independent research into normal and everyday England. In the field of normal *behaviour*, and in the whole of the working class, we ourselves (Mass-Observation) still stand and feel alone. Though the results which we have presented in this volume are clearly in many ways very inadequate, remember that this represents only a fraction of our total activity (four other books this winter), and that there's nothing better and no one else has so far tried to do this job at all. We have to keep ourselves and this large organisation without private means and on our own earnings, and in doing so have thus far received no help from any scientific or academic body.

H

9

BASIC IN BRITAIN

CERTAIN rights of the individual and sanctities of the home are basic in the pattern of British life. When Mr. Chamberlain in his broadcast from No. 10 Downing Street said that to "all those who love liberty" life would become intolerable when a rule of force prevailed, he was speaking in the British jargon. This country was prepared to go to war on that issue, for to the ordinary working man the Sudeten issue meant nothing, and Czechoslovakia was only unspellable. The Munich agreement has seemed to a great many to outrage the national tradition. Our sense of guilt has found expression in pæans of praise to God, extraordinary hero-worship of the Premier, a loan of £10,000,000 to the Czechs.

Basic in Britain is the right to say what you think or at the least think what you think, and express it privately through the secret ballot. This right of each adult is essential and total in democracy. It is also essential and total in science. On democracy plus science our industrial civilisation is now inescapably founded. And while we can in the future reject a good deal of the democracy, the material circumstances and consequences of science are inescapable.

This "Liberty" puts Home before State in normal circumstances. The other main alternative idea in modern Europe puts State always first, and in favour of the State and its leader disallows the right of the individual to differ. One result of our Liberty is that many individuals are in no sense participating in the

226

working of the State. Our culture has not been integrated with the changing times. Science has changed the material and economic conditions, but our social institutions, outside work, have gone on in the pre-scientific way. For example, Church, Politics, Art, Billiard Halls, Repertory Theatres. The present-day working of these institutions is described in Mass-Observation books to be published shortly, by Victor Gollancz:

The Pub and the People, by John Sommerfield and Bruce Watkin.
Politics and the Non-Voter, by Walter Hood and Frank Cawson.
How Religion Works, by J. L. Wilcock and others.
Blackpool: One Week a Year, by Herbert Howarth and Richard Glew.

These institutions were in full swing long before popular education or the popular vote. To a large extent they still continue to speak the language and use the techniques of pre-industrialism. In consequence, the ordinary man or woman or child to-day cannot get from the older institutions those satisfactions which modern technical considerations suggest or demand. Increasingly the older institutions get out of gear with a general public. And even the fundamental right of the vote is ignored, in municipal affairs by much above half of the adult population. Politicians have therefore inclined to call non-voters dumb-bells or fools. In fact, the non-voter is responding in a reasonable way to a situation in which politics seem to offer few solutions, and these worded and presented in a manner much less exciting or convincing than that of Hollywood or Littlewood. Obviously an enormous theme, we will go into it fully in the above-named publications. It is hardly necessary to emphasize here that many of the organs of our democratic society are dangerously sick.

If a dog or man is sick, a doctor or vet diagnoses the causes, suggests the cures; a vast body of facts ascertained by scientific experiment and objective analysis are available and indispensable for this purpose. But when a society is sick, loans, pacts, armies and conferences are the only offered diagnoses-cum-cures. Only when chaos is overwhelmingly obvious does Earl Baldwin say "Mobilise Industry" (October 4).

It is, of course, a job of science, which has caused so much of this chaos, to illuminate and analyse our own relations, forgetting all about ideals and abstractions, describing and arranging only ascertained facts. It is outside the realm of science to pass moral judgments: the scientist does not condemn the skunk for its smell.

To be any use, of course, this sort of social science has got to go on all the time, partly with a long-term endowed programme of research, partly with an immediate and constantly changing programme, coping daily with working problems. In principle, this need has been faintly recognised by the Trades Union Congress, which over a year ago announced the formation of a scientific advisory committee. Not till September 1938 was its personnel decided. Eleven eminents. None representing the social sciences, though Professor Winifred Cullis is the single representative both for physiology and psychology. There has been no suggestion that any non-eminents should get on with the simple job of obtaining facts upon which science could become more advisory in relation to the T.U.C.

Other groups who are not themselves scientific naturally feel antipathetic to the whole idea of a scientific approach to these problems. When they find themselves getting hopelessly out of touch with the literate masses they easily tend to blame the masses for not understanding them, for being too stupid or ignorant or escapist. Yet, if democracy as an ideal can function and survive, this great gap between the intellectual leader and the ordinary man has to be bridged. The poets more than any other intelligent group have shown contempt for this suggestion, and in a recent broadcast series on the Poet and the Public, summarised in the *Listener* (June 16), one eminent modern summed up the usual assumption:

"Those who heard or read last week's discussion in this series will remember that C. Day Lewis put forward the theory that to create the type of public to which the poet could appeal, it would be necessary for there to be some sort of social or political mass movement."

Thus neatly the poet inverts the responsibility, actually suggests that a new sort of public has got to be CREATED and ignores the numerous existing mass movements, like the weekly football pool, All-In or the Lambeth Walk. Religious leaders have also put the responsibility on the masses, as church attendances have steadily dropped since the Four-Years-War. Recently, however, they have recognised that their alleged enemy, science, has a technique to offer which they may exploit. Though nothing has yet been done, as long ago as May 2nd *The Times* carried a leader-page article headed THE MYSTERIOUS BARRIER:

"He would be a rash man who stated assertively that this country had grown less inwardly Christian in the last 30, or 40, or 50 years. There has been no outward sign of that in, for instance, our social legislation, . . . yet the number of empty pews in church or chapel has grown, and, in many places, is still growing. . . .

Those who would have the Churches meet the deep-seated needs of man are, therefore, at fault somewhere; it is unimaginable that Christianity itself can fail. . . .

An attempt is afoot to discover more precisely the nature of this gulf, and by so doing to throw light on true and proper means of bridging it. We all know that where outstanding personalities are found, the gulf vanishes. Beyond that, all or almost all is conjecture or unsystematic private opinion. It would seem unreasonable that the upholders of Christianity should make it the special business of nobody to probe troubles which in the medical or any other field would be deemed worthy of intensive, methodical, and devoted research. . . . To initiate research always implies an act of faith. In the greater things of life, if a plan is born of the utmost thought and sincerity it is hard to conceive that it will not be prospered."

The same sort of thing is slowly becoming recognised on many fronts. Now the British Association for the Advancement of Science has set up a section on the social relations of science. Still it does nothing about the social relations of cockneys or Jews. Foremost in promoting the feeling of science's social responsibility is vivid Launcelot Hogben. But his latest great work, *Science for the Citizen*, an enormous volume which aims to cover the whole field of scientific thought and method, has no place in its text or its extensive index either for anthropology or sociology, though anthropomorphism gets five separate references. No wonder a B.B.C announcer (August 24) introducing a talk on the British Associations 1938 meeting at Cambridge, described this as the scientists' regular opportunity for meeting each other "and making their yearly contact with the world outside science". Staggering especially has been the slowness of Social Psychology. Typical is a paper by E. J. Lindgren, a leading psychologist, in the *British Journal of Psychology* (Vol. xxv). In a very long discussion of "Fieldwork in Social Psychology", Dr. Lindgren nowhere suggests that any need be done in Europe. She does however suggest that we *might* train ourselves here in our own country for fieldwork among primitive people:

"Practical training in general observation needs, of course, only to be sought to be found, but it is extraordinary how few of us seek it near at hand. For those interested in shamanism and other religious phenomena, a study of spiritualist seances, revivalist and similar meetings, would be very relevant, as well as characteristically fatiguing.

By attempting to deal with such problems, even once or twice, at least a rudimentary technique is developed which is far better than nothing, and when a unique ceremony occurs—often during the very first days in the field—it does not find the investigator wholly unprepared."

Such is the scientific method and outlook of a prominent Social Psychologist, and the Doctor goes on, with characteristic naïveté and complete unawareness of contemporary problems:

"The prospective fieldworker should begin learning to note and describe many types of movements in the laboratory, but he must proceed to apply his knowledge to his surroundings as a more direct preparation for fieldwork. Thus he might attempt to describe the postures and paces of people taking dogs for walks; I mention this simple line of research because of its inoffensive nature and because it would take one a great deal into the open air."

Golly !

If there is any moral responsibility of the scientist at all, it is that he should spend a part of his time, or see to it that more than sufficient scientists should spend more of their time, in studying normal and everyday behaviour problems of our own lives, as actually lived in the houses and factories, pubs and chapels and shops in this sort of civilisation. Above all, it is the job of the scientist to find out, in this field, what people do want, do get, don't get and could get to want. It is on those points that the future of democracy, and indeed of any system, depends. It was not necessary to find it out so long as science had not developed. But today widespread scientific techniques are changing the circumstances of life and influencing the minds of people for the benefit of those who can pay to buy the services of a scientist or his discoveries.

Mass-Observation has in a very small way tried to cope with some of these points. We are not now criticising science for not doing something because we feel clever at doing it, or rather trying to do it in so far as we can. On the contrary, we ourselves responded to the situation which we have described, and in which it seemed to us improbable that people would go on indefinitely blathering about the masses and arguing about abstractions, making decisions which vitally affect the lives of everyone, without anyone thinking it necessary to provide facts. For several years Market Research has in a limited way been making factual investigations on behalf of advertising agencies. But the only object of these is to provide material enabling the advertiser to get more people to buy his particular product; and the results are not published or available to the social scientist. A number of important surveys of special areas, Tyneside, Merseyside and London, have been undertaken by University bodies. These have been based on statistical and census material, and on information invariably obtained from official sources, never by observation or contact with the great mass of people concerned—with the single exception of the section on the Pub in the London Survey, where personal observation was undertaken by B. D. Nicholson, subsequently inventor of the slogan NIGHT STARVATION.

One of the main objects of this sort of science should be to get its results out to the public, not bury them in specialist journals and special language, as is the custom, often necessary, in most branches of research. If social science means anything, that meaning can and should be made clear to the people that it is about. "Should" because then the people themselves can check the results and constantly control misunderstandings or falsifications. We hope that as many as possible of the readers of this book will be sufficiently impressed by this need to consider actively co-operating with

Mass-Observation, in work which they will find no burden, no cost, and increasing fascination. Anyone can help in this organisation of voluntary observers, and should they wish to do so, can write in to

MASS-OBSERVATION,
6 GROTES BUILDINGS,
BLACKHEATH,
S.E.3

It is immediately practicable to define. many basic British mental and social needs in the same sort of way as Sir John Orr and the British Medical Association have defined basic nutritional needs. For example, one of our recent Worktown investigations on sleeping, showed over 70% of the working-class people investigated got less than the recognised minimum hours of sleep for normal health. And in another Worktown research, into What is Happiness ?, people were asked to vote on which of ten factors they considered the most conducive to more happiness for themselves. The representative sample gave this result:

Security	.	129	
Knowledge	.	118	
Religion.	.	104	(personal or organised)
Humour	.	80	
Equality.	.	79	
Beauty .	.	34	
Action	.	23	
Pleasure	.	10	
Leadership	.	8	
Politics .	.	2	

The actual order of emphases from political leadership today are almost exactly the reverse of this series of needs, presumably basic in Britain.

Yes sir: Politics, 2. Security, 129. . . .

10

AFTERMATHS : POLITICS 2, OR I OZ. CHRISTIANITY

THE rapid kaleidoscope of the past few weeks in which the material for this book has been prepared and printed has brought up with unmistakable clearness the jagged and ill-fitting edges in the institutions of our Great Britain. We have seen that in this country, where nearly all our observations have been done, there is neither a democracy with a clear feeling that it has some common function, nor the alternative imposed un-animity which enables Hitler to make his big drives. So it is no wonder that since the crisis, newspapers and through them the advertisers and business interests have been pressing for conscription.[1]

They advocated forms of organisation which, to say the least, hinted a drastic change in our social organisa-tion. Typically the *Evening Standard* (October 7):

"In the event of war there would be no room for, no safety in, individual liberty. Uniform national service would be imperative.

[1] In an advertisement to a trade paper, Advertising Manager Tomlin of the *News Chronicle* stated (October 6): "As I was one of those who continued to preach optimism when the Crisis first began to look serious, I think I have a right to remind advertisers once more that there is plenty of room for development in this country. . . . I am, of course, quite well aware that confidence is the one thing which is supremely necessary for this expansion to begin. But confidence is in many ways synonymous with courage and no advertiser has ever succeeded without a generous measure of that quality."

An important member of the staff of one great paper told an observer: "I've had my Advertising Manager coming in every day and telling me, 'Look here, old boy, you can't possibly put that in, it'll scare off our advertisers!'"

234

To expect the nation to step unprepared from peace to war organisation is to court confusion. The country is eager to join unitedly in a mighty effort to make its security impregnable. It asks that the Government should co-ordinate and systematise the public spirit and energy at its disposal."

So we are back where we started this book from, at the invention of unanimous feelings for a "country", which in fact can only have such apparent unanimity under Fascism. In the absence of machinery for finding out what people do think, it is a natural and even unconscious tendency for leader-writers and leaders of all sorts to turn all the individuals into such a unity, and thus constantly to balance the scales a little more against democracy. There is therefore every excuse for a politician in power, who by judicious transfer of allegiances is in line for the premiership, to say, as the Chancellor of the Exchequer did in the Commons on October 5:

"A friend of mine in this House has expressed the view that it is deplorable that Parliament last week demonstrated what he regarded as a most lamentable exhibition of mass hysteria. I believe that to be an utterly false view. This popular assembly never in its history has more truly represented the sentiments of people outside (*Parliamentary cheers*)."

One Opposition leader did try to face the fearful task of finding out what a few everyday people are thinking; Miss Ellen Wilkinson with another Labour and three Conservative M.P.s "gave up one night to going the round of a number of cinemas casually selected". The result was "No cheering, a little clapping in some, on the whole the usual silence of the cinema, occasionally some booing, when Chamberlain came on the screen". Miss Wilkinson summed up this pathetically unsystematic observation—incidentally if one person in fifty claps in a cinema the impression obtained is that of considerable applause, and this was what was happening during most of the crisis—by saying that it "did not tell us much except that the ordinary people were feeling no special enthusiasm".

But there is no excuse for one speaking with the supposed authority of social science, Professor Launcelot Hogben, who the day before had started a letter to the *New Statesman*: "One result of the Crisis is obvious to any but the blindest adherent of the Labour Party. It is the immense popularity of Chamberlain and the complete lack of confidence in Labour." The threatened decay of democracy threatens especially the basic tenets of the contemporary scientist, artist, and Christian. For the first time in centuries these groups are gradually being forced publicly to take sides. In consequence their own internal unities are in turn threatened with new and important divisions. But to science it is really important that in taking sides the scientist should not then proceed to invent facts or make a magic out of science in the same sort of way as the poets have tried to make a magic out of poetry. Professor Hogben ends his letter by referring back to a previous point and stating: "Constructive pacification recognises this inescapable implication (that Empire Free Trade means war) and calls for biologists, chemists and engineers to draw a bold plan for creating collective farms under scientific management." This is his final word on the world crisis.

What was the actual situation at this week-end? At this last moment for Penguin printing we have only been able to receive the reports of four observers who in a few hours interviewed 83 working-class people in London. Result:

	Male	Female	Total
Pro-Chamberlain . . .	13	27	40
Anti-Chamberlain . .	25	9	34
Doubtful	3	6	9

This once again confirms the previously made point that a majority of men are strongly anti-Chamberlain, while the women are for him because they are for peace at any price.

The reactions of Christianity, or rather of religion, which continues to emphasise an intervening deity without reference to Christ, have been consistently higher mathematic. Of Munich the *Sunday Chronicle* asked: "How has the miracle been wrought?" and answered itself: "By the unswerving determination, resource, courage and faith in peace of the Prime Minister. The world to-day honours him." Beverley Baxter, M.P., in the *Sunday Graphic* gave a separate paragraph to his conclusion, "By a miracle the war was prevented." Hugh Redwood, (*News Chronicle*, October 6), developed this theme in his own way:

"One day perhaps, we shall hear the full account of that miracle. The word is not mine; it had been employed by those who knew the facts to describe the only possible means whereby disaster could be averted. And I am pretty sure that Mr. Chamberlain himself would be the last to disown it.

There is a story yet to be told of a telephone call to Downing Street late at night which gave the Premier a special assurance based on the people's prayers, and of his sudden awakening in the small hours with a clear conviction regarding his next line of action. He acted upon that conviction and the immediate peril passed. The wind changed.

There are thousands, and I am one of them, who believe that God heard and answered prayer. In so doing He gave us a new revelation of Himself. And, at the same time, He has shown us just where we are. That is the all-important fact of the present situation."

The Rev. W. H. Elliott had a crisis postscript: "I would add this—that the whole issue is on the plane of the spiritual. It is not a matter of armaments but of thoughts." But yet higher in hierarchy, the Bishop of

Chelmsford, said: "If a mad dog is roaming the streets, I think it is tempting Providence to walk about with bare legs. . . . One ounce of Christianity would solve every problem on the Continent of Europe in twenty-four hours."

Symbol of the Chamberlanic sky world was what the *Mirror* front-paged and main-headlined as LONDON AIR DEATH WEB (October 9). Fine day, light wind. Best estimate gave 38 blimps, only five of which broke adrift or fouled something—including an electric railway; trains held up half an hour. An observer saw and heard it:

"There is a hold up of the buses, the drivers and the conductors are leaning out to try and get a view of the balloons, there are five of them to be seen in a row across to the south-east, they are about 5 to 7,000 feet high. They are plainly to be seen, they are all below the cloud height.

People in the buses follow the drivers in turning round and looking through the windows to see what is being looked at, the busmen are smiling, one says to a passer: 'It's like a fat Jerry sausage, what a gag.'

Whenever people see the balloons they stop to look at them, some stop on the pavement and put hands to their eyes, shading the light. Three ex-service men say—

'They have to have a lot of wires between like they had in the war, they're no bloody good like that, it's to make us think it's O.K. . . . There 're not enough of 'em, anybody can see that . . . it's to put the wind up everybody . . . make 'em think there's going to be a bloody war, then they'll do something about it. . . . Say they're full of gas, so's when they hit it they get on fire. . . . Is it hell. . . . It's so as when they hit that wire they get a shock, there's electricity in 'em, that brings 'em down.'

Woman: 'There's not enough of them, they'll get over, it's easy to get in between too. They look nice though. Does anybody go up in them? I can't see the wire.'

Man: 'They can't tell me it's only for peace, it's as plain as my bloody face, it's to put the wind up everybody . . . it's a nice basin for anyone who wants it though.'

Man : 'Christ, it looks as though they knew more than they tell us . . . there's not enough of the blighters.'"

While Londoners looked up at their blimps with mixed optimism and doubt, 'planes were filming them from close quarters, circling and diving in among the wires in wild abandon. The Air Ministry refused information on the number of blimps and very naturally all aspects of our air defences have been obscured by secrecy. To the majority of ordinary people, however, the evidence has been unquestionable. All the essential arrangements and preparations for a state of aerial bombardment of the civil population has been grossly, flagrantly, neglected. London might have 38 blimps and some anti-aircraft guns. Birmingham had none. On the only opportunity which has been provided in recent months to obtain any information on these points, the sudden short October session of Parliament, Cabinet Ministers appeared almost deliberately to obscure issues and increase that state of public bewilderment which is in fact most dangerous to their own political security. Thus in reply to a question from Mr. Paling as regards the number of German divisions made available by the cession of Sudeten territory, the following passage of parliamentary words took place : the whole is worth reading and re-reading with care as an example of leadership and public representation. Here it is according to *Hansard* :

"*The Secretary of State for War* (*Mr. Hore-Belisha*): Until the final determination of the frontiers has been carried out by the International Commission in accordance with Article VI of the Munich Agreement, it is impossible to give even an approximate estimate.

Mr. Paling: Does the right hon. Gentleman mean to tell us that his Intelligence Staff has not informed him of the numbers likely to be added to Hitler's army because of this transfer? Has not a statement been published that it is likely to be about 400,000?

Mr. Hore-Belisha : My Intelligence Staff is too intelligent to proceed on such an assumption.

Mr. Paling : Am I not right in assuming that it is so intelligent that the Prime Minister asked its advice before he went to Germany ?

Mr. Mander : May I ask the Secretary of State whether the number of divisions, whatever it may be, is to be counted for us or against us ?

Mr. A. Henderson asked the Secretary of State for War whether he can give particulars and the number and size of guns, and the nature, quantity, and value of munitions of war surrendered under the Munich Agreement to the German Government ?

Mr. Hore-Belisha : My Department is informed that the Czechoslovak Government have been unable to estimate, even approximately, the value of guns and other munitions which may ultimately be involved in the transfer of ceded territory, pending delimitation of the new frontier and determination of the amount of material which can be evacuated.

Mr. Benn : Does the right hon. Gentleman mean to say that he has not been informed of that by the Prague Government, in view of the fact that an official, or semi-official, statement has been issued pricing these goods at from £25,000,000 to £30,000,000 ?

Mr. Hore-Belisha : I mean to say what I said. Of course it is impossible to put a figure upon the amount which will be lost, if any, until the transfer has taken place.

Sir Archibald Sinclair : What does the right hon. Gentleman mean by 'if any' ? Does he suggest that the International Commission will try to get some of these guns back ? What does he mean by 'if any' ?

Mr. Hore-Belisha : I have answered the question in its original form. Until it is known what, if any—and that is the usual phrase—has been transferred, it is impossible to estimate its value.

That's how information is *not* given to the people's representatives in Parliament by the Government leaders. The sealed-lips technique has become familiar to the British public in past years. On October 13 the

News Chronicle's A. J. Cummings announced the banning of a "March of Time" film on the crisis by the censor:

"It is understood that his view, after seeing the film yesterday, was that it might be 'dangerous'—though it has not been made clear who or what would be endangered.

The film is entitled 'Britain's Dilemma'. It starts with a short note on *Mein Kampf* and goes on to tell the story of China, Abyssinia, Spain, Austria and the last situation over the Czechoslovakian problem.

The film ends before the actual Munich settlement. Taking the *Mein Kampf* theme that Great Britain would not fight against Germany, it closes on a note of quiet interrogation on this point. . . ."

Such incidents support Winston Churchill's forecast that:

"In a very few years, perhaps in a very few months, we should be confronted with demands which may affect the surrender of territory or the surrender of liberty. The policy of submission would carry with it restrictions upon the freedom of speech and debate in Parliament, on public platforms and discussions in the Press. With every organ of public opinion doped and chloroformed into acquiescence, we should be conducted along further stages of our journey."

In the House of Commons Mr. Chamberlain stated categorically and at length the differences between the Munich terms and the Godesberg terms—the differences which had made him a hero. Despite Press reticence, a map in the *Daily Telegraph* and a B.B.C. News Bulletin on October 12 have made it clear that Hitler has now in fact virtually occupied all the areas of his Godesberg terms, and in several cases exceeded even these *without any protest* from the British Government. There is of course no reason why the British Government should protest. We have already suggested that the whole crisis between Godesberg and Munich was only forced on the Government by public opinion so outraged that uniquely it stormed the intellectual barriers and got through to the big shots before the leaders could settle anything.

Public opinion really did protest against Godesberg. Every day since Munich the relief then felt has been declining, the revulsion increasing. Our evidence strongly suggests that the consequences of the Prime Minister's relations with Herr Hitler will affect the whole future of this country, not only in terms of economics, politics and peace, but also within the minds of a great proportion of the community. Innumerable people feel in some vague way that the whole tradition of Britain has been broken. That tradition has always been some-what ephemeral, and much of our Empire history makes it look slightly fantastic. But the majority do not study history or go to the Empire. From Public School to coal-pit, certain phrases, and codes of behaviour which go much deeper, have crystallised around conceptions like "fair play", "honesty is the best policy", "the bottom dog", "an Englishman's word". There has been in these past weeks a vast increase in the readiness of ordinary people to consider as important what happens to little bits of far-off territory, on grounds of fair play. Said a young man in answer to an observer's question: "Well, I went to pictures last night, saw 'Under Two Flags'. That's Neville Chamberlain too." While one observer summarised a day's talking in a way which agrees with the experience of others: "Hitler is making himself the best hated man in England."

A woman aged 60 put the commonest female point of view:

"He did what he thought best. After all a good many things are obsolete and what he did was something new. There's a right and a wrong to everything, and he chose the lesser evil. Though some did say of course that he was creeping to Hitler. It seems strange that we should have to go to war to settle anything in these days. No one wants war, that's the point, though I think it took the gas mask to bring it home to people. It taught them a lesson. They, like myself for instance, are thinking more about things now."

While some people were thinking more, others deliberately were thinking less. A youth on a bus dramatically exclaimed to his neighbour: "Somehow I can't bear to think any more. The bottom of everything's dropped out this last month." And a woman: "The admiral I work for said he couldn't vote Conservative after this, but couldn't vote Labour either. He wants a new Party everyone could vote for."

New party alignments are indeed the subject of some intrigue at this moment. But other new parties have escaped the attention of politicians and intellectuals. Cads' College, Narkover, Littlewoods' Loyalists, Newark's Happy Family, for instance, number literally millions. Prototype is the now extinct Frothblowers which centred on alcohol and worked for charity. So, to take one modern example, does the Flute Club, already a roaring success in the U.S.A. and introduced into England by Clifford Whitley, Toot No. 1. Enrolling thousands a day through the *Sunday Pictorial*, the only advantage of membership as described in the Club's prospectus:

"Every member has a little flute. On entering a room he 'toots' the signature tune of the club—just eight notes up and down the scale—anybody can do it at once. At once, from different parts of the room come answering calls from fellow members.

When you have joined, there are special distinctions for enrolling new members. For twenty members you are presented with a special flute, and become a 'Big Toot'. Later you can become a 'Grand Toot', 'Super Toot' and finally a 'Grand Blast'."

In the same simple eight-note language as the Lambeth Walk, people participate together without any higher aim than the wish to fraternise. The same sense of unity is exploited in the Ovaltine theme song, "We are the Ovaltineys . . ." and in other songs such as one advertising a Yeast Vite product and ending "So join the happy members of the Beefox Brigade". At the head of most of these organisations is a dictator, Clifford Whitley, Will Hay, Gracie Fields, the Western Brothers. Football Pools specialise in this mechanism, the two biggest having respectively The Chief (Cecil Moores), and The Governor (Vernon Sangster). Each week "The Governor Chats With You", in a special publication, always with problems, cartoons and photos. He says this sort of thing: "So many spare coupons are passed to friends each week—so many names and addresses of friends are sent to Vernons on the special forms provided, that it is no wonder the Happy Family grows greater and forges stronger links of friendship week by week." While a brand of salmon has had posters all over the country graphically urging you to VOTE FOR PA PARSLEY! With these modern techniques and in a language distinctly different from that of the House of Commons, new and potentially powerful groupings are being formed, almost unnoted, throughout the structure of English society. And the Church has formed one too through the radio, The League of Prayer. Its leader, the Rev. W. H. Elliott, now claims 800,000 members, who pray each day at noon, and if they cannot do that have a special "Walking or Talking" Prayer, for any hour:

"God guide us.
God guard us.
God bring the nations together in one family.
God keep us in His peace."

In the carefully prepared and sub-edited commentary of a special Movietone News Reel celebrating all the stages in Chamberlain's diplomacy, the always-brilliant commentator uses worship metaphor:

"Our words of admiration are exhausted for the man who prevented another Armageddon."

In the atmosphere which the above organisations imply and which was vividly accentuated by Chamberlain's flights, it was for a few days possible for many to look on the Prime Minister as a new leader to bind together the disintegrating or novel loyalties. And, perhaps unfortunately for "democracy", science, art, church and mass-observation, the need still exists. Only an extremely vigorous and immediate intervention along new channels and with new techniques, by "democrats", "scientists", etc, can perhaps provide an alternative to this impending dictation. Above all, the language of a mass appeal must be common talk and thought. As Neville Chamberlain was getting into the aeroplane to fly to Munich, he spoke a few well-chosen words into Movietone's microphone, including a quotation from Hotspur, "Out of this nettle, danger, we pluck this flower, safety." Actually Hotspur is reading from a letter and the quotation goes on:

"'The purpose you undertake is dangerous; the friends you have named uncertain; the time itself unsorted; and your whole plot too light for the counterpoise of so great an opposition.'
By the Lord our plot is a good plot as ever was laid, our friends true and constant: a good plot, good friends, and full of expectation: an excellent plot, very good friends."

And in his "historic" statement to Parliament on his successful return from Munich, he dropped another right away, referring to the Czech request for a loan of £30,000,000 and to his proposal that they should have a third of that. *Hansard* reports it:

" . . . evidently this is one of those cases where the old proverb applies, that 'He who gives quickly gives twice.' (*Hon. Members :* 'Takes twice.') Would hon. Members opposite kindly allow me to continue this rather important part of my statement without those continual interruptions, which distract attention and make it difficult for the House to take in what I am saying?"

.　　.　　.　　,　　.

For the House: difficult.

Impossible for " the nation ", which is not made up of literati, but has 40,000,000 odd people who wouldn't even pretend to quote Hotspur,—they don't know or care who he is.